HEIDEGGER ON BEING UNCANNY

Heidegger on Being Uncanny

KATHERINE WITHY

Harvard University Press

CAMBRIDGE, MASSACHUSETTS & LONDON, ENGLAND

2015

First Printing

Excerpts from Martin Heidegger, *Introduction to Metaphysics*, trans.
Gregory Fried and Richard Polt, © 2000 Yale University Press.

Library of Congress Cataloging-in-Publication Data

Withy, Katherine.
  Heidegger on being uncanny / Katherine Withy.
    pages cm
  Includes bibliographical references and index.
  ISBN 978-0-674-41670-3
  1. Heidegger, Martin, 1889–1976. 2.   Uncanny, The (Psychoanalysis)
  I. Title.
  B3279.H49W534 2015
  193—dc23

                                                        2014035597

Contents

Abbreviations

EM   Introduction to Metaphysics *(Einführung in die Metaphysik)*

FCM The Fundamental Concepts of Metaphysics: World, Finitude, Solitude
     (Die Grundbegriffe der Metaphysik: Welt—Endlichkeit—Einsamkeit)

HI   Hölderlin's Hymn "The Ister" *(Hölderlins Hymne "Der Ister")*

SZ   Being and Time *(Sein und Zeit)*

WM   "What Is Metaphysics?" *("Was ist Metaphysik?")*

HEIDEGGER ON BEING UNCANNY

Introduction

THERE ARE MOMENTS when we are struck by a feeling of strangeness, as if there is something wrong with being human. Perhaps we sense the inadequacy of human knowledge in the face of the brute *that-ness* of the natural world; perhaps we feel an emptiness in the routines of daily social life; perhaps the familiarity drains away from ordinary objects, leaving only mute intruders. At such moments, it seems that we can never make our lives and our world fully familiar, fully meaningful. Any meaningfulness we win is haunted by meaninglessness. We feel that there is a dimension of human existence out of step with itself—unstable, out of joint, *unheimlich.*

Consulting dictionaries for foreign-language equivalents to '*unheim-lich,*' Freud assembles a list of English approximations: "[u]ncomfort-able, uneasy, gloomy, dismal, uncanny, ghastly; (of a house) haunted; (of a man) a repulsive fellow."[1] The standard English translation of both Freud's and Heidegger's '*unheimlich*' is 'uncanny.' This translation uses not the cognate 'home' *(heim)* but 'canny,' a word of Scottish origin carrying the senses, among others, of knowing and comfort, coziness. So what is *un*canny, according to the *OED*, is something "mysterious, weird, uncomfortably strange or unfamiliar."[2] The initial force of 'uncan-ny' (or *unheimlich*) is a sense of strangeness or, more strongly, eeriness.

'Uncanniness' is usually understood as an affective property. 'The un-canny' is an object that possesses this property, and 'the uncanny feeling'

---

[1] Sigmund Freud, "The Uncanny," *The Standard Edition of the Complete Psychological Works of Sigmund Freud,* Vol. 17, ed. and trans. James Strachey (London: Vintage, 2001), 221; Sigmund Freud, "Das Unheimliche," *Imago: Zeitschrift Für Anwendung Der Psycho-analyse Auf Die Geisteswissenschaften* V (1919): 297–324.

[2] "un'canny, adj." OED Online. Oxford University Press. Retrieved March 2014 from http://www.oed.com.proxy.library.georgetown.edu/view/Entry/210106?redirectedFrom=uncanny

is the corresponding affect. To understand uncanniness is to investigate uncanny objects and the uncanny feelings that they arouse and to determine what is distinctive about such objects and such feelings. We might go further and ask what such an experience reveals about us: what must the human condition be like, if the uncanny feeling is possible for us? Indeed, does experiencing this affect itself give us any insight into the human condition? To go even further, we might say that the human condition is itself an uncanny one—not because we are capable of experiencing the uncanny affect or because the human condition has the affective property of uncanniness (although it might), but because there is something inherently strange or unsettled about being human. What would this mean? What would it be not just to *feel* uncanny but to *be* uncanny?

As I read him, Martin Heidegger takes human existence to *be* uncanny. In this book, I pursue the idea of *being uncanny* by working out an interpretation of Heidegger's use of the concept.

In *Being and Time,* Heidegger's 'uncanny' seems to be simply 'how one feels' in the mood of angst.[3] In the mood of angst, things that were familiar and homely become strange. The world in which we make our home suddenly seems alien to us. It is, as Iain Thomson puts it, 'retroactively defamiliarised.'[4] Accordingly, we feel a sense of disquiet or unease—a strange or eerie feeling.[5] This feeling recalls the dissociative phenomenon of derealization, which has been described as involving a similar experience: "Familiar things look strange and foreign. I feel like

[3] Martin Heidegger, *Being and Time,* trans. J. Macquarrie and E. Robinson (San Francisco: Harper & Row, 1962); Martin Heidegger, *Sein und Zeit* (Tübingen: Max Niemeyer, 1979). Hereafter SZ. Page references in the text will be given in the form (SZxx) and refer to the Niemeyer pagination, which is included in the margins of English translations. I decapitalize Macquarrie and Robinson's 'Being' (*Sein*), substitute 'angst' for 'anxiety,' and substitute 'findingness' (and related words) for '*Befindlichkeit*' (and related words) when quoting from their translation.

[4] Iain Thomson, *Heidegger, Art and Postmodernity* (Cambridge: Cambridge University Press, 2011), 144, 145, 146.

[5] For example: "the uncanny feeling in which one feels no longer at home in one's familiar surroundings [. . .] " Eric Kligerman, *Sites of the Uncanny: Paul Celan, Specularity and the Visual Arts* (New York: Walter de Gruyter, 2007), 86. "To no longer feel 'at home' in the world does not mean that I am no longer able to identify things, recognize what they are called; rather, it means that things lose their *grip* on me. The normative force that they normally exert has dissipated; affordances have taken on the inertness of mere social facts." Steven Crowell, *Normativity and Phenomenology in Husserl and Heidegger* (Cambridge: Cambridge University Press, 2013), 219–220. "We experience uncanniness when our comfortable dealings with the normatively contoured everyday world are disrupted. Dasein is *in* its world, not by being physically contained by it, but by *living* in it and *being at home* in it. When our living is put into question because we cease to be at home in the world, our situation is disclosed as uncanny." Rebecca Kukla, "The Ontology and Temporality of Conscience," *Continental Philosophy Review* 35 (2002): 9.

an anthropologist from another planet, studying the human species. I look at things that once meant a lot to me, and I don't understand what I saw in them that made me love them. They're just shapes, objects, things, with no personal connection to me. My old coffee mug looks no more familiar than a baby with two heads. It's all just there and it's all strange somehow."[6] In Chapter 2, I am going to question this description of Heidegger's angst and how we feel in it. At the moment, I want to draw out an important difference between the psychological phenomenon of derealization and Heidegger's angst. For Heidegger, the experience of angst is not just a breakdown of familiarity but a breakdown that reveals something. Angst is not a pathological way of relating to the world (even if in it we cannot carry out our daily lives) because it is a genuine way of latching onto how things are—a special mode of access to the ontological.

There are at least two ways to understand this revelation. First, we might think that feeling uncanny reveals the fact that we normally feel at home. It makes accessible for the first time the 'normality' that we have lost. In this respect, the experience of angst is like the experience of illness: you never realize what it is to be healthy until you are not. So too with the uncanny feeling. For example, as Kukla has it: "[U]ncanniness, while it may not incapacitate us, reveals the way in which our situation is made up of normative *projects,* and it forces us to thematize our relationship to this situation."[7] We are now in a position to recognize and thematize what we ordinarily take for granted. Heidegger makes much of the way in which ontological revelations stem from withdrawals when he analyzes boredom in *The Fundamental Concepts of Metaphysics.*[8] On this kind of reading, the uncanny feeling reveals, through breakdown, those aspects of human life that we do not normally see.

Alternatively, we could say that such breakdown reveals the true human condition not by displaying what is taken for granted in daily life and then *lost* in breakdown but by displaying something that is covered

---

[6] Daphne Simeon and Jeffrey Abugel, *Feeling Unreal: Depersonalization Disorder and the Loss of Self* (Oxford: Oxford University Press, 2006), 80–81. Note that this is a composite description, collated from sufferers' reports.

[7] Kukla, "The Ontology and Temporality of Conscience," 9. Consider also Richard Polt's description: "We realize that we have been living in our own, familiar home; we are now capable of experiencing and perhaps appreciating that home as such, precisely because we are now alienated from it, because we are fish out of water." Richard Polt, *The Emergency of Being: On Heidegger's* Contributions to Philosophy (Ithaca, NY: Cornell University Press, 2006), 26.

[8] Martin Heidegger, *The Fundamental Concepts of Metaphysics: World, Finitude, Solitude,* trans. William McNeill and Nicholas Walker (Bloomington: Indiana University Press, 1995). Hereafter FCM. References will be given in the text in the form (FCMxx). I substitute 'entities' for 'beings' as a translation of '*das Seiendes*' when I quote from this text.

over in daily life and then *revealed* in breakdown. On this kind of reading, the uncanny experience is not a negative revelation of what everyday life has been like but a positive revelation of what the human essence is like. I will argue for this kind of reading later; for the moment, notice that Heidegger suggests something like it when he says that not being at home is a more primordial phenomenon than being at home (SZ189). Whatever uncanniness is for him, it is not the awkward vantage point from which we view everyday life. It is what underlies and in some sense makes possible everyday life. On this reading, the uncanny feeling is not analogous to the perspective gained in illness. Feeling uncanny is in some sense feeling what we are.

If we do not just feel uncanny but *are* uncanny then uncanniness is not just a window onto human life but itself belongs to the human essence. What could this mean? Uncanniness might be a deep-seated affective phenomenon—a repressed or unconscious emotion, perhaps—or a non-affective ontological structure named by analogy with the uncanny affect. (Compare Augustine's view that the natural condition of the human soul is misery. Is misery an unconscious emotion or a structural defect in the soul?) In either case, there is a doubling of the uncanny: the uncanny that describes how we feel and the uncanny in us that this feeling (and perhaps others) reveals. Thus the feeling of uncanniness has been said to reveal the "radical rootlessness" or ungroundedness of human practices, which means that "human beings can *never* be at home in the world" (Dreyfus); to show that "there is nothing about the structure of the self that can ever definitively tell us what to do with our lives" (Thomson); to suggest that "the dwelling places of the ontic are not There-being's true abode," such that to be human is to be "expatriate" (Richardson); to mirror the ontologically "primordial lack that constitutes the essence of humanity" (Ciaramelli); to be the "utter strangeness of action between two nothings" (Critchley); to be an invasion of a "disquieting strangeness" which "makes manifest the dispossession of the transcendental faculties of man" (Haar).[9] These formulations locate uncanniness as a feature of

[9] Hubert L. Dreyfus, *Being-in-the-World: A Commentary on Heidegger's* Being and Time, *Division I* (Cambridge, MA: The MIT Press, 1991), 37; Iain Thomson, *Heidegger, Art and Postmodernity*, 146 fn15; William J. Richardson, *Heidegger: Through Phenomenology to Thought*, 4th ed. (New York: Fordham University Press, 2003), 74, 81; Fabio Ciaramelli, "The Loss of Origin and Heidegger's Question of *Unheimlichkeit*," *Epoché: A Journal for the History of Philosophy* 1 (1994): 30; Simon Critchley, "The Null Basis-Being of a Nullity, or Between Two Nothings: Heidegger's Uncanniness," in *Interpreting Heidegger: Critical Essays*, ed. Daniel O. Dahlstrom (Cambridge: Cambridge University Press, 2011), 77; Michel Haar, "Attunement and Thinking," in *Heidegger: A Critical Reader*, ed. Hubert L. Dreyfus (Cambridge, MA: Blackwell, 1992), 171.

the human essence and describe it as some kind of "utter strangeness of being human."[10] But what, precisely? And where does Heidegger say any of this?

Heidegger's most explicit discussions of uncanniness occur after *Being and Time* and it is plain that, in these texts at least, uncanniness is not an affective property of things in the world but a feature of the human essence. In two later lecture courses, Heidegger analyzes the first choral ode from Sophocles's *Antigone*, the "Ode to Man," and uses '*Unheimlichkeit*' ('uncanniness') to translate Sophocles's '*to deinon*.' On this translation, the choral ode opens by naming the human being as the uncanniest entity: "Manifold is the uncanny, yet nothing / uncannier than man bestirs itself, rising up beyond him" (EM156/112).[11] 'Uncanniness' has graduated from a minor and largely affective concept to a key term that names "the basic trait of the human essence, into which every other trait must always be drawn" (EM161/116). (Is this a graduation or the first full recognition of a persisting status? Even in 1924, Heidegger holds that human existence *itself* is characterized by uncanniness, and that uncanniness is the ground of both uncoveredness and language)[12] In these texts, uncanniness is not to be understood in terms of "an impression made on our emotional states" (EM161/115); it is a wholly ontological concept.

But it remains unclear exactly what 'uncanniness' means. Heidegger's analyses in these lecture courses are difficult and interpretations of them tend to explain uncanniness in passing and without much argument. Uncanniness has been said to be the condition of the human being as "a

[10] Critchley, "The Null Basis-Being of a Nullity," 69.

[11] Martin Heidegger, *Introduction to Metaphysics*, trans. Gregory Fried and Richard Polt (New Haven, CT: Yale University Press, 2000); Martin Heidegger, *Einführung in die Metaphysik* (Tübingen: Max Niemeyer, 1998). Hereafter EM. Page references in the text will be given in the form (EMxx/xx), where the first page number refers to the Yale translation and the second to the Niemeyer edition pagination, which is included in the margins of the translation and of the *Gesamtausgabe* edition (Frankfurt: Vittorio Klostermann, 1983). I alter the translation to read 'entities' rather than 'beings' for '*das Seiendes*', 'being' rather than 'Being' for '*Sein*', and (usually) 'the human being' for '*der Mensch*'.

[12] "[. . . I]t can be a question of fear in yet another sense, what we designate as *anxiety* or *dread*: where it is *uncanny* for us, where we do not know what we are afraid of. If it is uncanny for us, we begin to discourse. That is an indication of how the *genesis of speaking is measured by being-there*, as speaking is connected with the basic determination of being-there itself, which is characterized by *uncanniness*." Martin Heidegger, *Basic Concepts of Aristotelian Philosophy*, trans. Robert D. Metcalf and Mark B. Tanzer (Bloomington: Indiana University Press, 2009), 175. "This phenomenon of [*Unheimlichkeit*] is the condition of possibility that something like *uncoveredness* [*Entdecktheit*] lies in existence"; "What we designate as *language* must also be explicated on the basis of this basic phenomenon of [*Unheimlichkeit*]" (Martin Heidegger, *Introduction to Phenomenological Research*, trans. Daniel O. Dahlstrom (Bloomington: Indiana University Press, 2005), 240).

'stranger in his own essence', deprived of any ontological 'at-homeness'"
(Haar); the condition of the human being as "a stranger [. . .] to his own
essence," but now in the sense that he is "basically a foreigner [. . .] to
his own *Unheimlichkeit*" (Derrida); the denial to the human being of
"any ultimate reliance on a constant and familiar order of things" (Geiman); "a name for being's enigma" (Fóti); the "tension between an authentic relationship to Being and a falling away from Being into the mere
appearances which make everydayness familiar and secure" (Taminiaux);
"the opening up of the very possibility of ownness," which opening "exceeds the order of the proper" (McNeill).[13] What these glosses have in
common is that they again take uncanniness to be a dimension of the
human essence associated with strangeness—a kind of "estrangement of
the human."[14] But of what kind, precisely? And do all these descriptions
describe the same phenomenon?

There are at least five reasons that it is difficult to understand what
Heidegger means by 'uncanniness.' First, Heidegger seems to use the
term in a peculiar way, appropriating it as an ontological term without
explaining how or why. (He does this often—famously, with the terms
'truth' and 'temporality.') Second, Heidegger sometimes uses the term
in a way that does *not* seem peculiar. For example, he will use the term
'uncanny' or 'uncanniness' to describe the alienation characteristic of the
public sphere and technology.[15] Are such occurrences non-technical uses
of the term or extensions of its technical sense? Which of Heidegger's

[13] Michel Haar, *Heidegger and the Essence of Man,* trans. William McNeill (Albany:
State University of New York Press, 1993), 184; Jacques Derrida, *The Beast and the Sover-
eign,* Vol. 2, trans. Geoffrey Bennington (Chicago: The University of Chicago Press, 2011),
288; Clare Pearson Geiman, "Heidegger's *Antigones,*" in *A Companion to Heidegger's
Introduction to Metaphysics,* ed. Richard Polt and Gregory Fried (New Haven, CT: Yale
University Press, 2001), 168; Véronique Marion Fóti, "Heidegger, Hölderlin, and Sophoclean Tragedy," in *Heidegger toward the Turn: Essays on the Work of the 1930s,* ed. James
Risser (Albany: State University of New York Press, 1999), 172; Jacques Taminiaux, "Plato's Legacy in Heidegger's Two Readings of *Antigone,*" in *Heidegger and Plato: Toward
Dialogue,* ed. Catalin Partenie and Tom Rockmore (Evanston, IL: Northwestern University
Press, 2005), 36; William McNeill, "*Heimat:* Heidegger on the Threshold," in *Heidegger
toward the Turn,* ed. Risser, 321.
[14] Philippe Lacoue-Labarthe, "Catastrophe: A Reading of Celan's 'The Meridian,'" *Oxford Literary Review* 15 (1993): 12.
[15] To give two examples: "Is there still an 'alternative' to the uncanny 'public sphere'? To
put it more clearly: *before* this chatter about 'alternatives', is there still a measure for essential things? What hells must man still endure before he realises that he is not his own creation?" Hannah Arendt and Martin Heidegger, *Letters: 1925–1975,* ed. Ursula Ludz, trans.
Andrew Shields (Orlando, FL: Harcourt Books, 2004), 139; "We do not know the significance of the uncanny increasing dominance of atomic technology. *The meaning pervading
technology hides itself.*" Martin Heidegger, "Memorial Address," *Discourse on Thinking,*
trans. John M. Anderson and E. Hans Freund (New York: Harper & Row, 1966), 55.

uses of the term are to be taken as contributing to its technical sense and which not? This is a problem whenever Heidegger uses an everyday word to name an ontological concept, for he may still use the term in a non-technical sense and we as readers have to determine in which sense he employs the term in any given case.

The third reason that uncanniness is a difficult concept to understand is that we ourselves are not always clear on what we ordinarily mean by the *Unheimliche* or the 'uncanny'—whether as a feeling or as the affective property that evokes it. How does the feeling differ from fear, surprise, uncertainty, or revulsion? Can we agree on what evokes the feeling—ghosts?—lifelike robots?—coincidences?—oddities? Is the uncanny the same as the strange?—the peculiar? If we turn to philosophical and literary accounts of the uncanny, we will not find much to help us. The concept has much contemporary currency in certain circles, owing in large part to the recent interest in Freud's essay "The Uncanny."[16] Freud's seminal essay takes the concept of *das Unheimliche* out of its prior aesthetic context and gives it a psychoanalytic interpretation. In circles influenced by Freud, there seems to be wide agreement about the general semantic field to which the uncanny belongs: it is associated with the destabilization and uncertainty of identity or the proper, because it is the power or presence of an Other or Stranger that secretly haunts the sphere of one's own, estranging one from oneself and yet nonetheless requiring hospitality.[17] In sum: "Uncanny is a certain indecidability which affects and infects representations, motifs, themes and situations, which [. . .] always mean something other than what they are and in a manner which draws their own being and substance into the vortex of signification."[18] This undecidability is a general structure, force, or process of instability and uncertainty. But one can be forgiven for finding in contemporary analyses only a kind of hyper-abstraction and conceptual play that does little to clarify what is happening when I feel uncanny or what something

[16] Mladen Dolar helps to explain this interest by describing postmodernism as "a new consciousness about the uncanny as a fundamental dimension of modernity." Mladen Dolar, "'I Shall Be with You on Your Wedding-Night': Lacan and the Uncanny," *October* 58 (1991): 23. For a full conceptual history of the uncanny, see Anneleen Masschelein, *The Unconcept: The Freudian Uncanny in Late-Twentieth-Century Theory* (Albany: State University of New York Press, 2011). Masschelein traces the development of the concept from Freud's essay through its appropriation by Derrida and Lacan, to its dissemination throughout recent European and Anglo-American thought.

[17] For a summary of representative appropriations of the uncanny, see Nicholas Royle, *The Uncanny* (New York: Routledge, 2003).

[18] Samuel Weber, *The Legend of Freud,* exp. ed. (Stanford, CA: Stanford University Press, 2000), 233–234.

must be like in order to be uncanny. One can also be forgiven for getting quite lost in the conceptuality of the uncanny. For instance, if the
uncanny is a play of strangeness and familiarity, does it encompass both
the strangely familiar and the familiarly strange? Are all combinations of
strangeness and familiarity uncanny?

Perhaps such questions are not fully answerable. The thought would
be that the concept of the uncanny, and so any investigation of it, is
itself uncanny and so resists full understanding. Even Freud's essay on
the uncanny has been shown to undo itself in multiple ways.[19] We might
generalize from this and reach Derrida's conclusion about the uncanny:
"It is less a question of [. . .] trying to master the *Unheimliche* or the
uncanny so that it becomes simply the familiar, than it is of the opposite
movement."[20] The opposite movement presumably consists in leaving the
Unheimliche as it is, in its own essential unfamiliarity. This would be a
fourth difficulty in determining the concept of the uncanny: the concept
is shot through with uncertainty and ambiguity, and necessarily so. The
uncanny or the unhomely, we might think, cannot be domesticated.

If the project of determining the uncanny is inappropriate to the phenomenon, then we must cease attempting to pin it down. Perhaps the
appropriate way to treat the uncanny is to let the phenomenon play itself
out in our text. We find thematic resonances, rhyme concepts and terms,
and allow meanings to shift and become unfamiliar.[21] This may appear
to be a lack of clarity in exposition, but—we might claim—it is the only
honest approach to the uncanny, for it brings us to unhomeliness and
uncertainty. We *show* or *perform* uncanniness by producing an interplay
of familiarity and unfamiliarity in the investigation.

There are two assumptions here. The first is that the concept of the
uncanny is itself uncanny, and the second is that 'the uncanny' always
refers to a perpetual interplay of familiarity and unfamiliarity. In the
case of Heidegger's uncanny, both of these will turn out to be (roughly)

---

[19] Kofman, for example, has argued that "The Uncanny" is "a text dominated by an
investigation which is not, at any moment, complete without being immediately invali-
dated." Sarah Kofman, *Freud and Fiction*, trans. Sarah Wykes (Cambridge: Polity Press,
1991), 121.

[20] Jacques Derrida, *The Ear of the Other: Otobiography, Transference, Translation:
Texts and Discussions with Jacques Derrida*, ed. Christie McDonald, trans. Peggy Kamuf
(New York: Schocken Books, 1985), 156.

[21] This approach is exemplified by David Farrell Krell in *Archeticture: Ecstasies of Space,
Time, and the Human Body* (Albany: State University of New York Press, 1997); Jacques
Derrida, especially in *Specters of Marx: The State of the Debt, The Work of Mourning, and
the New International*, trans. Peggy Kamuf (New York: Routledge, 1994); and Royle, *The
Uncanny*.

true, but neither can be assumed at the start. Even if the uncanny is an undecidable interplay of familiarity and unfamiliarity, the own and the foreign, it remains a question whether the concept of the uncanny is itself like this. Is the concept of the uncanny itself uncanny? The answer is not obvious. Compare the concept of nonsense. Nonsense cannot be made sense of without destroying it, just as the uncanny cannot be known or made familiar without destroying it. But we can still understand what nonsense is, for the concept of nonsense is not nonsensical. We can grasp what it takes for something to be nonsense without destroying the phenomenon of nonsense and without resorting to nonsensical analyses to illuminate it by performing it. Perhaps the same is true of the uncanny. This remains to be determined through a clear exposition of Heidegger's uncanny. Heidegger's concept of uncanniness must *turn out* to be uncanny, and there will be much to pin down definitively about it before we reach this point. As even Derrida reminds us, one must not "turn oneself over, bound hand and foot, to the *Unheimliche*."[22]

The second assumption is that Heidegger's uncanniness is a perpetual, undecidable play of familiarity and unfamiliarity—that is, a version of Freud's uncanny. This also cannot be assumed at the outset. Freud argues that what is distinctive about the uncanny feeling is that it is not merely a sense of *un*familiarity but a sense of unfamiliarity that *includes* a sense of familiarity. Something *unheimlich* is something that is strangely familiar. Freud understands this as a 'return of the repressed': some psychic item used to be familiar, then became unfamiliar through repression, and now an event or experience prompts it to return to the conscious mind, where it disrupts or haunts the realm of the familiar like a ghost from an old world. The experience of this is the uncanny feeling. The uncanny is thus a certain kind of interplay between the familiar and unfamiliar, in which the realm of familiarity is disrupted.

Approaching the uncanny primarily through Freud is a final—yet often first—source of confusion in understanding Heidegger's concept of the uncanny. What warrant do we have to read Heidegger through Freud? It is certainly *tempting* to listen to Heidegger's talk of uncanniness and to hear Freud's voice speaking through it. Such channeling gives us a way to make sense of what Heidegger says, and it further offers the pleasure of experiencing an instance of Freud's uncanny: Heidegger's talk of uncanniness appears strangely familiar by virtue of the Freudian presence haunting it. This may be the uncanny return of Heidegger's Freudian repressed, disrupting the Heideggerian familiar! In the most sustained discussion of

---

[22] Derrida, *The Ear of the Other*, 156.

Heidegger's concept of uncanniness to date, David Farrell Krell has explored this uncanny entwining of Heidegger and Freud.[23] Krell finds various instances of uncanny hauntings and doublings in Heidegger's work, as well as an uncanny Freudian presence. Noting a link between Freud's concepts of return and repression, on the one hand, and Heidegger's concepts of unconcealment and concealment, on the other, Krell comments that "[o]f all Freud's essays, this is the one that Heidegger—the thinker of concealing and self-showing—must have read most closely. In secret. Closely closeted."[24]

As Krell recognizes, it is unlikely that Heidegger read Freud's essay, and it is certain that he did not hold Freud in high esteem.[25] So why think that the ghost of Freud is present in Heidegger's work? Perhaps Freud is present in Heidegger only because he is present to us as we read. We might now—noticing that Freud is haunting *us*—explore our own uncanniness as readers of Heidegger and Freud, as well as the uncanniness of the experience of reading about uncanniness. But this takes us farther from our goal of attempting to understand what Heidegger means by uncanniness. It is true that some kind of convergence of familiarity and unfamiliarity belongs to the sense of the term '*unheimlich*,' even apart from its Freudian interpretation. But, as I have noted, it is also true that Heidegger regularly uses ordinary words in unexpected ways. While there must be some dimension of the ordinary sense of the term '*unheimlich*' that Heidegger wants us to hear, it is not thereby the case that he wants us to pick up on the same resonances that Freud finds salient. It is also not necessarily the case that what Heidegger wants to do philosophically with these resonances is the same as what Freud does with them psychoanalytically. It must be established what relation Heidegger's uncanniness bears to Freud's. To do this, we must first read Heidegger without Freud. We cannot assume that the two are talking about the same thing in the same way.

[23] Krell, *Archeticture*. See especially Section III, "Unhomelike Places: Archetictural Sections of Heidegger and Freud." (Note that the play on the spelling of 'architecture' is deliberate.) Krell's broader project in this text concerns the uncanniness of space, bodies, and homes, and so belongs to the more general architectural application of the concept of the uncanny. On this, see also Anthony Vidler, *The Architectural Uncanny: Essays in the Modern Unhomely* (Cambridge, MA: The MIT Press, 1992), and various articles in the volume of *Research in Phenomenology* dedicated to the topic "Deconstruction and the Architecture of the Uncanny." *Research in Phenomenology*, Vol. 22, ed. John Sallis (Atlantic Highlands, NJ: Humanities Press International, 1992).

[24] Krell, *Archeticture*, 101.

[25] Ibid., 99, 101.

Given all these difficulties, is it still worthwhile to attempt to get clear on the concept? Uncanniness is a minor and irregular theme in Heidegger's corpus, and its attraction for contemporary commentators can be traced largely to an interest in Freud's treatment of the uncanny. Yet even though Heidegger never unambiguously adopts 'uncanniness' as a key term in his philosophy, he keeps returning to it. Each time he takes it up, it becomes more central to his account of human being. Derrida claims that Heidegger has "frequent, decisive, and organizing recourse" "to the value of *Unheimlichkeit*, in *Being and Time* and elsewhere," and that this reliance on uncanniness has been overlooked.[26] It seems to me that this remains true despite the recent attention to the concept. This is a scholarly reason to pursue clarity in our understanding of Heidegger's concept.

The non-scholarly—human and ethical—reason to pursue Heidegger's uncanniness is that it promises to illuminate something about what it is to be human, something that perhaps has been insufficiently noted or insufficiently described in philosophy to date. If we have an intuition that there is something fundamentally unsettling about human life, and in particular something out of joint about our attempts to make the world meaningful, then perhaps Heidegger can help us to clarify this intuition and to figure out how to live well in this unsettled condition.

[26] Derrida, *Specters of Marx*, 174.

1

Feeling Uncanny

Iᴛ ᴜsᴇᴅ ᴛᴏ be the case that the first point of reference for evoking and discussing the uncanny feeling was ghosts or hauntings. Nowadays, we are more likely to talk about humanoid robots. The reason is that the uncanny has been adopted as a technical concept by roboticists. In 1970, robotics professor Masahiro Mori wrote a paper describing what he calls "the uncanny valley."[1] The uncanny valley is the sudden and dramatic dip in our felt affinity for an object as its resemblance to human beings increases. Rather than showing up as familiar and comforting, the object shows up as eerie or strange: uncanny. Mori populates this uncanny valley with corpses, zombies, and prosthetic hands, and he warns roboticists that they need to seriously confront and understand this phenomenon if they are going to build humanoid robots.

Mori's brief description of the uncanny valley raises a number of important initial questions about how the uncanny feeling arises and the conceptual space it occupies. First, it is not obvious why affinity should drop as similarity increases. Why does affinity not increase straightforwardly? In a footnote, Mori suggests that the valley may be based on a survival instinct "that protects us from proximal, rather than distal, sources of danger."[2] Such proximal sources of danger include "corpses, members of different species, and other entities we can closely approach."[3] The uncanny affect thus resembles the feeling of disgust and is strongly associated with death and disease.

But Mori's primary intuition seems to be that affinity drops as we revise our opinion about where an object falls on the similarity axis: "once

[1] Masahiro Mori, "The Uncanny Valley," trans. Karl F. MacDorman and Norri Kageki, *IEEE Robotics and Automation Magazine* 19 (2012): 98–100. Originally published, in Japanese, as M. Mori, "The Uncanny Valley," *Energy* 4 (1970): 33–35.

[2] Mori, "The Uncanny Valley," 100.

[3] Ibid., 100.

we realize that the hand that looked real at first sight is actually artificial, we experience an eerie sensation. [. . .] When this happens, we lose our sense of affinity, and the hand becomes uncanny."[4] The story, I take it, is this: we believe that the hand is a human hand but then realize that it is artificial. Upon this realization, our sense of affinity drains away and we feel uncanny. But this story raises a number of further questions. First, it seems that what we are doing here is correcting ourselves. To correct ourselves is to reposition the object on the similarity and affinity axes. How does this repositioning bear at all on whether affinity drops as similarity increases? Further, it is not obvious that such a correction would produce an uncanny feeling. It might, of course, produce a sense of shock, surprise, or fear—heightened, of course, in any non-ideal epistemic environment, such as darkness: "If someone wearing the hand in a dark place shook a [person's] hand with it, the [person] would assuredly shriek!"[5] But why should a shock or/and a negative sense of affinity involve an eerie feeling? Why is an eerie feeling produced by making a mistake—and a mistake about the degree of human likeness in particular? Why do we not just correct the mistake and move on? It is not obvious that what we have here is either uncanny or a valley.

Even if we could explain how such mistakes produce a dip in affinity, and one which is uncanny, it is not clear why the dip should be a valley rather than an uncanny cliff. The other side of the curve (which makes the valley) signals increased human similarity and positive affinity. Mori situates ordinary dolls here. But we might have expected that with increased similarity comes an increase in mistakes and so a deepening rather than lessening of the uncanniness. Further, such mistakes should be a temporary phenomenon and need not concern robotics indefinitely. The mistaken identification, and so the uncanniness, should pass with time, insofar as time and exposure increase our familiarity and our sensitivity to relevant distinguishing features. Over time, we should find it harder to confuse robots and humans. The uncanny valley should vanish.

All this suggests that tying uncanniness to mistaken identification is extremely problematic. Mori also appeals to movement, saying that when something is in motion it heightens the severity of the valley. Why should animateness accomplish this, as opposed to merely increasing the degree of human likeness? Does animateness, as a fundamental category, somehow figure in the explanation of the eeriness of negative affinity? Does it distinguish those classes of mistakes that produce the

[4]Ibid., 99.
[5]Ibid., 99–100. 'Person' replaces 'woman.'

uncanny feeling from those that do not? The idea of machines come to life does indeed seem to get at something of uncanniness, since such coming to life is associated with horror, which in turn is associated with uncanniness. (Mori: "If the mannequins started to move, it would be like a horror story.")[6]

Mori's essay and the subsequent discussions of the uncanny in robotics serve to raise the question of what the uncanny feeling is and how it arises. None answers the question. We know that the uncanny feeling is related to horror, surprise, fear, and disgust. It seems to arise when we make mistakes—especially in the dark, and especially about what is living and what is dead. In this chapter, I want to clarify the domain of the uncanny feeling. However, my aim will not be to identify a single set of conditions that make for uncanniness. Rather, I want to draw out and loosen up our sense of the semantic field surrounding the uncanny so that we may be sufficiently limber to adapt ourselves to Heidegger's novel and robustly ontological use of the term. I begin where Mori's essay leaves off, at the beginning of a philosophical exploration of the uncanny feeling.

Jentsch's Uncanny

In his 1906 essay "On the Psychology of the Uncanny," Ernst Jentsch identifies the psychical condition of possibility of the uncanny affect as a lack of orientation or a psychical uncertainty.[7] This uncertainty is a difficulty incorporating something into your 'ideational sphere': not being able to fit that thing into the world that you know and the life that you lead. 'Lack of orientation' suggests that this uncertainty is more basic than a lack of conceptual knowledge; it points to experiences where we *just don't get* what to do with something or how to stand with respect to it. Jentsch speaks as if this uncertainty causes the uncanny affect, although he leaves the precise relation unclear. In any case, his claim is that in situations of uncertainty there will generally follow a feeling of the uncanny. The conditions of the uncanny, then, are more or less the conditions of uncertainty. By considering Jentsch's examples, however, we will be able to specify this further: the uncertainty that produces the uncanny feeling must be an irresolvable uncertainty.

---

[6] Ibid., 100.

[7] Ernst Jentsch, "On the Psychology of the Uncanny," trans. Roy Sellars, *Angelaki: A New Journal in Philosophy, Literature and the Social Sciences* 2(1) (1996): 7–16.

Jentsch splits the world into things old, known, and familiar and things new, foreign, and hostile. Uncertainty emerges 'naturally' in relation to the latter, since we have to work to figure out what kind of thing this novel object is and so how to fit it into our 'ideational sphere.' Jentsch suggests that literature often makes use of this kind of uncertainty in evoking the uncanny affect, since such uncertainty relies on ignorance about what the entity is, and an author can reliably produce and manipulate our ignorance. The uncertainty is more pronounced the more it has to do with the most basic distinctions that we make in organizing our world—for instance, that between the animate and inanimate. Thus the uncanny feeling is associated with apparently inanimate objects becoming animated and *vice versa*. The uncertainty is dispelled when we determine what kind of thing we are dealing with and thus incorporate it into the realm of the familiar. With the novel rendered familiar, the uncanny feeling is replaced by whatever affect is appropriate to the actual state of affairs.

Jentsch gives the example of a traveler: "someone sat down in an ancient forest on a tree trunk" (presumably a fallen tree trunk, or a root or branch) and "to the horror of the traveler, this trunk suddenly began to move and showed itself to be a giant snake."[8] At first, the traveler sees only what she expects to see; she locates the 'tree trunk' in her ideational sphere quickly and without difficulty. In doing so, the traveler fails to acknowledge those features of the entity that would allow her to recognize it as a snake. Suddenly, one of these—motility—bursts into her experience and the traveler is forced to revise her identification of the entity. In the gap before she does so, the traveler experiences the inadequacy of her initial discovery and so finds herself suspended in doubt, uncertain as to whether the movement she has perceived is the movement of the tree or that of some living entity. She feels uncanny. As soon as she grasps the entity as a snake, the traveler has made the entity familiar again and experiences the appropriate affect: fear.

Jentsch's way of thinking about the uncanny is obviously similar to Mori's, which also traffics in surprises about animateness. But I disagree with both, for I do not think that Jentsch's example, as described, is a case of the uncanny affect—precisely because it is a story about a mistake. (Mori's examples may yet be uncanny, but they will be so for a different reason.) On Jentsch's story, the traveler mistook a snake for a fallen tree trunk. What makes this kind of error uncanny for Jentsch, given that not all errors are? Jentsch implies that we might attribute the specifically uncanny quality of this experience to an ambiguity of in/animateness,

[8] Ibid., 11.

arguing that this is the kind of uncertainty that is most often uncanny. But he does not explain why this is so, or how such an uncertainty works to produce the uncanny feeling in this example. At first, we might think that what is significant about an ambiguity of in/animateness is that it involves an uncertainty regarding categories that are eminently significant for living and acting in the world. The traveler herself is at stake in her grasp of the entity as either animate or inanimate; mistaking the snake as a tree puts her in real danger (presumably in a way that misidentifying the snake as some harmless animal would not). When an entity shifts between our most basic organizing categories, we find ourselves at risk in an uncertain world. The more central an entity or way of understanding entities is to our lives, the more its instability affects us.

But is this what makes us feel uncanny? If identifying entities as either animate or inanimate is crucial to leading a human life, then having to reassess such an identification is important; it matters to us that we get it right. If we get it wrong, we must revise—and this revision will be a significant event. In the tree/snake case, we can no longer be complacent and comfortable but must flee or fight. In this transition, we may be at a loss as to how to behave towards the entity, but the affect that we experience is not the uncanny feeling. It is surprise or confusion. This may seem like the uncanny feeling because, in this case, it transitions to fear—of which Freud holds the uncanny to be a species and which Jentsch makes no effort to distinguish from the uncanny feeling.[9] (Indeed, he describes the traveler's affective condition as 'terror,' which is plausibly fear mingled with surprise.)[10] Either such a case of mistaken identification does not involve the uncanny feeling or the uncanny feeling is simply fear mixed with surprise and confusion.

Jentsch's other examples of the uncanny ambiguity of in/animateness are significantly different from the tree/snake case and suggest that the uncanny affect is something other than the affect experienced by the traveler. Jentsch mentions automata and epileptics during a seizure.[11] Both of these present an ambiguity of in/animateness—but, importantly, one that cannot be resolved (even if it becomes familiar and so ceases to be uncanny; more on this situation in the next section).[12] Even if an automaton

[9] Sigmund Freud, "The Uncanny," *The Standard Edition of the Complete Psychological Works of Sigmund Freud,* Vol. 17, ed. and trans. James Strachey (London: Vintage Books, 2001), 219.

[10] Jentsch, "On the Psychology of the Uncanny," 11.

[11] Ibid., 12 and 14, respectively.

[12] For conditions under which an unresolvable ambiguity of in/animateness can become familiar, see ibid., 15.

is known to be mechanical, and the epileptic seizure to be a manifestation of 'mechanical' bodily processes, both remain disquieting. Our doubts persist and no amount of evidence or argument can do away with them. (Jentsch brings his tree/snake example closer to this kind of case when he suggests that it is more uncanny when the doubt is obscure and so harder to recognize and resolve.)[13] Jentsch hypothesizes that the persistence of doubt and of the feeling of uncanniness is due to either "semi-conscious secondary doubts" or a "lively recollection of the first awkward impression lingering in one's mind."[14] But here he seems to miss the point. If we have doubts, they persist because the 'resolution' that assigns the entity to the category of either animate or inanimate is never final. This, in turn, is because the entity in question *does not fit cleanly into these categories.* For many of us, the automaton or the epileptic having a seizure has features that cannot fully be accounted for by the category of 'inanimate' or 'mechanical.'

I suggest that an ambiguity of in/animateness is uncanny when this ambiguity calls the very distinction between animate and inanimate into question. Consider ghosts, which do the same for the distinction between living and dead (or past and present). A ghost is neither living nor dead, neither past nor present—and so *both* living and dead, past and present. Ghosts are uncanny because they ambiguously span different categories, belonging to both and neither. Experiences of such anomalous phenomena reveal that the 'ideational sphere' or the set of categories in terms of which we make things familiar is not adequate to some entities. The very category of 'ghost' marks this failure, since it is a category for a certain kind of anomaly. (Thus the vocabulary of ghosts and haunting is often used to evoke the structure of uncanniness, especially by Derrida.)[15] Ghosts, epileptic seizures, and automata straddle the gaps between the joints in our ways of making sense of the world and in doing so reveal that these joints do not match up perfectly with the way that the world is jointed. Thus Hamlet, haunted by his father's ghost, is not uncertain whether his father is alive or dead. He is uncertain about how, or whether, to apply these categories in this case. Of course, Hamlet expresses his concern more basically, seizing not on in/animateness but on the fundamental categories of time. Is his father present or past? It is unclear. "The time is out of joint" (Shakespeare, *Hamlet,* I.V).

[13] Ibid., 11, 13.
[14] Ibid., 12.
[15] Jacques Derrida, *Specters of Marx: The State of the Debt, The Work of Mourning, and the New International,* trans. Peggy Kamuf (New York: Routledge, 1994).

The uncertainty associated with the uncanny affect is not a temporary confusion about how to categorize an object (tree or snake?) but an irresolvable uncertainty about the applicability of the very categories that we use (neither/both past nor/and present, living nor/and dead). As I interpret them, Jentsch's most persuasive cases of ambiguous in/animateness show this, although the tree/snake case does not. The reason is that the tree/snake is *either* animate or inanimate rather than *both* and *neither*. To experience the uncanny affect, the traveler would have to have cause to wonder whether the entity is in fact a snake-tree (or tree-snake, as it were). The mistaken identification of the snake as a tree involves only the experientially similar affect of surprise and confusion resolving into fear. Freud gives another example: a table carved with crocodile figures that seem to roam the house at night, "wooden monsters come to life in the dark."[16] Is it a table, or a nest of crocodiles? It is both and neither. This is uncanny. Similarly for Mori's examples: simple mistakes about whether this hand is prosthetic or not will not involve an uncanny affect. Those objects that do reliably produce an uncanny affect are those that (seem to) span the distinction between animate and inanimate, like zombies and extremely lifelike robots.

So Jentsch's uncanniness of the unfamiliar, as illustrated in the tree/snake example, fails to capture the uncanny feeling because it involves a resolvable uncertainty, the locus of which is the entity itself rather than the categories in terms of which we make sense of it. The unfamiliar is not itself uncanny but merely waiting to be made familiar. Thus Freud argues that Jentsch's account of the uncanny feeling is "fertile but not exhaustive" because it does "not get beyond this relation of the uncanny to the novel and the unfamiliar."[17] Freud objects, as I have, that not everything unfamiliar or uncertain is for that reason uncanny. "Something has to be added to what is novel and unfamiliar in order to make it uncanny."[18] I have suggested that what must be added is that the unfamiliar thing be radically anomalous, in the sense that it calls the jointing of our 'ideational sphere' into question. But is this the whole story? Surely sometimes even the most familiar things can become anomalous in this way. What happens when familiar things become uncanny?

Although his essay focuses on the uncanniness of the unfamiliar, Jentsch allows that we can lack orientation, and so feel uncanny, in the face of even the most familiar and ordinary things. He argues that this

---

[16] Freud, "The Uncanny," 245.
[17] Ibid., 219 and 221, respectively.
[18] Ibid., 221.

is possible only if our usual conflation of the known or familiar with the self-evident is revealed to us. Ordinarily, what is familiar shows up to us as self-evident: as not requiring any explanation or investigation. But what shows up in this way may nonetheless be "remarkable and inexplicable."[19] Such a thing may *seem* to be self-evident, but only because familiarity or habit covers over the uncertainty that it evokes: "disorientation remains *concealed* for as long as the confusion of 'known/self-evident' does not enter the consciousness of the individual."[20] So while we are uncertain about even the most familiar things, the fact that they are familiar and belong to the realm of the habitual *masks* the disorientation or uncertainty that we feel with respect to them. Jentsch gives the example of the sun: "No-one in the world is surprised under usual circumstances when he sees the sun rise in the morning, so much has this daily spectacle crept into the ideational processes of the naive person since early childhood as a normal custom not requiring commentary."[21] But the sun is a perplexing entity and its behavior is far from self-evident. This becomes apparent, and the sun becomes the locus of the uncanny feeling, when we suspend the everyday familiarity of the sun and come to see that, at bottom, we do not understand it: "It is only when one deliberately removes such a problem from the usual way of looking at it—for the activity of understanding is accustomed to remain insensitive to such enigmas, as a consequence of the power of the habitual—that a particular feeling of uncertainty quite often presents itself."[22]

On the face of it, this experience of uncertainty resembles the experience of Socratic *aporia*. Everyday familiarity with, for example, justice and piety leads us to think that we understand what justice and piety are. But Socratic questioning suspends this familiarity and leads us to see that at bottom we do not understand. Justice may be a familiar phenomenon in human behavior and the law courts, but what it *is* is not thereby evident to us. Here, something familiar becomes uncanny (perhaps) when we realize that its familiarity is merely apparent and that at bottom we do not know it. Is this the uncanny feeling that Jentsch has in mind?

It seems not, for Jentsch identifies the uncertainty otherwise. In the case of the sun, one becomes uncertain and feels uncanny "when one remembers that the rising of the sun does not depend on the sun at all but rather on the movement of the earth, and that, for the inhabitants of the earth, absolute movement in space is much more inconsequential

---

[19] Jentsch, "On the Psychology of the Uncanny," 8.
[20] Ibid., 9. My emphasis.
[21] Ibid., 8–9.
[22] Ibid., 9.

than that at the centre of the earth, and so forth."[23] About what are we uncertain here? We are not uncertain about what is moving. It is not the case that we lack knowledge about the sun's true behavior or about how the earth's rotation gives the appearance of the sun rising. We are not uncertain about why it seems to us that the sun moves. This makes the case different from Socratic *aporia,* since we know the truth behind the everyday appearance as well as how the two are related. We are not uncertain about our perceptual experience or our scientific knowledge or how the two are consistent. I suggest that we are instead uncertain about which orientation we are to inhabit. We 'lack orientation' not because we have no way of making sense of the sun's rising but because we have a surplus of orientations. The sun's rising fits into our world in two different, yet equally valid, kinds of ways. This renders us unable to "assimilat[e . . .] the phenomenon in question into its proper place" in our ideational sphere, since both places are equally proper.[24]

The sun case is markedly different from the tree/snake case. The sun becomes strange and we feel uncanny not because we are unsure about how to identify it (as *either* animate or inanimate) but because we find ourselves with two distinct ways of discovering this single entity (as *both* rising and stationary). Our uncertainty is not resolved by finding out the truth of the matter—by opting for the orientation that captures the entity as it really is. *Both* ways of making the entity familiar reveal it as the entity that it is, but neither does so fully and finally. Each leaves out something about the sun that the other way of making it familiar captures. (Although we can account for the perceptual experience of the sun rising when we inhabit the scientific orientation, the latter does not properly include the former.) This is a consequence of the fact that the sun's behavior is not self-evident, for in grasping the sun as either stationary (scientific perspective) or moving (perceptual experience) we render the entity familiar but do not get it entirely in our grip. So when we have both ways of grasping the sun simultaneously in view, we vividly experience the fact that its familiarity does not render it self-evident. This makes us feel uncanny.

Like the ambiguity of in/animateness (as I interpreted it), this experience calls into question the adequacy of our ways of making sense of the world. But it calls this into question in a different way because the locus of the uncanny feeling is different. The ambiguity of in/animateness is located in an entity that spans two categories within an ideational sphere

[23] Ibid., 9.
[24] Ibid., 8.

(animate, inanimate). It shows that the joints in our ideational sphere need not match up with the way that the world is jointed. In the sun case, the ambiguity is located across two ideational spheres (or, if you like, two distinct portions of a single ideational sphere): the perceptual and the scientific. The entity can be grasped in terms of either sphere but not in terms of both simultaneously, and so never fully. This shows that each of our ways of making familiar need not capture an entity entirely. Our uncertainty in this case is possible because there is a gap between the sense that we make of the entity and the entity itself.

Jentsch implies that the gap is always there. It is not a feature of *some* way of making something familiar, or of *our* ways of making things familiar, which we might avoid by finding a better way to grasp the world. It belongs to the constitution of familiarity itself that something familiar is not thereby entirely captured. Jentsch puts this by distinguishing the known and the self-evident, which he thinks we surreptitiously conflate in the process of making familiar. "That which has long been familiar appears not only as welcome, but also—however remarkable and inexplicable it may be—as straightforwardly self-evident."[25] (This is why the expert for whom epileptic seizures are a commonplace need not be troubled by an ambiguity of in/animateness.) Making familiar rests upon the pretense of full knowledge: the concealed assumption that what is known or familiar is thus self-evident or fully manifest. This is "the power of the habitual."[26] For familiar objects, then, "disorientation remains concealed for as long as the confusion of 'known/self-evident' does not enter the consciousness of the individual."[27] Here Jentsch suggests that all familiarity involves a conflation of the known and self-evident. Put differently: the assumption that what is familiar is self-evident is never warranted. It follows that, according to Jentsch, familiarity is always grounded in a more basic unfamiliarity. The uncanny feeling marks our experience of this more basic unfamiliarity, which renders the familiar perpetually unstable and able to show up as perplexing or recalcitrant. It shows that the way that we make sense of things is never adequate to the world.

Since the uncanny feeling is here grounded in a concealed, primitive unfamiliarity, the uncanniness cannot be resolved. Unlike the tree/snake case, we do not resolve the uncertainty and pass to the appropriate affect. The uncertainty is constitutive for familiarity and so cannot be solved at all. Uncanniness *is* the appropriate affect. But the uncertainty cannot be

[25] Ibid., 8.
[26] Ibid., 9.
[27] Ibid., 9.

lived with as an orientation to the world, so we must cover it over by re-turning to the familiar and the habitual. We resume our normal business and re-assume the conflation of the known and self-evident, allowing the habitual to conceal our lack of orientation. What we gain from our expe-rience is not some new fact about the world (for example, by identifying the tree as a snake) but the awareness (even if dim) that familiarity does not go all the way down.

What is common to the uncanniness of the familiar and the ambiguity of in/animateness is an uncertainty that is irresolvable and which is so because it is a product not of ignorance but of the nature of familiarity. Is this essential irresolvability the 'something else' that Freud considers Jentsch to have missed, which bridges the distance between the merely unfamiliar and the uncanny? This may be the case if the sun example is indeed an instance of the uncanny feeling. It is not yet clear that it is so. Let me turn to Freud's account of the uncanny to establish what he thinks Jentsch has overlooked and to work through our intuitions about whether the sun case is uncanny.

Freud's Uncanny

According to Freud, Jentsch's account misses the pre-history of the unfa-miliarity involved in producing the uncanny affect, and with it the role of familiarity. Something unfamiliar is uncanny not because it is unfamiliar but only if its unfamiliarity is ambiguous by virtue of being tied up with a prior familiarity. Consider E. T. A. Hoffmann's story "The Sandman," which Freud analyzes in detail.[28] Jentsch would hold that the uncanny ef-fect of this story is centered on an uncertainty about whether the lifelike doll, Olimpia, is inanimate (a doll) or animate (a person). Freud disagrees on two points. First, Olimpia is not the primary locus of the uncanny feeling in the story, and second, if Olimpia is uncanny, it is not because

---

[28] E. T. A. Hoffmann, "The Sandman," *The Golden Pot and Other Tales,* trans. Ritchie Robertson (Oxford: Oxford University Press, 1992). Much has been said about Freud's reading of "The Sandman"; see, for example: Hélène Cixous, "Fiction and Its Phantoms: A Reading of Freud's *Das Unheimliche* ('The Uncanny')," *New Literary History* 7 (1976): 525–548, 619–645; Neil Hertz, "Freud and the Sandman," *The End of the Line: Essays on Psychoanalysis and the Sublime* (New York: Columbia University Press, 1985), 97–121; Sarah Kofman, "The Double Is/and the Devil: The Uncanniness of the Sandman," *Freud and Fiction,* trans. Sarah Wykes (Cambridge: Polity Press, 1991); Nicholas Rand and Ma-ria Torok, "The Sandman Looks at 'The Uncanny': The Return of the Repressed or of the Secret; Hoffman's Question to Freud," in *Speculations after Freud: Psychoanalysis, Philoso-phy and Culture,* ed. Sonu Shamdasani and Michael Münchow (London: Routledge, 1994).

of uncertainty about her in/animateness. Freud allows that a living doll may produce an uncanny affect but insists that there is nothing particularly unsettling about a living doll *per se;* many children wish that their dolls would come to life and do not find this prospect distressing.[29] Such an occurrence is unsettling only if we consider it to be impossible but are not entirely confident in this belief. What makes for the uncanny feeling, according to Freud, is that our flirtation with the belief in Olimpia's animateness resonates with a primitive or infantile belief in animism that we have only ostensibly overcome.

Freud posits an animistic phase in the development of humanity and of the individual, in which we wish or believe that inanimate entities are imbued with a life force or spirit. This primitive or infantile belief is surmounted in later stages of development but not entirely surrendered. 'Traces' or 'residues' remain such that the non-animistic beliefs we now hold are unstable and can be revealed as such: "we do not feel quite sure of our new beliefs, and the old ones still exist within us ready to seize upon any confirmation. As soon as something *actually happens* in our lives which seems to confirm the old, discarded beliefs we get a feeling of the uncanny."[30]

Freud's account does not do away with the role of uncertainty in the uncanny feeling but displaces it. An ambiguity of in/animateness is uncanny for Freud not because it is unclear whether the entity is animate or inanimate but because this ambiguity itself introduces a further uncertainty—what Freud calls a "conflict of judgement."[31] This is an uncertainty attaching not to entities and their characteristics but to our belief systems. We once believed in the reality of animism but no longer do; an ambiguously animate entity like Olimpia casts our new beliefs in doubt. This crisis of belief is an uncertainty about whether our old belief in animism might in fact be legitimate and our current beliefs inadequate. So if Olimpia evokes the uncanny feeling it is not because we are uncertain about whether she is animate or inanimate, and so because she is unfamiliar. Rather, she is familiar—but in an unfamiliar way. As ambiguously in/animate, Olimpia is both familiar (in terms of the allegedly abandoned animistic belief system) and unfamiliar (in terms of the current non-animistic belief system). It is this play of familiarity and unfamiliarity around a single entity that makes for the uncanny feeling, and it is grounded in the play of old and new belief systems.

[29] Freud, "The Uncanny," 233.
[30] Ibid., 247–248.
[31] Ibid., 250.

If Freud is right, then Jentsch's account of the ambiguity of in/animate-ness (as I have interpreted it) has indeed missed something. I argued that, on a Jentschian picture, an uncertainty about in/animateness is uncanny if the entity spans these two categories in a way that calls their distinction into question. Thus Olimpia would be both familiar and unfamiliar since the ambiguity of her in/animateness consists in the fact that she both fits and does not fit each of these categories. Both Freud and Jentsch (as I have interpreted him) agree that Olimpia is simultaneously familiar and unfamiliar. The difference lies in where they locate this play. Jentsch locates it across categories within a single ideational sphere or belief system, while Freud locates it across different belief systems.

This difference makes manifest an explanatory gap in Jentsch's account, which Freud's account fills. Freud explains *how* this play of familiarity and unfamiliarity is possible while Jentsch does not. For Freud, Olimpia can call the distinction between animate and inanimate (in our current belief system) into question only because her ambiguous in/animateness revives our latent belief in animism. Although Freud does not note it, Jentsch does mention that an "important factor in the origin of the uncanny is the natural tendency of man to infer [. . .] that things in the external world are [. . .] animate in the same way" as he is.[32] But Jentsch does not afford this animistic tendency pride of place and also grounds the possibility of the arising of the uncanny affect in primitiveness, childhood, ignorance, and various weakened psychological states. In mentioning these factors, Jentsch makes a cursory effort to fill the explanatory gap. But he does not confront the question of how an ambiguity of in/animateness can make the jointing of our ideational sphere questionable and so does not explain how our uncertainty about it can arise in the first place.

Jentsch seems to think that a phenomenon like Olimpia can simply show up as ambiguously in/animate—that our ideational sphere allows for the appearance of anomalies, and so is open to its own destabilization. But without a prior animistic belief system for a phenomenon like Olimpia to invoke, an ambiguously in/animate entity cannot be a possible object of experience for us. The entity would always show up in terms of the categories of our ideational sphere—as *either* animate or inanimate. At most, then, we could experience only an uncertainty like that of the tree/snake case: namely, the uncertainty attending temporary misidentification. If experiences of anomalies are to be possible, there must be something in us prepared to receive them. Freud recognizes that

[32] Jentsch, "On the Psychology of the Uncanny," 13.

something else needs to be in place for anomalous experiences to be possible, and he identifies this as the second, prior belief system. Strictly, then, it is this prior belief system that provokes our uncertainty and not the entity. Olimpia is the occasion for this uncertainty and not its ground.

Jentsch skirts the issue of how the uncanny affect can arise, but this is merely a symptom of what Freud thinks that Jentsch has missed. To see why, consider the sun case, which comes even closer to Freud's account and so throws the difference between Freud and Jentsch into sharp relief. In this case, the play of familiar and unfamiliar that produces the uncanny affect spans not opposed categories but two ideational spheres (or two portions of a single ideational sphere): the perceptual and the scientific. The uncertainty concerns which ideational sphere or belief system to inhabit, just as on Freud's account we are uncertain about whether to take up our old animistic beliefs or to remain with our current non-animistic beliefs. But there is a crucial difference: for Jentsch, we simultaneously have two equally legitimate and compatible ways of relating to the sun, and we do not need to reject one in favor of the other (even though we cannot inhabit both at once). For Freud, we have already rejected one of the belief systems and cannot hold it concurrently with the new. Our animistic beliefs have been surmounted, even if imperfectly. Freud's picture is of a diachronic uncertainty while Jentsch speaks of a synchronic uncertainty.

The temporal difference is significant because Freud wants to hold that it is this temporal dimension rather than the uncertainty itself that makes for the uncanny feeling. Uncertainty is not a necessary constituent of Freud's uncanny affect. It enters the picture only because what is at stake in this kind of uncanny experience is our adherence to particular beliefs and whether we hold these securely or not. But this explanation is "incomplete" since the uncanny feeling may arise in a completely different way.[33] Jentsch, Freud thinks, has no intimation of this second species of the uncanny, which shows the full role of time in the uncanny affect.

Freud distinguishes (i) the uncanny that is related to surmounted infantile or primitive beliefs and wishes, and (ii) the uncanny that is related to repressed childhood complexes. The latter is more rare in real life but Freud seems to think that it is more paradigmatic. His second criticism of Jentsch is that Jentsch's account misses the phenomenon of the uncanny in a story like "The Sandman" because he misses this kind of uncanniness. The uncanny motif in the story, according to Freud, is not the doll Olimpia but the figure of the Sandman, who threatens loss of

[33] Freud, "The Uncanny," 221.

eyes. The uncanny effect of the Sandman cannot be explained in terms of uncertainty but is instead due to the return of repressed childhood complexes—in this case, the castration complex.[34] We feel uncanny because we are reminded of this remnant of our past and such remembering involves neither belief nor uncertainty. Yet this uncanny experience has the same structure as the other species of the uncanny (that stemming from surmounted beliefs like animism). It must be this structure, then, that unites various instances of the uncanny under a common banner, and it is this that Jentsch has missed entirely. Freud calls this structure "the return of the repressed." The uncanny affect arises when an entity or experience prompts that which has been surmounted or repressed to express itself. Uncertainty is thus a contingent aspect in the genesis of the uncanny affect and belongs to only one species of it.

The return of the repressed can be captured by speaking of a splitting in the self, but I would like to bring out its temporal dimension.[35] When the repressed returns, the clean, linear progression of psychic development is disrupted. We are reminded of, or regress to, earlier stages of development. Since the act of repression converts any emotion attending what is repressed to anxiety, the return of what is repressed brings anxiety with it. Thus the association of the uncanny feeling with fear. But this feeling is also, and primarily, associated with strangeness. It is so because the repressed content that returns is ambiguously familiar and unfamiliar. It is familiar insofar as it belongs to an earlier stage of development but unfamiliar insofar as we have already passed through this stage and left it behind (either by repressing a complex and estranging it from the conscious mind or by surmounting a primitive belief system in favor of a new one). A loose analogue is the experience of hearing the sound of one's own alarm clock on television. Such an experience is palpably uncanny, but it is not so because it introduces an uncertainty as to whether or not I am asleep. I know full well that I am awake. What makes it uncanny is that a remnant of the condition of sleep is brought into the domain of wakefulness, where it does not belong. So too with the emergence of surmounted or repressed elements from one's pre-history in the present time. The uncanniness is not a matter of uncertainty but a matter of time.[36] As far as Freud is concerned—and following him, Derrida—if his father's ghost is uncanny for Hamlet it is not because Hamlet is uncertain whether it is living or dead but because it is neither and both past and

---

[34] Ibid., 231.

[35] For Freud's description in terms of a split self, see ibid., 234.

[36] This suggests that there is a close connection between Freud's uncanniness and *déjà vu*. See the section on *déjà vu* in Nicholas Royle, *The Uncanny* (New York: Routledge, 2003).

present.[37] It disrupts Hamlet's own timeline. What is out of joint about a ghost is not life but time.

So what Jentsch's uncanny is lacking, according to Freud, is the presence of the past in the present—a history that never remains past but which irrupts into the present and destabilizes it. This is what makes for the uncanny affect. Uncanniness involves uncertainty only when that which intrudes upon the present is a past set of beliefs, which intrusion disrupts our present set of beliefs. Jentsch's error stems from focusing on the role of uncertainty in such cases and neglecting the more fundamental temporal phenomenon. This leads him to offer cases of uncertainty that involve no obvious temporal disruption—not only the tree/snake case but also the rising of the sun. Recall that I deferred discussion of whether the sun example is an instance of the uncanny feeling. If this example does not involve the intrusion of a past upon a present, then either it is not uncanny or Freud's account is incomplete or mistaken. If Freud is right about uncanniness and the sun's rising can indeed be uncanny, then this example must manifest the temporal structure of the return of the repressed. What could the return of the repressed be in Jentsch's example?

Freud's account primes us to look for a past that belongs to infancy or, by extension, primitive stages in the development of humankind. We find no such past in the sun case. What shows up is not our past but the fact that familiarity involves a conflation of the familiar with the self-evident. But note that this feature of familiarity is usually concealed from us; we feel uncanny when it is revealed.[38] This is structurally similar to Freud's return of the repressed, which is the reappearance of repressed or surmounted—that is, concealed—infantile or primitive modes of thought. But the revelation of something concealed is not necessarily uncanny. (If it were, then finding out a secret would spark an uncanny feeling.) Freud's claim is that this revelation must be a disruption of temporality. What is concealed must be past and its revelation must disrupt the present. It is easy to see what this might involve in a Freudian story about the origin and development of the psyche. What could it mean in Jentsch's sun example, which is an episode in a story about familiarity?

In Jentsch's example, the past that irrupts into the present is not the pre-history of the individual or of the human race. It is the pre-history of familiarity. The conflation of known and self-evident is something that

---

[37] Derrida makes much of Hamlet's utterance "the time is out of joint" in his *Specters of Marx*. In "The Uncanny" (250), Freud explicitly denies that the ghost in *Hamlet* is uncanny for the reader, but this does not mean that it is not uncanny for Hamlet—and so that it would not be uncanny for us were we to encounter such a ghost in real life.

[38] Jentsch, "On the Psychology of the Uncanny," 9.

must take place 'before,' as it were, any familiarity or making-familiar. Such a pre-history does not take place in time and so is easy to overlook as something that belongs to the past. The past to which it belongs is that of an ontological or conceptual, rather than temporal, pre-history. Since it tells of a past that never took place, the story of familiarity as grounded in the concealed conflation of known and self-evident amounts to an origin myth of familiarity. (Indeed, Freud's own story of psychic development may be understood as a similar kind of origin myth. Freud is ambivalent—or at least, his interpreters are—about whether his primal histories are myths that tell the essence of the psyche or stories of actual historical events.) So while 'prior' for Freud is the prior of our infantile or primitive history, in Jentsch's sun example it is the 'prior' of a conceptual structure.

This pre-history of familiarity is 'repressed' or 'surmounted'—Jentsch says "concealed"—in the following sense.[39] The conditions of possibility of everyday familiarity do not themselves show up within everyday familiarity and so are not themselves familiar. While we are busy living in the realm of the familiar, we see only *what* is familiar and not that upon which familiarity is itself built. Jentsch holds that this concealment is necessary for familiarity, just as Freud holds that repression or the surmounting of primitive and infantile modes of thought is necessary for the development of the psyche. This similarity reveals the sense in which the pre-history of familiarity (the concealed conflation of the known and self-evident) is 'previously familiar.' The claim is not that it had been previously made familiar or recognized as such, since 'past' and 'previous' here do not refer to past experience. The concealed conflation is 'previously familiar' in the sense that it has already happened to us, where this means that it is always already at work behind, beneath, or before all making-familiar. Another way to put this prior familiarity is thus to say that we take familiarity and its ground for granted.

It follows that the revelation of the pre-history of familiarity is a disruption in our timeline of a special sort. When we grasp something about how familiarity works (as we do in the sun case), we experience our *essential* past while in the midst of our lives. Put differently, the conditions of familiarity (past) intrude into familiarity (present) itself. Such an experience is perhaps more vividly expressed in a spatial metaphor than in a temporal one: the (view from the) outside irrupts into the (view from the) inside. The spatial metaphor serves because at stake is a non-historical temporality. Extending Freud's temporal picture, then, allows us to fit

[39] Ibid., 9.

Jentsch's sun case into the structure of Freud's return of the repressed. We can identify (i) a 'prior' that accounts for the arising of the uncanny affect (primitive belief system/the essence or pre-history of familiarity), (ii) the concealment or repression of this 'prior,' and (iii) the return of this 'repressed,' understood as the irruption of the past (of the essence) in the present (of the living of it).

To complete this reading of Jentsch's picture, it would be necessary to interpret the uncanniness of the unfamiliar (especially as an ambiguity of in/animateness) in terms of the return of a similar *a priori* or mythical past—in this case, the jointing or articulation of familiarity. But I am not concerned to develop a complete and coherent reading of Jentsch on the uncanny—or of Freud on the uncanny, for that matter. Instead, I want to pursue the idea that I have built out of the confrontation between Freud and Jentsch: that the uncanny does or can belong to an encounter, within everyday life, with what lies before, outside, or beneath it.

Lear's Ironic Uncanniness

Jonathan Lear's 'ironic uncanniness' pushes Freud's uncanny in a direction similar to the one in which I have pushed it, but in a way that further extends our conceptual arsenal.[40] Lear appropriates Freud's concept to characterize what he calls 'the ironic experience,' in which I find myself committed to an ideal—say, being a teacher—but no longer have a sense for what living up to this ideal would look like. Received understandings of what it takes to be a teacher no longer seem adequate to the ideal itself. I am, we might say, profoundly struck by the question "What is it to be a teacher, anyway?" Lear takes pains to distinguish this ironic uncertainty from ordinary reflection on the adequacy of our practices, conceiving it as a very special kind of breakdown. I will touch on this later, but in general the details of Lear's picture will not concern me any more than is necessary to see how Lear makes use of Freud's uncanny. Recall that for Freud:

(a)   something familiar (and prior) (e.g., belief in animism)
(b)   undergoes a process of defamiliarization (e.g., is surmounted)
(c)   and returns to awareness—in such a way that it is marked by both the familiarity (a) and the unfamiliarity (b).

---

[40] Jonathan Lear, *A Case for Irony* (Cambridge, MA: Harvard University Press, 2011).

Now consider how Lear describes the experience of ironic uncanniness:

> [A] person gives a familiar designation to himself. He takes on a practical identity. As the irony unfolds, not only does the designation become weirdly unfamiliar; one suddenly experiences oneself as called to one-knows-not-what.[41]

> When irony hits its mark, the person who is its target has an uncanny experience that the demands of an ideal, value, or identity to which he takes himself to be already committed dramatically transcend the received social understandings. The experience is uncanny in the sense that what had been a familiar demand suddenly feels unfamiliar, calling one to an unfamiliar way of life; and yet the unfamiliarity also has a weird sense of familiarity; as though we can recognize that this is our commitment.[42]

As I understand it, the experience has the following structure, which Lear captures with the name 'pretense-transcending aspiring':

  (i)   Pretense: a familiar identity ('teacher'), to which I am committed (social role)
  (ii) Transcending: . . . suddenly becomes unfamiliar; I experience it as transcending the available social understandings of it (irony)
  (iii) Aspiring: . . . but in such a way that it remains oddly familiar since I remain committed to it (Eros)

Pretense-transcending aspiring—the experience of irony—offers itself to be described as 'uncanny' because of its play of familiarity and unfamiliarity. It looks like we have the Freudian uncanny: x is familiar at one point, then unfamiliar, then both together. What takes the place of repression in the ironic experience is my transcendence of the received social pretense. What the two share is that they each serve to defamiliarize. We see a 'return' of this 'repressed' insofar as my commitment to the ideal persists despite this defamiliarization: I remain committed to being a teacher, despite not knowing what this commitment should look like— that is, how to be a teacher.

This experience, as described, does not cleanly fit Freud's structure. Notice, first, the difference between (iii) and (c). One way to get at this difference is to say that what is oddly familiar in ironic uncanniness is not quite the same thing that was originally familiar. Step (i) speaks of

[41] Ibid., 16.
[42] Ibid., 25.

the familiar pretense (the socially available ways to put oneself forward as a teacher) but (iii) involves the familiarity of the ideal itself, which the pretense or social role purports to fill out. The center of this tension can be seen in (ii), in which the reference of 'it' is ambiguous. The 'it' that becomes unfamiliar is 'being a teacher,' but is this the transcendent ideal or the socially available pretense or both? Does the distinction cease to matter here? Or does the distinction first open up at this point? This latter strikes me as most plausible: the role/ideal suddenly comes to fall short of itself, and it is to express this self-undermining move that we distinguish an ideal from its expression in a social role. The splitting of self that is accomplished in Freudian repression is here accomplished as a splitting of the practical identity in terms of which I understand myself.

Yet for Freud, it must be the same thing that is originally familiar and that returns or persists. This is what produces the simultaneous familiarity and unfamiliarity. Lear's picture would have to look like this:

(i) An ideal is familiar to me, because I am committed to it (aspiration) *and* live it out in terms of received social understandings (pretense, social role),

(ii) but it becomes unfamiliar because I experience it as transcending the social pretense,

(iii) although it remains familiar since I am still committed to it (aspiration).

This revision makes plain that there are two senses in which the ideal is familiar. The revision works by shifting the original problem—that of having two distinct objects in (i) and (iii)—onto this doubled familiarity—marked by the 'and' in (i). First, an ideal is familiar insofar as I am committed to it; second, an ideal is familiar insofar as I know how to go about living it. In ironic uncanniness, the former persists and the latter does not. Are we still entitled to describe this as a simultaneous familiarity and unfamiliarity, given that the ideal is familiar in one way and unfamiliar in a distinct way? It seems that the split here is intractable because what happens in (ii), the moment of defamiliarization, is that a divorce is produced within my understanding of how to go about being a teacher. The split is between being committed to such going about and knowing how to do it (two senses of familiarity) and correspondingly between the ideal to which I am committed and the social role through which I express this commitment. It is this divorce that characterizes the ironic experience and which, presumably, distinguishes it from ordinary reflection on our practices and practical identities, which address only the social role. It is also this divorce that distinguishes ironic uncanniness from Freud's uncanny and garden-variety uncanny experiences.

Lear himself situates the persistent commitment to the ideal (iii) beyond Freud's uncanny. He describes it as "erotic":[43]

> [I]n an ordinary experience of the uncanny, there is mere disruption: the familiar is suddenly and disruptively experienced as unfamiliar. What is peculiar to irony is that it manifests passion for a certain direction. It is because I care about teaching that I have come to a halt as a teacher. Coming to a halt in a moment of ironic uncanniness is how I manifest—in that moment—that teaching matters to me. I have a strong desire to be moving in a certain direction—that is, in the direction of becoming and being a teacher—but I lack orientation. Thus the experience of irony is an experience of *would-be-directed* uncanniness. That is, an experience of standard-issue uncanniness may give us goose bumps or churn our stomachs; the experience of ironic uncanniness, by contrast, is more like losing the ground beneath one's feet: one longs to go in a certain direction, but one no longer knows where one is standing, if one is standing, or which direction is the right direction. In this paradigm example, ironic uncanniness is a manifestation of utter seriousness and commitment (in this case, to teaching), not its opposite.[44]

Lear is perhaps adverting to our common understanding of 'uncanniness' rather than to Freud's technical use of the term, but he seems to be attempting to solve the problem that I have identified. In effect, Lear tries to entwine the two senses of familiarity by showing that the loss of one manifests the other. He says that the unfamiliarity of not knowing how to go on in light of an ideal is a manifestation of familiarity *qua* continued commitment to an ideal. What it is to have a commitment, then, is to be serious about finding or having a way to manifest that commitment in our social lives—and so, to make it familiar in the ordinary sense of knowing where it fits or how to go about it. But the commitment itself is associated with familiarity in a different way. It is familiar insofar as it is *mine*, proper to me (L. *proprius*: one's own, personal, private, peculiar, etc.). This is what I want to bring out: a new resonance for the 'familiar,' which will be important for us later.

Using this new vocabulary, we can gloss Freud's uncanny in this way:

    (a)   something that is *mine* (e.g., belief in animism)

    (b)   is alienated from me, rejected (surmounted, repressed)

    (c)   but then returns to me, as both *mine* and *not mine*.

[43] Ibid., 20.
[44] Ibid., 19.

This is a common way to think about the dynamics of the psyche and particularly the act of repressing as an act of disowning. The gloss relies on the thought that what is familiar is not only what is known or understood but also what is *recognized,* plus the thought that what I recognize first of all is what is *mine.*

But even in this vocabulary, Lear's picture does not quite map onto Freud's—especially in the second step: repression or transcendence. Transcendence works as an equivalent to repression only if the sense of familiarity or unfamiliarity at this step is different from what it is in the first and/or third step. This is because transcendence is the opening up of the distinction between the ideal and its expression in social practices, which Lear needs but which introduces a new kind of familiarity/unfamiliarity. So I am inclined to disagree with Lear's assessment that the *erotic,* directed, and serious, aspect of ironic uncanniness is not present in Freud's uncanny. Either it corresponds to the return of the repressed (the part of the picture to which it is supposed to correspond) or Lear's picture is not a picture of Freudian uncanniness.

The real difference between Lear's ironic experience and Freud's uncanny lies in the temporality or the kinetic structure of each. For Freud, what is originally familiar belongs to the (often distant) past, as does its repression. (If we think of repression—as we should—as an ongoing activity, then it is the initiation of this activity that we locate at a prior point in time.) The return of the repressed can occur at any time and when it does so it is a sudden return. Thus:

(a)   (more or less distant) past
(b)   (more or less distant) past (or ongoing)
(c)   now, all of a sudden

On Lear's picture, in contrast, what is equivalent to repression (defamiliarization) is what *happens* in the experience rather than the condition for it, and the 'return' of what is thus repressed is less a return than a continuation. What is moving and what is staying still are entirely different from what is moving and what is staying still on Freud's account. For Lear:

(i)   past/ongoing
(ii)   now, all of a sudden
(iii) ongoing

We could possibly say that (ii) and (iii) both happen now and all of a sudden, if my continued commitment to the ideal is in fact a reaffirmation of my commitment despite its defamiliarization. There are interesting issues here surrounding the temporality of commitment. Notice, in this regard, that (i) does not mark a literal past or a temporal priority. It is not even a conceptual or essential priority. Rather, what makes my commitment to an ideal 'prior' to its defamiliarization is the foundational character of that commitment. Being committed to being a teacher, say, is 'below' or 'before' any particular event in my life. It is *always already* there. It precedes any experience I might have as teacher, including my loss of the sense of what it is to go on as a teacher. This introduces a new kind of temporality in terms of which to think about the uncanny, in addition to those that we have seen before.

What happens in the experience of irony is that this 'past' of an ongoing commitment, which is normally 'below the surface' of our lives, forces its way up to us as a question. As such, ironic uncanniness remains a disruption of temporality—or, strictly, priority. Usually, in being committed to an ideal, *what* it is that one is committed to is largely settled *before* one goes about trying to live up to it, in the sense that it is the foundation for such going about. In ironic breakdown, however, one is committed to an ideal and experiences a desire to go about living up to it but lacks any idea of how to do this. As Lear puts it: "one longs to go in a certain direction, but one no longer knows where one is standing."[45] This is the ironically uncanny version of what it is like to have the timeline of psychic life disrupted. Recall that it is this disorder of time that distinguishes the Freudian uncanny proper from mere uncertainty. So too for Lear, we might say, it is the ideal itself (and not the social pretense) coming into question that distinguishes irony from ordinary reflective assessment of practices. The ideal itself, which usually recedes beneath daily life, comes to the fore.[46]

A related point is that what occasions an experience of ironic uncanniness is not some external event but the ideal itself. Ideals disrupt themselves. This is why Lear rejects the metaphor of the 'outside' irrupting into the 'inside,' which I have used (and will continue to use). In response

[45] Ibid., 19.

[46] This way of thinking about the temporality of commitment suggests an alternative route that one might take to map this experience onto Freud's uncanny: we take on an ideal, which retreats into the background (the priority of a commitment) and can then irrupt into ordinary life when it becomes questionable. The problem with this reading is that it is likely false of commitments and ideals that we take them on consciously; Lear in particular is committed to rejecting this (see especially the second lecture, "Ironic Soul," in Lear, *A Case for Irony*).

to Christine Korsgaard, Lear writes: "Insofar as there is a narrative here, I do not think it is captured by the image of inside and outside. Rather, the image is of a form of life and a moment of breakdown *internal* to that form of life."[47] There is nothing external, alien, or other that intrudes upon the ideal and my life with it. Rather, ideals are self-undermining. Although for Freud the uncanny feeling is possible because repression, as a part of psychic development, is not a perfect mechanism, it remains the case that he requires something to 'set off' the return of the repressed. Something has to get into the crack that the imperfection of repression has produced and wedge it open. For Lear, ironic uncanniness is possible because ideals are inherently unstable and can manifest this instability at any point without any particular catalyst.

Lear explains that if ideals or practical identities must be expressed in particular social practices, and if these practices never exhaust or fully express the ideal, then there is always a possibility of this gap showing up to us.[48] Such disruption does not require the intrusion of any third party or the appearance of any third term. We can put it actively by saying that I must be able to transcend received social understandings of an ideal, or passively by saying that the ideal manifests itself to me as exceeding these.[49] The metaphor most appropriate to this experience may thus be not 'inside/outside' but 'depths/surface' or 'background/foreground.' It is not that something external intrudes but that something submerged comes to the surface or that I reach a new height of perspective.

Much depends, however, on how we identify the 'inside' and 'outside.' I think that there are ways of using this vocabulary that avoid the misleading impression that Lear is worried about. If the 'inside' is ordinary daily life, then an explicit encounter with one's commitments and ideals is indeed an intrusion from the 'outside'—not in the sense of what is not mine or foreign to me but in the sense of what makes possible and shapes the inside. Here, the 'inside' is what is ordinarily familiar, the everyday. It is only when we identify 'the inside' with 'what is mine' that this vocabulary is misleading. Once again, it is important to keep these two senses of familiarity distinct.

[47] Ibid., 116.

[48] Ibid., 22.

[49] Lear also allows (or this may be the same thing) that the experience of irony can arise from a confrontation between one's conscious practical identity and one's unconscious practical identity. See the second lecture, "Ironic Soul," especially ibid., 60–61.

In any case, because ironic uncanniness is not occasioned by something other than me and my commitments, what is revealed to me in it is something about me and my commitments—namely, the instability of the latter. For Freud, what shows up in the uncanny experience is the object that occasioned it (e.g., the Sandman, the crocodile table) and only secondarily (on reflection or for the analyst) what it is about me that makes this experience possible. So too for Jentsch: we do not simply grasp the gap between our ways of making familiar and the things that are made familiar; we experience this gap *through* a particular entity—for example, the sun. In ironic uncanniness, we are directly exposed to the instability of our ideal rather than to some consequence of this instability. Lear continues the passage I quoted earlier:

> But, as I shall argue, a stronger claim is warranted: namely, developing a capacity for ironic disruption may be a manifestation of seriousness about one's practical identity. It is not merely a disruption of one's practical identity; it is a form of loyalty to it. So, my ironic experience with teaching manifests an inchoate intimation that there is something valuable about teaching—something excellent as a way of being human—that isn't quite caught in contemporary social pretense or in normal forms of questioning that pretense. [. . . I]t is a mistake to think that if we just got our social practice—say, of teaching—into good shape, there would no longer be room for ironic disruption of practical identity. It is constitutive of our life with the concepts with which we understand ourselves that they are subject to ironic disruption.[50]

The instability of our ideals is not a failure or defect that we ought to seek to remedy. It is part of what it is to have ideals, and so facing up to this risk is part of what it is to have ideals *well*. We are essentially erotic creatures whose lives are unstable, risky, and subject to breakdown. The ironic experience depends upon these features of human life and exposes us to them. This latter claim may be going beyond Lear, but it seems to me that what the ironic experience reveals to us is nothing other than the instability that makes it possible. To no longer know what it is to be a teacher is to see that this ideal transcends the social roles that represent it, and for the ideal to transcend the social roles that represent it is for it to be at risk of disruption. The ironic experience directly reveals crucial features of human nature, including that we are erotic and finite: committed, transcending, and vulnerable.

---

[50] Ibid., 22.

The Absurd Feeling

Lear's ironic, uncanny experience reveals the inherent instability in human life that brings about such an experience. The experience includes the moment of defamiliarization, which Freud identifies as a condition of, rather than part of, the uncanny feeling. I have used Lear's account to add the sense of 'the own' or 'the proper' to our talk of 'the familiar' and to extend the range of non-historical pasts at stake to include not only the conceptual pre-history or essential pre-history but also the background of a foundational commitment. We feel uncanny when the *seemingly* unfamiliar past, outside, background, or basis destabilizes the everyday, familiar present, inside, foreground, or surface.

Like Lear's ironic uncanniness, Albert Camus's and Thomas Nagel's respective absurd feelings reveal a fundamental instability in human life. Both describe this as our essential absurdity, again pairing the feeling with the feature of us that it reveals and which makes it possible. Indeed, the absurd feeling is strikingly similar to the uncanny feeling. It is typically attributed to the experience of the essential past from within the midst of everyday life. We feel absurd when we take a 'step back' from our ordinary lives and see them from the outside for what they 'really' are.

Camus catalogues various loci of the absurd experience: "the stage sets collapse" on my daily routine and I see it *as* a play; I am "seized" by the "horror" of the passage of time and the fact that I "belong" to it; I sense that the natural world "is foreign and irreducible" to me; a slice of a stranger's life appears as nothing more than a "meaningless pantomime."[51] The most common absurd experience is perhaps that occasioned by the natural world: "perceiving that the world is 'dense', sensing to what a degree a stone is foreign and irreducible to us, with what intensity nature or a landscape can negate us. At the heart of all beauty lies something inhuman. [. . .] The world evades us because it becomes itself again. That stage scenery masked by habit becomes again what it is. It withdraws at a distance from us."[52] This distance, and so the strangeness of the natural world, obtains when the world's 'aspects' "lose the illusory meaning with which we had clothed them."[53] Ordinarily, we make the natural world familiar by understanding it in human terms—whether in terms of our activity ('this is the hill that I walk up on the way to work'), our needs ('this riverbank is a good location for a

---

[51] Albert Camus, *The Myth of Sisyphus and Other Essays*, trans. Justin O'Brien (New York: Vintage Books, 1991), 12, 13, 14, and 15, respectively.

[52] Ibid., 14.

[53] Ibid., 14.

photograph'), our perception ('the sun rises in the East'), or the rules of logical thought (e.g., the principle of non-contradiction). To make things familiar is to humanize. "Understanding the world for a man is reducing it to the human, stamping it with his seal. [. . . T]he mind that aims to understand reality can consider itself satisfied only by reducing it to terms of thought."[54] But this satisfaction does not satisfy because it fails to achieve what the mind desires. Specifically, it necessarily fails to get at the world as something apart from human beings with its own principle of unity. Thought misses its object, grasping it only as it is reflected in thought itself and its laws.

This self-impeding of thought is revealed in the absurd experience. In the absurd experience, our ways of knowing cease to stick to the world and so show their inadequacy to the world as it is in itself. As in Jentsch's sun case, this is an experience of an essential gap or discrepancy between our ways of making sense of things and the things themselves. The difference is that, for Camus, the revelation of this discrepancy is not sparked by simultaneously making sense of the world in two different ways. The Jentschian experience, with its multiplicity of ideational spheres, is cacophonous; Camus's absurd experience is quite silent. We encounter the world itself in its mute and naked otherness and so directly experience it as escaping any conceptualization. This strikes me as closer to Lear's ironic uncanniness, at least insofar as the ideal that we encounter in this experience is similarly silent. In these experiences, there is *less* to hold onto than before, whereas for Jentsch the problem is that there is too much to grasp at once. And just as for Lear ironic uncanniness reveals that social practices will never exhaust the ideal, so too for Camus the absurd experience reveals that the ways we make the world familiar do not capture it. They are nothing more than crude and impoverished metaphors. This is the Jentschian insight, won in a different way.

The term 'absurdity' is used for this experience and for the dimension of the human essence that it reveals because an absurdity is a kind of contradiction or discrepancy.[55] Although Camus wavers on it, the discrepancy in question is not properly that between the mind and the world. It is a self-contradiction internal to the mind, which desires to know the world as it is in itself but must employ means incommensurate to that end (namely, humanizing thinking). That we must employ such means—not only to satisfy our desire but in order to be at all—distinguishes absurdity from mere disappointment. Attempts to satisfy our desire to understand

---

[54] Ibid., 17.
[55] Ibid., 29.

are inherently self-undermining. This feature of human nature makes the human being itself—rather than the human-world relation—absurd.

Thomas Nagel also takes human nature to be absurd by virtue of a discrepancy, although for him it is a discrepancy between our ordinary, everyday self-understanding and a skeptical self-understanding.[56] Specifically, there is a discrepancy between the pretension or aspiration embodied in our everyday self-understanding and the reality of our everyday self-understanding as it is revealed in the skeptical perspective. In our everyday action, we purport to be fully rational in the sense that we take our actions to be backed up by reasons. This is part of what it is to understand oneself as a rational agent. But when we take a 'step backwards' (or a "transcendental step") and view our actions from the outside, we see that we are not rational all the way down.[57] Our reason-giving runs out in a set of basic reasons for which we can give no further reasons. These are "responses and habits that we never question," such as seeking comfort and avoiding pain.[58]

Nagel understands the absurd experience by analogy with epistemological skepticism, which has the same structure: in everyday life, we count ourselves as having knowledge only when our true beliefs are justified. Yet when we consider human knowledge as a whole, we find that it rests on a set of unjustified beliefs or assumptions. Everyday knowledge works by excluding certain possibilities (such as evil demons) and taking certain things for granted (such as the veracity of our senses). So for both knowledge and action, there is a discrepancy between how it shows up in the midst of life (as justified or rational at every step) and how it shows up from the outside (as finitely justified or rational). This is a discrepancy between two different ways in which we can understand ourselves and our own knowledge or agency. The absurd experience is an experience of this discrepancy.

Ultimately, Nagel's absurd experience depends on the fact that we can take different perspectives on our lives. We can view human life both from the inside, as we are living it, and from the outside, from which perspective we can determine its structure and see how it works. These two perspectives show us different and conflicting things about human life. When we inhabit both simultaneously, we experience the discrepancy between what they show—and we feel absurd. That we simultaneously dwell in two different perspectives on a single entity makes this like

---

[56] Thomas Nagel, "The Absurd," *Mortal Questions* (Cambridge: Cambridge University Press, 1991), 13.

[57] For the phrase "transcendental step" see ibid., for example 21.

[58] Ibid., 15.

Jentsch's sun example, as does the fact that for Nagel the absurd feeling is resolved when we resume our everyday perspective and return to our lives 'ironically.'[59] Further, Nagel's absurd experience reveals that our familiar self-understanding works by covering over the finitude of justification, just as for Jentsch familiarity works by covering over the finitude of knowledge, which does not attain self-evidence. Similarly for Camus, for whom the absurd experience reveals that our everyday familiarity with the world is an illusion grounded in the concealment of the fact that knowledge does not succeed in knowing the world. The difference between Camus, on the one hand, and Jentsch and Nagel, on the other hand, is that the latter two take this covering over to be how knowledge *works,* while Camus takes it to be how knowing *fails.*

There are many significant differences between the two accounts. However, , both can be seen to fit Freud's structure of the return of the repressed. Camus and Nagel both take the absurd experience to reveal how familiarity is constituted: the essential structure of knowledge (or rational action). Both take this to be necessarily covered over as a condition of that very knowledge, as in Jentsch's concealed conflation of the known and self-evident. For Camus, this is the habitual illusion that knowing grasps the world itself, and for Nagel it is the pretense that reasons go all the way down. For all, we feel absurd or uncanny when the veil drops and we see what it takes to have knowledge or to dwell in the familiar. The constitutive structure of familiarity is revealed; the repressed returns.

Since what is 'repressed' or concealed here is the essential rather than the historical past, the disruption that marks its return is better expressed in a spatial than a temporal metaphor: the outside is brought into the inside. The 'inside' is our going about in the midst of everyday life and the 'outside' is the essential structure of such familiar, everyday life. (So this is not quite the 'outside' to which Lear objects.) The outside is what 'returns' and its return does not remove us from the 'inside' of the midst of life but takes place within it. Nagel puts this well: "[W]hen we take this [outside] view and recognize what we do as arbitrary, it does not disengage us from life, and there lies our absurdity: not in the fact that such an external view can be taken of us, but in the fact that we ourselves can take it, without ceasing to be the persons whose ultimate concerns are so coolly regarded."[60] We do not feel uncanny or absurd because we are viewing ourselves from the outside (i.e., because the constitution of familiarity is manifest to us). Rather, we feel uncanny or absurd because

[59] Ibid., 20.
[60] Ibid., 15.

this 'outside' is manifest to us from the 'inside.' We simultaneously stand inside and outside our lives, living them *and* watching how they operate. (Since we cannot genuinely act when we are spectators of our lives, nothing can happen in this absurd experience and it cannot be maintained as a way of living in the midst of life.) This simultaneity of inside and outside is the same as the simultaneity of past and present in Freud's uncanny.

What Camus and Nagel add to our thinking of the uncanny is the resemblance of the absurd or uncanny experience to a skeptical experience. This resemblance is explicitly noted in Nagel's essay and manifest in Camus's vocabulary and examples. Both distinguish the practical absurd experience from the experience of the mind reflecting on its own operation, but for both the model of the absurd experience is clearly skeptical: we step back from everyday knowing and going about, reflecting on the adequacy of this everyday knowing and going about to its own pretensions. We find ourselves falling short, at odds with ourselves: there is a discrepancy between our desires and claims to know (or to have reasons) and the fulfillment of those desires and claims.

The skeptical model encourages us to see the absurd experience as an exercise of a detached rationality—dissociative and depersonalized. Nagel speaks of observing and spectating our lives "with that detached amazement which comes from watching an ant struggle up a heap of sand," and viewing our commitments as do anthropologists: "as no more than a curiosity, like a ritual of an alien religion."[61] This is one reason that Lear rejects Nagel's model as inappropriate to the ironic experience, which "by contrast, is a peculiar form of *committed* reflection."[62] Nagel's picture implies that the 'outside' to which the 'transcendental step' leads me really is outside of my life—a genuinely third-personal standpoint. But if it is also the case that we remain *inside* our lives while inhabiting this outside perspective, we might wonder whether it is possible to take up such a thoroughly third-personal perspective.

Indeed, we might wonder with Lear whether there is an 'idealization of reflection' in this picture.[63] Perhaps Nagel and Camus have purified— and so misunderstood—skepticism. Consider Stanley Cavell's description

[61] Ibid., 15 and 21, respectively.

[62] Lear, *A Case for Irony*, 21. Note that Lear rejects the model of reflection for other reasons also. Consider his response to Korsgaard: "There is no way to account for irony as a manifestation of reflective distance, no matter how special. The experience of irony is a peculiar form of *breakdown* of the reflective structure that Korsgaard describes. And the breakdown of a structure is not another instance of it." Ibid., 94. This is an enormously complicated point, and I await more from Lear on it.

[63] Ibid., 21.

of the skeptical impulse: "The skeptic does not gleefully and mindlessly forgo the world we share, or thought we shared; he is neither the knave Austin took him to be, nor the fool the pragmatists took him for, nor the simpleton he seems to men of culture and of the world. He forgoes the world for just the reason that the world is important, that it is the scene and stage of connection with the present: he finds that it vanishes exactly with the effort to *make* it present."[64] The skeptical 'step backwards' is a manifestation of commitment and passion—pathological, to be sure, but necessary nonetheless. The skeptic may appear to be a detached and neutral spectator but she is in fact a desperate seeker who longs to know and fears failure. Camus himself may be the most transparent of the skeptics in philosophy: he plainly manifests the intense passion and crushing disappointment of skepticism, which culminate for him in the live question of suicide. Encountering a hiccup in the normal operation of things, Camus concludes that the entire enterprise of knowing is a failure and asks whether it is possible to continue living. Such reflection is skeptical, but it is not detached.

Nagel will have none of this. He says to Camus that absurdity "need not be a matter for agony unless we make it so" and that "[s]uch dramatics, even if carried on in private, betray a failure to appreciate the cosmic unimportance of the situation."[65] This is why the absurd experience is for him merely a telling oddity from which we return to our lives, the only difference being that we now have a sense of ironic distance from ourselves. But if Nagel holds on to such detachment, then his absurd experience becomes significantly less interesting. Without my commitments and passions, the person who inhabits the 'outside stance' is not me but merely some shadow of me. And if it is not me who is thus outside, then the outside does not intrude into and disrupt my everyday life. It is merely a shift in perspective, as when we notice the camera angle chosen when watching a film. Without intrusion and disruption, the absurd experience is a mere curiosity and not an experience that is noteworthy or philosophically interesting. It is certainly not similar to Freud's uncanny, which requires the past that returns to be genuinely mine and exert a real pull on me. If the past that returns is the past of the essence, then this too must exert a pull on me—it must stand as an ideal or standard, to which I am committed and so the satisfaction of which *matters* to me.

---

[64] Stanley Cavell, "The Uncanniness of the Ordinary," *In Quest of the Ordinary: Lines of Skepticism and Romanticism* (Chicago: University of Chicago Press, 1994), 173.
[65] Nagel, "The Absurd," 23.

The Uncanniness of the Ordinary

The uncanny feeling may arise in a broadly skeptical way, but only on a Cavellian understanding of skepticism. However, Cavell differs from our other authors, and from Heidegger, in his understanding of what this feeling reveals. For Cavell, the uncanny feeling reveals the everyday that we have lost, just as being ill first makes health—which was previously transparent—manifest. This experience does not reveal our essence to us, much less as an uncanny or absurd essence. And yet we might wonder whether the skeptical impulse itself does not belong to or manifest something like an essential uncanniness. Let me explain.

Start with ordinary, familiar, everyday life. We manage to go about our business by and large successfully. But we possess a tendency to disrupt this everyday and to make the ordinary extraordinary or uncanny. This drive to self-disruption is paradigmatically manifest in philosophical skepticism, so Cavell calls it 'the skeptical impulse.' For example, the skeptical impulse might seize on an ordinary failure of communication—someone withholds information, does not accurately express herself, or is misunderstood. The skeptic is *horrified* by this failure and realizes "that I may be suffering when no one else is, and that no one (else) may know (or care?); and that others may be suffering and I not know, which is equally appalling."[66] The skeptic is so afraid of this situation and so desperate to know and be known that she overreacts. Our ways of knowing about other people's feelings and experiences come to seem grossly inadequate; she worries that perhaps she never *really* knows whether someone else is suffering or not. With this 'really,' we have full-blown skepticism.[67]

The skeptical move makes the ordinary extraordinary or uncanny. The ordinary or everyday is a condition of unproblematic familiarity: an original "intimacy" with things. The skeptical move denies or repudiates the adequacy of this everyday—for instance, the adequacy of ordinary knowing or communication. It is a movement of transcendence that posits an overinflated ideal (e.g., of knowing) in comparison with which the everyday is lacking. (Note that this is very different from Lear's ironic

[66] Stanley Cavell, "Knowing and Acknowledging," *Must We Mean What We Say?: A Book of Essays* (Cambridge: Cambridge University Press, 2002), 247.

[67] "At some stage the skeptic is going to be impressed by the fact that my knowledge of others depends upon their *expressing themselves,* in word and conduct. That is surely an essential fact to be impressed by. And then he realizes that the other may not in fact express himself, or that his expression may be falsified (deliberately or in some other way); and that again is undeniable. It follows that in such a case I would not know what is going on in the other. So the skeptic adds, supposing himself to express that fact, 'But still, *he* knows.'" Ibid., 254.

experience, in which the transcendent ideal does not have accessible content.) We can understand this as a repression, exclusion, or rejection of our original intimacy and familiarity. In our disappointment at this failure, the everyday first appears to us. It is retrospectively recognized, as lost.[68] Our everyday intimacy and familiarity with things is no longer our simple habitat but shows up to us, and it does so as strange and alien. The ordinary has become strange.

We recognize in Cavell's picture the familiar idea that we see our lives only when they stop working, or that the activity of looking at our lives alienates us from them and causes them to break down. As with the absurd experience, we can see this as an original familiarity repressed or rejected that returns to us as rejected and so no longer as our own. The ordinary or everyday, on this story, can *only* appear under the mark of the uncanny. But it is unclear exactly what Cavell means by this uncanniness or the extraordinariness of the ordinary. Is the ordinary uncanny because it is lost and so no longer familiar but nonetheless our own? Is it uncanny or strange in comparison to the skeptical ideal? Is it that we come to be amazed, from the skeptical perspective, that we ever unproblematically inhabited the everyday? Cavell insists that there is an uncanniness here, but the details are never spelled out.

Cavell spends most of his effort diagnosing the skeptical move that produces uncanniness in the first place. In the case I described above, the skeptic has vividly experienced the fact that people are separate or distinct and so must express themselves to one another. Like Camus, the skeptic takes this distance to be a failure of knowledge or language: "a metaphysical finitude as an intellectual lack."[69] She concludes that there is something important that she cannot do but ought to be able to do, and she sets about finding a way to achieve it. Our metaphysical separateness becomes an epistemological isolation that needs to be remedied but cannot be. This is an understandable, and very human, reaction. But it is no less pathological for that. According to Cavell, what we should take away from experiences of the limits of knowledge or failures of communication is that our separateness and the difficulties that it can produce place an ethical demand and responsibility on us to understand one another as best we can and to respond appropriately. That understanding one another does not always come easily or happen perfectly

---

[68] Cavell attributes this insight about skepticism to Wittgenstein, who "takes the drift toward skepticism as the *discovery* of the everyday, a discovery of exactly *what* it is that skepticism would deny." Cavell, "The Uncanniness of the Ordinary," 170.

[69] Cavell, "Knowing and Acknowledging," 263.

does not mean that it is impossible but only that we have an obligation to make an effort.

So the skeptical move beyond the ordinary and everyday is a falsified or distorted view on the world. We need to learn to cope with and compensate for it—as if it were a chronic illness—but we cannot or should not seek to avoid it. The skeptical impulse is part of our broadly philosophical—and so human—nature (so that the ordinary or everyday is "something that the very impulse to philosophy, the impulse to take thought about our lives, inherently seeks to deny, as if what philosophy is dissatisfied by is inherently the everyday").[70] As human beings, we cannot rest unproblematically in the everyday but must make the skeptical move. At best, we can 'resettle' the everyday and learn to appropriately mourn its loss.[71] But because such self-disruption is necessary, "an irreducible region of our unhappiness is natural to us but at the same time unnatural."[72]

This is a somewhat tragic picture of human nature. Cavell sees skepticism as "a place, perhaps the central secular place, in which the human wish to deny the condition of human existence is expressed"; it is "an argument internal to the individual, or separate, human creature, as it were an argument of the self with itself (over its finitude)."[73] The human being, then, is "inherently strange, say unstable, its quotidian [. . .] forever fantastic."[74] What is the human such that it is essentially driven to deny the condition of its own existence? What is it about our human powers that puts us at odds with our own finitude? Is there not something strange, perhaps even uncanny, in a creature thus constituted? Perhaps it is only an uncanny being that can make its ordinary life extraordinary. There are hints that for Cavell, it is not the ordinary so much as we ourselves who are uncanny.

The suggestion is that the feature of human life that makes it possible for us to feel uncanny also makes us be uncanny. Insofar as the uncanny feeling reveals to us those features of ourselves that bring it about, the uncanny feeling will reveal an essential uncanniness.

I have explicitly brought out this deeper revelation in Cavell's and Lear's accounts. Camus speaks of the discovery of absurdity, as if absurdity belonged to the human condition independently of the absurd

---

[70] Cavell, "The Uncanniness of the Ordinary," 170–171.
[71] Ibid., 176, 172.
[72] Stanley Cavell, "The Philosopher in American Life," *In Quest of the Ordinary*, 9.
[73] Both quotes are from Cavell, "The Philosopher in American Life," 5.
[74] Cavell, "The Uncanniness of the Ordinary," 154.

experience.[75] If absurdity lies in the conflict between the mind's desire and the means that it employs to fulfill this desire, and if both are essential to the mind, then absurdity must belong to the mind itself. It will be revealed in the absurd feeling but will characterize us independently of that feeling. Similarly for Jentsch, who not only says that we feel uncanny when the conflation between the known and self-evident comes to our awareness but also suggests that we *are* uncanny by virtue of this conflation. He says, "disorientation remains concealed for as long as the confusion of 'known/self-evident' does not enter the consciousness of the individual."[76] What is this concealed disorientation? Jentsch understands the uncanny feeling as an experience of disorientation or uncertainty. If the conflation of known and self-evident amounts to a disorientation, and if this disorientation is uncanniness, then uncanniness will belong first of all to the constitution of familiarity and only secondarily to the revelation of this in the uncanny feeling.

On the other hand, it seems that for Freud the uncanny is nothing but an affective property, and that for Nagel the absurd feeling is a condition of an essential absurdity rather than *vice versa*. Since absurdity consists in the discrepancy between our pretension (to have full justification) and the reality (that we have finite justification), absurdity obtains only when we experience the discrepancy. We are absurd only when we take the step beyond our lives, and so we are absurd only when we feel absurd.[77] And yet—what of this essential finitude in knowledge or justification? Being finite is a way of being limited and implicitly a way of failing. Is there perhaps an essential discrepancy internal to justification, which seeks to give reasons but which runs out at some point? Similarly for Freud. We are receptive to the affective property, uncanniness, because of the imperfection of the mechanism of repression, which opens the possibility of something repressed returning. But is there not something uncanny in our constitution as creatures who are imperfectly self-alienating?

There may be sense to be made of the idea that human beings are essentially uncanny because of some concealment, gap, lack, discrepancy, excess, finitude, or self-disruption. Such uncanniness would belong to the human essence as part of the human project of making familiar or making sense of things. We may be uncanny because we make things familiar by covering over the gap between known and self-evident (Jentsch), because justification is finite (Nagel), because the mind's means are inappropriate

[75] Camus, *The Myth of Sisyphus*, 23, 25, 30, 34, 94, 95, 122.
[76] Jentsch, "On the Psychology of the Uncanny," 9.
[77] Nagel, "The Absurd," 23.

to its goal (Camus), because our ideals exceed our practices (Lear), because repression is imperfect (Freud), or because we are self-repudiating
(Cavell). These may all point to different features of human nature or
to the same fundamental feature. Our essential uncanniness may be, as
Jentsch has it, ordinarily concealed from us. It may be revealed to us
through the experience or feeling of uncanniness, which would then be
not merely the uncanny return of the repressed but the uncanny return of
a repressed uncanniness. In the next chapter, I outline Heidegger's version
of such being uncanny.

2

Feeling Our Being Uncanny

I F WE BOTH are and feel uncanny, then it is tempting to think that it is
when we feel uncanny that we are exposed to the fact that we are
uncanny. This would produce a certain doubling of the uncanny, of the
kind that we find in Jentsch's picture. We seem to find a similar doubling
in Heidegger's discussion of the uncanny in SZ. Heidegger talks about
both the uncanniness of Dasein (roughly, human existing) (SZ189) and
the uncanniness of "everyday familiar being-in-the-world" (SZ342). We
might take the latter to be the feeling that attends familiar things becoming strange and identify this event as the experience of angst—in which,
as Heidegger says, "one feels '*uncanny*'" ["*ist einem* 'unheimlich'"]
(SZ188). The former, then, is a different and more essential uncanniness
in Dasein itself and it is revealed when the familiar becomes strange. So
there is an uncanniness that we feel and an uncanniness that we are.

But there is no such doubling of uncanniness in SZ. The uncanniness
of 'everyday familiar being-in-the-world' is the same as Dasein's essential
uncanniness, and it is revealed in angst because angst exposes Dasein to
its own being. To understand this uncanniness, we need to pursue angst
and what it reveals at length. Ultimately, we will see that angst—like uncanniness—must be understood at the level of essence rather than at that
of experienced feeling. This will in turn situate uncanniness at the very
ground of human existing.

The Methodological Role of Angst

It is not obvious what Heidegger has in mind by 'angst.' Is it what we
know as anxiety? Is it depression? Or is it existential angst of the sort that
characterizes a midlife crisis or a significant life change? The text seems
to bear any and all of these interpretations. Perhaps a more productive

way to approach angst is to ask why Heidegger analyzes it. Heidegger says that the analysis of angst plays a methodological role (SZ181, 182, 184, 185, 190). Since he analyzes this mood only as much as he needs to in order to achieve his broader goal, Heidegger does not have a completely worked out phenomenology of it. This is why it is not obvious which mood he is talking about. Our best approach is to identify the methodological role of angst.

Typically, angst is taken to deserve its place in SZ by virtue of its connection to authenticity or ownedness. Angst is the mood that brings us to our authentic being, and an authentic existence is one that either experiences angst or is ready for such an experience. Angst thus belongs to the story told in Division II of SZ about anticipatory resoluteness, alongside the accounts of the call of conscience and being-towards-death. Yet Heidegger analyzes angst in Division I. Why? The peculiar location of the analysis of angst is rarely acknowledged; it is often denied or dismissed.[1] The analysis of angst comes hard on the heels of Heidegger's account of falling; it allows him to transition from the analysis of Dasein's everydayness to the characterization of the unity of Dasein's being. It is needed for this transition because the analysis of angst solves a very particular problem.[2]

The problem that the analysis of angst is supposed to solve is that it belongs to everydayness that we fail to see our own being. This failure to grasp our being is falling. Falling is our being amidst *(bei)* entities or our openness to them (SZ175). (Elsewhere, Heidegger uses 'falling' differently, to name unowned or inauthentic being amidst entities. I leave this unowned falling aside for the moment.) Despite the term's theological heritage, 'falling' *(Verfallen)* names not a fall from grace but something like an ontological 'motion' (SZ180). Talk of motion metaphorically grasps the dative structure of our openness to being or meaning. Such openness is distinctive of Dasein, and it is always an openness *to* entities, in their being. This *to which* can be grasped as a motion: openness is pulled or drawn out *towards . . .* ; 'falling' captures this opening out. Extending the metaphor, opening *out* can be expressed as a motion *from . . .*

---

[1] Dreyfus, for instance, imaginatively moves the analysis of angst out of Division I, reserving discussion of it for his treatment of Division II. Hubert L. Dreyfus, *Being-in-the-World: A Commentary on Heidegger's* Being and Time, *Division I* (Cambridge, MA: The MIT Press, 1991). He acknowledges that angst plays a methodological role in SZ (176) but does not explore it, citing a confusion in the notion of falling (226).

[2] For a more detailed analysis of the methodological role of angst in SZ, see Katherine Withy, "The Methodological Role of Angst in *Being and Time,*" *Journal of the British Society for Phenomenology* 43:2 (2012): 195–211.

and accordingly described as a 'flight': openness 'flees' *from* something *to* entities. (The vocabulary of flight will be significant later, when we see that falling is a flight from uncanniness.)

From the side (as it were) of entities, the movement of falling is called 'absorption.' Openness gets caught up in or absorbed in that *to which* it is open: entities. This absorption requires a correlate covering over of openness itself. Compare ordinary absorption in an activity, which involves a blindness to one's surroundings and especially to the conditions of possibility of the activity. For example, being absorbed in playing the piano involves being blind to the internal mechanism of the instrument, as well as to the motion of one's fingers in relation to the keys and one's feet in relation to the pedals. Similarly, falling absorption in entities allows entities to show up but in doing so overlooks or looks through the very openness that makes this possible. We lead our lives, we deal with entities; we pay no heed to what it *takes* to lead a life and to deal with entities. Falling (absorption) is an openness to entities that brings *entities* into salience and obscures *openness*. Entities are revealed in their being and this revelation itself withdraws.

The point is that when entities show up, our being (as openness) withdraws. We can put the same point differently by saying that when entities show up, *their* being withdraws. That is, we dwell with intelligible entities and not with intelligibility (being) itself. Or again: we dwell with present things and do not access their presencing itself. Being, presencing, or intelligibility is necessarily backgrounded; it is self-effacing.

This falling presents a methodological difficulty for the analysis of openness and being. If openness to entities requires the covering over of openness itself—if entities show up only when being is backgrounded—then Heidegger faces the unenviable challenge of analyzing something that must remain hidden from us. To access it, we need an experience in which what is hidden from us is brought to light, even if only *as* hidden. The mood of angst is such an experience and so a 'distinctive disclosure': "in angst Dasein gets brought before itself through its own being, so that we can define phenomenologically the character of the entity disclosed in angst, and define it as such in its being" (SZ184). Angst brings to the fore the openness that falling obscures. In angst, entities recede into insignificance and so our absorption in them is suspended (but not surrendered). As suspended, our absorption is manifest—and with it, the withdrawn openness that made it possible. In other words, angst is a breakdown in the living of a daily life that allows us to see that life in operation and so reveals how a life works. (In this respect, it is similar to the absurd feeling.) Angst obscures the entities *to which* we are open and reveals *that* we are open. Thus angst disrupts falling or 'brings us back' from it (e.g., SZ189). If we analyze what the experience of angst reveals, then we can explore the openness that is constitutively hidden from us.

This way of reading Heidegger's analysis of angst differs in emphasis from many other readings. One common way to read the analysis is to focus on the personal significance of angst's revelation of the human situation: angst is an epiphany. Experiencing angst, I come to recognize that I have thus far failed to live my life authentically or ownedly—I have not been leading it as *mine,* in some significant sense. The mood brings me back to my own self. It is this dimension of angst that we usually have in mind when we think of 'existential angst.' In getting a clear view on the human condition, we get a clearer view on what really matters to us and what does not.

From this perspective, the analysis of angst can be seen to overcome a further methodological difficulty. Falling, as the backgrounding of our openness so that entities can show up, tends to exacerbate or intensify itself. By concealing our being, it encourages us to understand ourselves not as distinctively open but as just like the entities that are ordinarily in view for us—as kinds of tools, objects, or natural entities. This is a misunderstanding because such entities, through which we lead human lives, do not themselves lead human lives. They are not similarly open. So in this aggravated mode of falling, our openness is not merely hidden from us by entities showing up to us; it is forgotten or displaced by a self-misunderstanding in terms of entities unlike us. This self-misunderstanding is unownedness or unowned falling, and it is a second impediment to the analysis of openness. Like the first, it is overcome by the mood of angst—although in this case, not by analyzing but by experiencing this mood and so becoming authentic.[3] Since angst reveals our absorbed or fallen openness to us, it shakes us out of our inauthentic self-misunderstanding.

But Heidegger does not analyze angst primarily to determine how we become owned. Becoming owned is discussed two chapters later in the analysis of the call of conscience. The analysis of angst serves a different role—a purely methodological one. It does so because angst has ontological significance. Angst is a self-experience in which the distortions and distractions of everyday life slip away and so an experience in which I come face to face with the openness that I am. Angst offers genuine ontological insight—and it does so as an experience within a life. Heidegger

[3] The distinction between analyzing a ground mood like angst and experiencing it is not as clear as one might expect. Heidegger capitalizes on this in his analysis of boredom; see Katherine Withy, "The Strategic Unity of Heidegger's *The Fundamental Concepts of Metaphysics,*" *The Southern Journal of Philosophy* 51:2 (2013): 161–178.

needs such an experience in order to move forward in his analysis of Dasein, and this is why he analyzes angst in Division I rather than in Division II. It follows that to understand angst, we need to understand how it disrupts falling and reveals my being—that is, how angst is structured as a withdrawal and revelation.

The Four-Part Structure of Ground Moods

Moods are ways in which things show up to us as what they are and as mattering to us in some particular way. Moods are not subjective colorings laid over our commerce with entities and our relations to ourselves but are part of what it is for us to encounter anything at all. Most moods are backgrounds. Like soundtracks or climates, they set the stage for our immersion in our lives. Such moods saturate our experiences and typically go unnoticed. But there are also moods that pick us up from the midst of our lives and throw us back on ourselves. These strike us without warning and allow us to strike ourselves in new ways. Angst is such a mood.

Although Heidegger mentions some of the more familiar features of an experience of angst—it "stifles one's breath" (SZ186), can arise at any time (SZ189), is associated with darkness (SZ190)—his focus is on its distinctive revelatory or disclosive character. Moods like angst are structured as revelations and withdrawals. The particulars of our lives withdraw into the background or slip away and in this withdrawal is revealed something about me, about human life, or about the world as such. Ordinary life withdraws in the sense that the general hubbub and busy-ness of the day-to-day recedes into the background, becoming less salient. What, then, shows up to us? In anxiety, we may be hyper-aware of certain potential threats from the environment or of our own physical condition. In contrast, what we call 'existential angst' is 'existential' because in it we are aware of something 'bigger': something that lies underneath the ordinary life that we have slipped out of. We are aware of human life *itself*, either in general or as specifically mine. Life shows up as something that I have to take up and continue on with somehow. In both, what is revealed to me is revealed as a burden: I feel the *weight* of being human. This might be the burden of having to make a particular life decision or the burden of having to lead a human life at all.

The best way to analyze moods like angst is to explain how the world and I myself withdraw and to identify what stands revealed about me and about the world in this withdrawal. In brief, angst reveals the world in its worldhood, Dasein as being-in-the-world, and Dasein's being as care. Thus it also reveals Dasein's possibilities of owning itself or not: ownedness and unownedness. This revelation is specifically anxious because there is a threat lying in Dasein's being. This threat is unlike any ordinary, ontic threat from within the world (which would be revealed in fear). Usually, this threat is covered over by Dasein's engagement with entities and its worldly self-misunderstanding. But angst disrupts all this. Brought face to face with itself in angst, individualized as the kind of entity that it is, Dasein must confront the threat in its being. It is precisely this revelation that Heidegger needs at this point in SZ if he is to continue his hermeneutic and phenomenological analysis of Dasein's being. It is because angst is this specific combination of withdrawals and revelations that Heidegger analyzes it in SZ.

If all moods involve both a revelation and withdrawal, each with respect to both self and world, then we can analyze moods in terms of this schema. Of course, these dimensions are not genuinely distinct. Withdrawal and revelation are not separate events but two ways of describing the same thing. (Compare bringing something into focus, which always takes something else out of focus.) Self and world are likewise not opposed but are two ways of describing the same thing: Dasein's being-in-the-world. Nonetheless, we can distinguish these four dimensions of the mood and bring each into salience in our analysis: self-withdrawal, self-revelation, world-withdrawal, and world-revelation.

	Withdrawal (Angst disrupts falling)	Revelation (Angst is ontologically significant)
Self		
World		

Different accounts of angst tend to highlight or emphasize one or the other dimension of angst. Those that associate angst with depression focus on the 'withdrawal' column to express the sense of breakdown and loss of meaning, while those that understand angst as a way of becoming owned or as a kind of epiphany focus on the 'revelation' column—particularly the 'self-revelation' cell. There are good reasons in particular contexts to emphasize one or more of these dimensions, and any account will necessarily imply and touch on all aspects of angst. But it is useful to have an explicit understanding of all four dimensions and how they hang together, which is what I want to work towards now. The ultimate goal will be to accurately locate Heidegger's 'uncanniness' within this schema.

It will turn out that uncanniness is part of our essence that is revealed and is not, as is often thought, an affective consequence of the withdrawal of the world.

World-Withdrawal

Nagel describes the absurd experience as one of standing out from the midst of life, viewing it as would an alien anthropologist. He is expressing the *world withdrawing* moment of the absurd experience. Things become unfamiliar not so much in that they become unidentifiable but in that we lose our investment in them, seeing our lives as a series of ultimately meaningless gestures rather than as products of our values and commitments. This may—but need not—involve strangeness of the sort that the older psychological literature called *jamais vu*, the counter-concept to the more familiar *déjà vu*. In *déjà vu* we feel a familiarity with a situation that is unfamiliar. In *jamais vu* the familiar feels unfamiliar to us; it becomes strange. We can provoke *jamais vu* by, for example, repeating the same word until it becomes nonsense or staring at ourselves in the mirror for a long time. Typically, *jamais vu* is localized, affecting only how some particular thing shows up to us. Globalized *jamais vu* is something like what psychologists now call derealization.[4]

Along with depersonalization (a form of self-withdrawal), derealization is a dissociative phenomenon that is sometimes experienced in conjunction with anxiety and depression but which can also arise on its own. Sufferers often use the metaphor of being in a movie or being detached observers of their lives and world. DSM-5 describes depersonalization as "characterized by a feeling of unreality or detachment from, or unfamiliarity with, one's whole self or from aspects of the self" and derealization as "characterized by a feeling of unreality or detachment from, or unfamiliarity with, the world, be it individuals, inanimate objects, or all surroundings (Criterion A2). The individual may feel as if he or she were in a fog, dream, or bubble, or as if there were a veil or a glass wall between the individual and world around."[5] Here is the first-personal description I quoted in the Introduction, compiled from sufferers' own reports: "Familiar things look strange and foreign. I feel like an anthropologist

---

[4] For a more complete consideration of varieties of senses of reality and unreality (in a different argumentative context), including derealization, depersonalization, and Capgras syndrome, see Matthew Ratcliffe, *Feelings of Being: Phenomenology, Psychiatry and the Sense of Reality* (Oxford: Oxford University Press, 2008).

[5] American Psychiatric Association, *Diagnostic and Statistical Manual of Mental Disorders,* 5th ed. (DSM-5) (Arlington, VA: American Psychiatric Association, 2013).

from another planet, studying the human species. I look at things that once meant a lot to me, and I don't understand what I saw in them that made me love them. They're just shapes, objects, things, with no personal connection to me. My old coffee mug looks no more familiar than a baby with two heads. It's all just there and it's all strange somehow."[6]

Some people undergo this experience continuously for years. Such persistent derealization is considered a disorder. Depersonalization/derealization disorder is also diagnosed when experiences of derealization are recurring. But fleeting or transitory experiences of derealization that do not recur are quite normal; some studies suggest that as many as 70 percent of the population have experienced transitory derealization at some point in their lives, often in stressful or frightening situations.[7] If a transitory experience of derealization is an experience of detachment, then it will surely resemble Nagel's absurd experience. If it involves a definite experience of strangeness, then it will recall *jamais vu* in addition. The world-withdrawal in Heidegger's angst is, I suggest, somewhere in the vicinity of these phenomena.

What withdraws in angst is the world. The world is a public network of meaningful relationships, in terms of which entities are intelligible as the entities that they are. For instance, a hammer is what it is by virtue of its place in the context of other entities such as nails and wood. Heidegger calls the network of all such relations 'the totality of involvements' *(die Bewandtnisganzheit)*. In angst, "the totality of involvements of the ready-to-hand and the present-at-hand discovered within-the-world is, as such, of no consequence; it collapses into itself; the world has the character of completely lacking significance" (SZ186). What is this collapse of the totality of involvements? There are at least two options.

First, the collapse might be things ceasing to hang together: hammers no longer refer to nails and wood, for instance. At the local level, this resembles Jentsch's uncanniness of the unfamiliar: the hammer is not located in relation to other things in our ideational sphere. We would be left staring at the hammer, unable to make sense of it. When it lacks a place in the totality of involvements, an entity is only potentially intelligible.

---

[6] Daphne Simeon and Jeffrey Abugel, *Feeling Unreal: Depersonalization Disorder and the Loss of the Self* (Oxford: Oxford University Press, 2006), 80–81.

[7] Simeon and Abugel, *Feeling Unreal*, 14. Simeon and Abugel cite E. C. Hunter, M. Sierra, and A. S. David, "The Epidemiology of Depersonalization and Derealization: A Systematic Review," *Social Psychiatry and Psychiatric Epidemiology* 38:1 (2004): 9–18. Note that if 70 percent of the population experience derealization, as much as 30 percent of the population will never have this kind of experience at all. To such people, there is little that one can say to evoke the experience or to motivate its philosophical investigation.

But when this totality collapses globally, there is no totality at all. This experience must be something like Sartre's nausea: the world loses its articulation and everything slips into an undifferentiated mass. "[T]he root, the park gates, the bench, the sparse grass, all that had vanished: the diversity of things, their individuality, were only an appearance, a veneer. This veneer had melted, leaving soft, monstrous masses, all in disorder—naked, in a frightful, obscene nakedness."[8] This is a very serious collapse; it is barely recognizable as a human experience.

Heidegger's angst cannot be as extreme as the collapse of the totality of involvements in this sense. It is not the experience of everything coming apart at the seams. Instead, it is a loss of "consequence" (SZ186): "[t]he 'world' can offer nothing more" (SZ187). I take the collapse of the totality of involvements to be more properly expressed as the lack of significance: "the world has the character of completely lacking significance" (SZ186). 'Significance' *(Bedeutsamkeit)* is one of Heidegger's technical terms, and it names the reference of the totality of involvements to human practices and concerns. Hammers not only hang together with nails and wood (i.e., involvement), they also hang together with human practices like building and human goals such as seeking shelter. This latter 'hanging together' is significance. To lack significance, then, is for the totality of involvements to come apart from human goals. Thus the totality of involvements collapses in the sense that it falls *away* from us and not in the sense that it falls apart.[9] In this collapse, I know what things are, but I cannot see how to incorporate them into my own practices and life. This is what we see described in reports from derealization sufferers. At the local level: I know *that* this is a coffee mug—and indeed, *my* coffee mug—but it does not figure in my life as it used to or is supposed to. "It's all just there and it's all strange somehow."[10]

There are stronger and weaker ways of reading such a loss of significance. On a strong reading, the totality of involvements comes apart from human practices and goals entirely. I look at things and know what they are but I do not see that or how they connect to life. This is what it

[8] Jean-Paul Sartre, *Nausea,* trans. Lloyd Alexander (New York: New Directions, 2007), 127. For a cinematic representation of this kind of experience, see Terry Gilliam's film *Fear And Loathing in Las Vegas* (Universal Pictures, 1998), which is based on Hunter S. Thompson's *Fear and Loathing in Las Vegas: A Savage Journey to the Heart of the American Dream* (New York: Vintage Books, 1998). In this book, Thompson frequently references mescaline, a psychedelic drug which Sartre experimented with. Sartre implies that his experiences with mescaline inspired the descriptions in *Nausea;* see John Gerassi, *Talking with Sartre: Conversations and Debates* (New Haven, CT: Yale University Press, 2009), 79.
[9] Dreyfus uses the phrase "collapses away" in *Being-in-the-World,* 179.
[10] Simeon and Abugel, *Feeling Unreal,* 81.

would be for the world to *lack* significance, and Heidegger does say that this is what happens in angst (SZ186). However, this picture strikes me as implausible, both as an interpretation of Heidegger's angst and as a description of an experience. For tools in particular, there is no way to understand what they are without understanding how they are implicated in human life. I cannot understand what a coffee mug is or how it relates to coffee, kitchens, and cafés if it has come apart from the human goal of *consuming beverages recreationally;* I cannot understand what a hammer is independently of *construction* and *carpentry* as human practices. So it is not clear to me that the world can break down in this way, at least without the collapse of the totality of involvements in Sartre's sense.

A weaker reading is more plausible.[11] Instead of significance and the totality of involvements coming apart entirely, their bonds become more difficult for me to traverse. Things cease to matter to me; they become 'of no consequence' or 'lacking in significance' in the ordinary sense of these terms. Heidegger draws out this phenomenon when he analyzes boredom a few years after SZ: "Dasein which is thus attuned can no longer bring itself to expect anything from entities as a whole in any respect, because there is not even anything enticing about entities any more. They withdraw as a whole" (FCM147). This is to say that entities no longer solicit me to engage with them. As Heidegger puts it, they leave me *empty*. So, I see *that* this is a hammer and *that* it is for hammering nails and building houses. But sheltering from bad weather, the ultimate goal of such activities, does not exert a *pull* on me. I have lost my investment in that way of going about in the world. Since angst is global, I have lost my investment in going about in the world *entirely*. *Nothing* calls me to engage with it; no human goals motivate me. "The 'world' can offer nothing more" (SZ187).

In FCM, Heidegger calls this withdrawal 'indifference' *(Gleichgültigkeit)*: "[t]he indifference of entities as a whole manifests itself" (FCM139); entities "*show themselves precisely as such* in their indifference" (FCM138). I suggest that this is the same as the insignificance *(Unbedeutsamkeit)* in angst. To say that entities are indifferent to me and do not draw me out is to say that the connection between the totality of involvements and significance has faded for me. The significance of the world is not lacking but has *withdrawn*. What is suspended is not the relationships that situate things with respect to one another and so

---

[11] William Blattner offers what I take to be roughly the same interpretation, and for the same reasons, in his *Heidegger's Temporal Idealism* (Cambridge: Cambridge University Press, 1999), 79, and "The Concept of Death in *Being and Time*," *Man and World* 27 (1994): 61.

that structure and articulate the world, and not the figuring of these relationships in the broader context of human practices. Angst suspends my
investment in these human practices, making engagement in them (and
so, daily life) impossible.

It is because angst includes this loss of investment that it has been
associated with depression. William Blattner, for example, argues that
"some of the core phenomena of what Heidegger calls 'anxiety' are characteristic of what we today call *depression*. What sufferers without the
language of Heidegger, Dostoyevsky, and Kierkegaard call a 'hopeless-
ness,' 'intense boredom,' 'living under a dark cloud,' and which clinicians
call 'flat affect' and 'anhedonia,' are symptoms of a depressive disorder.
In such a condition, one withdraws into isolation, loses interest in the
world around one, stops taking pleasure in everyday life, loses motiva-
tion to carry on. Heidegger's descriptions of what he calls 'anxiety' fit this
model quite well: the world 'has nothing to offer,' and neither do others;
one cannot understand oneself anymore; one feels uncanny and not-at-
home."[12] This reading comes very close to capturing Heidegger's angst,
because the phenomenon that I think Heidegger is getting at is one that
often accompanies depression: derealization. I suggest that it is the way
that things cease to matter in derealization, rather than the way that they
cease to matter in depression *per se,* that is closest to the way that things
cease to matter in Heidegger's angst.

Derealization and depersonalization differ from depression in that they
consist in a detachment (hence the classification of depersonalization/de-
realization disorder as a dissociative disorder rather than as a mood disorder). One way to think about derealization and depression separately
is to think of depression as my withdrawal from the world ('the world
can offer nothing more to *me,* but it might to others') and derealization
as the world's withdrawal from me ('the world can *offer* nothing more
to me, because it is just a curiosity and I am just an observer').[13] Another
is to think of depression as a leveling of affect and derealization as an
intensifying of strangeness. Not all cases of derealization seem to involve
a strong sense of strangeness, and derealization is often associated with
hypoemotionality, so the contrast is not as crisp as I would like. But my
claim is only that angst *resembles* derealization—and that it resembles
this more than it resembles depression. It does so because the loss of significance involves detachment and strangeness.

---

[12] William D. Blattner, *Heidegger's* Being and Time: *A Reader's Guide* (New York: Continuum, 2006), 141–142.

[13] With this phrase, I do not intend to imply anything about a sufferer's agency in or
responsibility for her depression.

Indeed, angst involves a threat. This is what makes it angst as opposed to, say, melancholia.[14] To identify this threat, we need to explore what is revealed in the loss of significance. This revelation is not the negative revelation of what is lost, as it is for Cavell's skeptic. It is the positive revelation of something found: "entities within-the-world are of so little importance in themselves that on the basis of this *insignificance* of what is within-the-world, the world in its worldhood is all that still obtrudes itself" (SZ187).

World-Revelation

Psychology tends to focus on the de- or withdrawing moment of dereal-ization, emphasizing its dissociative dimension. But, as Heidegger stress-es in his analysis of boredom, refusals or withdrawals are telling: they reveal something to us (e.g., FCM139). Even the collapse of the world in Sartrean nausea is telling or revealing: "And then all of a sudden, there it was, clear as day: existence had suddenly unveiled itself. It had lost the harmless look of an abstract category: it was the very paste of things."[15] In derealization we can also find a revelation. Sufferers often report a proto-philosophical awareness: "It's like I'm too aware of certain larger aspects of reality."[16]

In many cases, this insight is an experience of what Heidegger would call the presence-at-hand in what is ready-to-hand, which he argues is revealed in cases of tool breakdown (SZ72–76). When a piece of equip-ment ceases to work—say, my computer monitor goes blank—it is no longer a transparent implement. Whereas previously I had used the moni-tor without attending to it, now I must turn my attention from my work to the tools that make it possible. The monitor shows up as a physical object with certain properties. But it never becomes a *merely* present ob-ject; the monitor always retains its previous and potential future utility. This is clear from the fact that some of the properties of the physical ob-ject demand modification: the object is in *need* of *repair* and so must be a tool. Heidegger says that the presence of the monitor shows up *within* its handiness or usefulness (SZ74).

Sartre's nausea seems to reveal presence without the context of lost utility, although some of his descriptions come close to what Heidegger

---

[14] Note that Blattner acknowledges this dimension of angst and suggests that what Hei-degger "really has in mind [is] what is sometimes called 'agitated depression.'" Blattner, *Heidegger's* Being and Time: *A Reader's Guide,* 142.

[15] Sartre, *Nausea,* 127.

[16] Simeon and Abugel, *Feeling Unreal,* 7.

describes here.[17] Reports of derealization resemble Heidegger's description more closely. Recall the example of the coffee mug: "My old coffee mug looks no more familiar than a baby with two heads. It's all just there and it's all strange somehow."[18] Instead of showing up as to-drink-from, my old coffee mug shows up as *just there*—as present. But it is not *simply* present; it is still a coffee mug, and it is still mine. It shows up as *something present that would otherwise be meaningful to me*. The coffee cup shows up as there in the context of its previous familiarity. Its presence is revealed within its familiarity.[19]

Since familiarity or utility persists, it is also revealed along with mere presence—revealed as what is lost. Further, since familiarity and usefulness are not simple properties of a thing but a function of its place in a context, the entire context is illuminated: "When an assignment to some particular 'towards-this' has been thus circumspectively aroused, we catch sight of the 'towards-this' itself, and along with it everything connected with the work—the whole 'workshop'—as that wherein concern always dwells. The context of equipment is lit up" (SZ74–75). We see the world—the totality of involvements and context of significance—in which the particular tool had its place. This is explicitly revealed for the first time in breakdown, although it was always disclosed to us (else we could not operate within it, making things familiar as what they are). The background context, which was previously transparent, comes to the fore along with the broken or missing tool. As with Cavell's skeptical breakdown, the world is revealed *only* as lost.

In analyzing angst, Heidegger uses language that implies that angst is a global version of practical breakdown. But it is analogous to a very particular kind of tool breakdown, which is unlike that which we have just considered. This difference is what distinguishes angst from derealization. Heidegger says that the world in its worldhood "obtrudes itself" (SZ187), just as tools are "obtrusive" when the further tool needed to use them is missing (SZ73). If the analogy holds, then the withdrawal of the world will be analogous to a tool being missing and the revelation of the world to the obtrusiveness of everything *else*. Thus

---

[17] "I lean my hand on the seat but pull it back hurriedly: it exists. This thing I'm sitting on, leaning my hand on, is called a seat. They made it purposely for people to sit on, they took leather, springs and cloth, they went to work with the idea of making a seat and when they finished, *that* was what they had made." Sartre, *Nausea*, 125.

[18] Simeon and Abugel, *Feeling Unreal*, 81.

[19] It is this awareness of how things used to be or should be that makes derealization more like tool breakdown and less like a psychotic break or drug experience. Psychologists put this by saying that in derealization, reality testing remains intact: sufferers know that what they are experiencing is not normal.

when the totality of involvements falls away from significance and we lose our investment in things, what is revealed is precisely *not* what is lost but instead what *remains:* the world, in its worldhood. This is to say that what becomes lit up when the totality of involvements collapses away from us is precisely the totality of involvements and the context of significance from which it falls away. A strictly analogous case of practical breakdown would be the following: if the link that holds two things together is missing, those two things stand out. When the totality of involvements and the context of significance come apart, they both show up: the world is revealed.

There is another, deeper, respect in which this revelation is different from that in ordinary practical breakdown. Both reveal the world but in angst the world is revealed *in its worldhood*—that is, *as* a meaningful context in which we dwell and in terms of which things are useful, familiar, and meaningful. The world is an ontic phenomenon; it is always the world of the workshop, the public world, the world of advertising, and so on (SZ65). The way that things are organized in a totality of involvements and how they hook up with a context of significance in these different worlds can be studied by anthropologists, ethnographers, and sociologists. The *worldhood* of the world, however, is an ontological-existential concept. The worldhood of the world is the principle or structure governing how the totality of involvements hangs together, how the context of significance hangs together, and how they hang together with one another. To study worldhood is to study the logic of these meaningful relationships. Thus Heidegger discusses in-order-to relationships, references or assignments, involvements, for-the-sake-of relationships, and significance—and not: how hammers hang together with nails, wood, and shelter. The world shows up in its worldhood when it shows up *as* a set of in-orders-to, references, for-the-sakes-of, and so on—and not as hammers hanging together with nails, wood, and shelter. In angst, the world shows up with its logic or structure on display. Angst reveals what it takes to *be* a world.

Angst is thus a specifically ontological revelation. There is an ontological dimension to the revelations in nausea, derealization, and tool breakdown, since they reveal the presence and the familiarity or utility of particular things. Tool breakdown reveals in addition the local context or world in which those things gain their familiarity or utility. But only in angst is the revelation *global*. The global scope of angst produces a qualitatively different kind of revelation. That angst is global means that the *whole* world—and not just the local world of the workshop—shows up. But this *wholeness* is not that of a sum totality; it is wholeness in the sense of a *unity*. The world shows up as a unified whole—as it hangs together, or in its logic. So what is revealed to us is not merely some particular ready-to-hand tool or some particular context of equipment but the very contextuality that makes contexts of equipment, and so particular tools, possible: "[w]hat oppresses us is not this or that, nor is it the summation of everything present-at-hand; it is rather the *possibility* of the ready-to-hand in general" (SZ187).

To summarize in a slightly different vocabulary: when the totality of involvements collapses away from the context of significance, both become obtrusive. What shows up in this obtrusiveness is not any particular involved or significant thing (e.g., the monitor), and it is not some particular involvement or significance (e.g., *for the sake of viewing the contents of my hard drive*). What shows up are involvement and significance themselves: the world as a network of mutually referring in-orders-to and for-the-sakes-of. This is not to say, however, that we grasp in a flash how everything in our world is connected—that and why all things hang together in the particular ways that they do. The insight is less ontic. We grasp *that* everything is connected and that things hang together *in these kinds of ways*. The expansiveness of angst is that of ontological depth rather than ontic scope.

If angst involves this ontological insight, then it cannot be maintained within a life. Living a life requires that particular involvements and significances be in view for us, so that we can engage with meaningful things in the world. These are not salient in angst. Further, if we are to live a non-derealized life, the totality of involvements must hook back up with the context of significance so that we can *meaningfully* engage with meaningful things in the world. Angst involves the kind of withdrawal and revelation that must be transitory; it can only be lived as a crisis experience. This makes angst unlike the moods that Heidegger otherwise seems most interested in: those that pervade our experience and attune it as does an atmosphere (FCM68). It also makes angst importantly unlike depression and derealization. The source of this difference is that angst is a deep ontological revelation. It is not a pathology but a source of legitimate ontological insight.

Self-Withdrawal

Heidegger does not say much about the self-withdrawing dimension of angst. One might take the world- and self-withdrawal in angst to be roughly of the sort that Lear analyzes in *Radical Hope:* the breakdown of my culture or world on the basis of the impossibility of the *telos* that provided my practical identity and deep self-understanding.[20] Lear considers the cultural devastation experienced by the Crow tribe when their traditional way of life became impossible in light of their move to a reservation and the U.S. government's ban on intertribal warfare. For a nomadic tribe, the life of which is organized around boundary-setting and boundary-defending warfare, the impossibility of courageous acts in battle is a profound loss of the activity and associated excellence around which life is organized.

This collapse is different from those that we have considered. It is not the loss of the integrity of the totality of involvements (nausea) and it is not this totality coming apart from significance (derealization, absurdity)—and not this as well as the illumination of significance and involvement themselves (angst). Instead, it is the loss of the integrity of the context of significance. Significance is the ordering of things to human goals or *for-the-sakes-of-which*. The ultimate for-the-sake-of-which is what Aristotle called the highest human good. As he explains at the beginning of the *Nicomachean Ethics,* this goal or *telos* organizes and gives meaning to our activities and the things that we use in them.[21] When this *telos* becomes impossible—when the Crow can no longer perform courageous acts in battle—the coherence of a life organized *for the sake of* this goal is undermined and that life breaks down. This will reverberate through the context of significance and generate a breakdown in the totality of involvements (although it will be unlike nausea). Further, if that ultimate goal is what holds together a community or world, then the breakdown is world-collapse, as well as the subjective 'death' of those who live in that world.

Insofar as angst involves a self-withdrawal, we might be tempted to read it as a similar kind of breakdown, at a personal level: a breakdown in my personal identity produced by the withdrawal of the goal that grounds my practical identity. If this goal becomes practically impossible, then my life is unlivable as a human life, and it and my world each cease to hang together intelligibly. I *die* as the kind of person that I am. This kind of breakdown is extremely rare. If my *telos* is to become practically impossible in the literal sense, then this breakdown—unlike angst—depends on very specific kinds of external factors as catalysts (in the case of the Crow, the U.S. government's forbidding of nomadic life

[20] Jonathan Lear, *Radical Hope: Ethics in the Face of Cultural Devastation* (Cambridge, MA: Harvard University Press, 2006).

[21] Aristotle, *The Nicomachean Ethics,* trans. W. D. Ross, rev. J. O. Urmson, in *The Complete Works of Aristotle: The Revised Oxford Translation,* Vol. 2, ed. Jonathan Barnes (Princeton, NJ: Princeton University Press, 1995).

and traditional warfare). Alternatively, my life could break down in the sense that the *telos* around which I organize my life comes apart from my other activities and the things in my world. This would be Lear's experience of irony: I hold on to *being a teacher* but it is no longer clear to me what all the various aspects of my practical identity—lecturing, grading papers, writing on the blackboard—have to do with that goal. As before, this 'collapsing away' could be more or less severe. At its most severe, my practical identity could become completely unhinged from my *telos* and so my self-understanding. This should spark a significant life change, since what it means to be committed to *teaching* now means something other than 'lecturing (and so on) at an accredited educational institution.' Less severely (and I think it is these cases that Lear has in mind with irony), the connection between my *telos* and everything else that I do in my world becomes more difficult to traverse. In the ironic experience, the question arises how we get from one to the other: "what does any of *this* have to do with being a teacher?"

These possibilities mirror (more or less) those that we explored in considering world-withdrawal. Self-withdrawal is the correlate of world-withdrawal, but it is so not merely in the sense that when the totality of involvements falls away from the context of significance, the context of significance also loses touch with the totality of involvements. That is, self-withdrawal and world-withdrawal name the same phenomenon but are not merely different ways of saying the same thing. Talk of self-withdrawal brings out a dimension of the phenomenon that we could never grasp if we spoke only of world-withdrawal: my life, my goals, my commitments somehow or in some sense fall away from me. The context of significance itself loses its grip on me, and along with it my goals and ordinary self-understanding. So in addition to the totality of involvements collapsing away from me and entities leaving me indifferent, my life collapses away from me and leaves me indifferent. This will be like Lear's ironic experience only if I remain committed to my most fundamental *telos* in some sense.

Losing my grip on myself and my life resembles the self-withdrawal that we find in depersonalization. Depersonalization is the self-withdrawing counterpart to the world-withdrawal of derealization.[22] Sufferers of de-

---

[22] As in angst, the self/world distinction is more a matter of emphasis than of real difference. Ratcliffe, for example, uses his notion of 'existential feeling' to argue for this: "it seems plausible to suggest that some of the feelings reported in depersonalization are what I call 'existential feelings'; modifications of the self-world relation. In describing them, either side of the relation can be emphasized. The world might be described as looking unreal or the person as feeling strangely different. But although different descriptions have different

personalization lose the sense of being a 'me' as opposed to just some 'one.' Consider this description: "Before, he *knew* who he was. Now, inexplicably, the knowledge that he was an individual person was there, but not a clear feeling of 'I.'"[23] Occasionally, sufferers will describe this in a way that suggests a self-withdrawing version of Sartrean nausea: mystical experiences of unity in which all distinctions between self and other dissolve.[24] But usually sufferers attempt to capture the experience of depersonalization using metaphors of automation and self-spectatorship; they feel like "mechanisms, automatons, puppets—what they do seems not done by them, but happens automatically."[25] One reports: "I look at my mind from within and feel both trapped and puzzled about the strangeness of my existence. My thoughts swirl round and round constantly probing the strangeness of selfhood—why do I exist? Why am I me and not someone else? At these times, feelings of sweaty panic develop, as if I am having a phobia about my own thoughts. At other times, I don't feel 'grounded'. I look at this body and can't understand why I am within it. I hear myself having conversations and wonder where the voice is coming from. I imagine myself seeing life as if it were played like a film in a cinema. But in that case, where am I? Who is watching the film? What is the cinema?"[26]

We have seen such self-spectatorship and self-distancing in Nagel's absurd feeling, and it is this that marks its major difference from Lear's irony. On which side is angst located? Heidegger's description of angst seems to situate it between these two visions: it is committed and passionate like Lear's ironic experience but dissociated from ordinary life like Nagel's absurd experience. The reason that it can be both lies in angst's self-revelation.

Self-Revelation

Angst reveals the ontological or existential dimension of human life—the human essence, if you like. It is to this that we are committed (because we are 'thrown into' it). It is our most fundamental *telos* and the core of

---

explicit referents, 'self' and 'world', this need not imply that they are descriptions of different experiences." Ratcliffe, *Feelings of Being,* 184.

[23] Simeon and Abugel, *Feeling Unreal,* 25.

[24] For example: "I feel like the 'I', for lack of a better term, is now somehow situated across many moments. My identity is scattered everywhere; as if I am everyone, and everything, and the spaces between things. [. . .] It's like the reflection of the sun being split into shards of light on the sea. I have dissolved, into a kind of 'oneness' with all that exists, but it's a fragmented oneness." Ibid., 46.

[25] Ibid., 59.

[26] Ibid., 15.

our self-understanding, not as individuals but as human beings. Our essence or our being is "so close to us that we have no distance from it that would allow us to catch sight of it" (FCM284). We achieve this distance in angst—but not through self-spectatorship, self-dissolution, or the collapse of our practical identities. Instead, the self-withdrawal paired with this revelation is a self-suspension.

In angst, my ordinary, everyday life falls out of view for me; it ceases to matter in the sense that it ceases to be salient. Thus "it is not as though 'you' or 'I' feel uncanny; rather, it is this way for some 'one.'"[27] As in depersonalization, there is no concrete 'I' implicated in the experience, since my ordinary self or life has slipped out of view. The 'subject' of angst is not me, in my particular life, but some 'one.' The *myself* from which I slip away is my particular existence in its concrete, worldly concerns. When this withdraws, "pure Dasein is all that is still there" (WM88–89).

That the totality of involvements has become insignificant or collapsed away from the context of significance contributes to this self-withdrawal, since it suspends my engagement with entities and so my worldly projects and concerns. My possibilities for going about in the world are deactivated, as a whole. With this global suspension of ordinary life, I no longer confront the particular possibilities that have been given to me. As with world-revelation, the global character of angst shifts its revelation from the ontic to the ontological. I confront my possibilities as a whole—where, again, this does not mean in their sum totality but in their very possibility. It is revealed that I am the kind of entity that *has* possibilities at all—that I am in a human way, that I am as a case of Dasein. Just as angst revealed what it is to be a world (involvement, significance, and so on), angst reveals what it is to be a self and that I am such a self.

Heidegger puts this by saying that angst is an experience of individualization or individuation (SZ187, 188). What kind of individualization can this be if the particulars of my life have slipped away? Usually when we talk about individualization or individuality we are talking about those features of my life and my personality that distinguish me from others and so make me an 'individual.' If this were the kind of individualization at issue in angst, then angst would be a personal epiphany experienced by someone lost in society, in which she is called to 'be authentic' or to 'be herself.' Angst shakes us out of complacency and conformity to society and reveals us to ourselves as free and self-determining. But it is

---

[27] Martin Heidegger, "What Is Metaphysics?," trans. David Farrell Krell, *Pathmarks,* ed. William McNeill (Cambridge: Cambridge University Press, 1998), 89. Hereafter WM. Page references in the text will be given in the form (WMxx).

hard to see why Heidegger should be interested in this kind of revelation in SZ, much less at this point in the text. (I discussed this earlier when I defended the methodological role of angst.) I suggest instead that the kind of individualization that Heidegger has in mind is better termed 'individuation.'

In angst, I am individuated as a case of Dasein and so as a sense-maker. Cases of Dasein are distinguished from other entities by the fact that they understand being or make sense of the world. Cases of Dasein have a world or are being-in-the-world. In our ordinary everydayness, we tend not to understand ourselves in these terms. We tend to grasp ourselves implicitly as the same kinds of things as animals, tools, or natural objects. This is a misunderstanding of what it is to be human—of the ultimate *telos* of human life as sense-making. Heidegger calls this misunderstanding a 'dispersion' (e.g., SZ129, 390). In misunderstanding ourselves, we disperse ourselves amidst other ways of being. Angst disrupts this misunderstanding by revealing to us that we are cases of Dasein. By coming to grasp ourselves as the kind of entity that we are, we grasp ourselves as ontologically distinct from other kinds of entities. With this self-understanding, we become individuated as the kind of entity that we are.

Further, angst reveals that this being is *mine to be it*. Sense-making is a *telos* to which I am bound and so to which I am committed. (This is what makes the revelation of angst similar to Lear's ironic experience.) Being a case of Dasein is a task that I am responsible for executing. But it is also a burden with which I am simply saddled: I cannot not take on being a case of Dasein. I must be a sense-maker; things must hang together meaningfully. We see the same responsibility revealed in the revelation of the world (as we should, since Dasein is being-in-the-world and world-revelation and self-revelation should thus be two sides of the same coin). Dasein is a sense-maker, and the world is that in terms of which it makes sense of things. Thus Dasein is responsible for involvement and significance—for arranging things in relationships of in-orders-to and for-the-sakes-of-which. (This does not mean that each case of Dasein can do so at will; the point is that meaningful relationships depend on sense-making.) So when significance and involvement show up in angst, they show up as my burdens, my responsibility. This is the sounding of the imperative to be a sense-maker, to let things hang together—to explicitly adopt myself, as Dasein, as my *telos*. Obviously, this is the ontological-existential version of the call to 'become what you are,' where 'what you are' is not some unique inner self but a human being. Such a call individuates me because responsibility is inherently individuating: the task falls to me and not to anyone else. The responsibility to make sense of things is mine and I must take over this *telos*.

So angst calls us to ourselves as sense-makers, insofar as we are cases of Dasein rather than particular, concrete individuals. Thus the 'subject' of angst is always a 'me' but is never any particular 'me.' It is me, stripped of anything that distinguishes me from you, stripped down to my being as Dasein and my individuating responsibility to be that. We can understand this experience as a self-withdrawal of a kind similar to Nagel's absurd experience, and as a self-revelation that reveals a profound commitment of the sort that we find in Lear's ironic experience.

Of course, the major influence on Heidegger's analysis of angst is Søren Kierkegaard.[28] For Kierkegaard, angst reveals the freedom to choose that is essential to us and with which we are burdened. This revelation counts as specifically anxious because the freedom to choose is terrifying. Similarly, Heidegger calls the revelation of our being 'angst' because it is threatening. The revelation is threatening because our being contains a threat to itself. 'Uncanniness,' I will argue, is Heidegger's name for this threat. It is this threat that Dasein flees when it falls, and so it is this threat that grounds or explains our being-amidst-entities. To identify uncanniness, we need to identify this threat. To identify this threat, we need to explore the being that is revealed to us in angst. Pause to notice, however, that if this is right then uncanniness does not belong to the withdrawing moment in angst but to its revelatory dimension:

	Withdrawal (Angst disrupts falling)	Revelation (Angst is ontologically significant)
Self	My everyday life is suspended, including my self-misunderstanding.	I am revealed as (individuated as) a case of Dasein or being-in-the-world, which I must be. In this lies a threat: uncanniness.
	Compare depersonalization, Nagel's absurdity.	Compare Kierkegaard's angst, Lear's irony.
World	The totality of involvements becomes insignificant—it collapses away from the context of significance.	World is revealed in its worldhood.
	Compare derealization.	Compare tool breakdown.

[28] Søren Kierkegaard (as Vigilius Haufniensis), *The Concept of Dread: A Simple Psychological Deliberation Oriented in the Direction of the Dogmatic Problem of Original Sin*, trans. Walter Lowrie (Princeton, NJ: Princeton University Press, 1957).

On this reading, uncanniness does not belong to the breakdown of everyday life. It is not a way of describing things that have lost their intelligibility and become unfamiliar and strange. It is also not a way of describing how I feel in a situation of world- and self-withdrawal—my feeling of lacking a secure and stable home in the world. My suggestion is that uncanniness belongs to what it is to be Dasein and so is revealed in angst insofar as angst discloses Dasein's being to it. Associating uncanniness with our being rather than with an experienced loss of meaning is what primarily distinguishes Heidegger's deployment of the 'uncanny' from other uses of the term. Uncanniness is what we find when we have genuine insight into what we are, not how we feel when our lives break down. The connection to the latter appears in Heidegger only insofar as having genuine insight into our lives requires that our lives break down—that is, that angst disrupt falling. It remains, then, to locate uncanniness in Dasein's being, as it is revealed in angst.

Thrownness

Angst reveals 'the Dasein in me,' or me as a case of Dasein. "The Dasein in us manifests itself" (FCM283). "[I]n angst Dasein gets brought before itself through its own being, so that we can define phenomenologically the character of the entity disclosed in angst, and define it as such in its being" (SZ184). As Heidegger uses it, 'Dasein' is a difficult term to understand and to translate. In ordinary German it means the same as 'existence,' but Heidegger uses it to pick out specifically human existence. Further, it picks this out in a specific way. Heidegger says that 'Dasein' picks out the entities that we are and that it picks us out with regard to our being: "we have chosen to designate this entity as 'Dasein', a term which is purely an expression of its being" (SZ12). So 'Dasein' is a peculiar, ontico-ontological term: it designates an entity but with regard to its being.

Insofar as 'Dasein' refers to the entities that we ourselves are, we might be tempted to mentally substitute for it a term like 'person' or 'human being.' The problem is that, while these words designate the same entity, they pick it out in ways that Heidegger wants to avoid. 'Human being' picks us out with regard to our humanity as opposed to animality or divinity, and 'person' picks us out in terms of our agency, consciousness, and/or personality. While these ways of understanding us do get at genuine features of us, they nonetheless obscure that aspect of us that Heidegger is interested in: our openness to being. Heidegger uses the term

'Dasein' to pick us out as being *(Sein)* there *(da)*, where by 'there' or *'da'* Heidegger means what we might call the space of intelligibility or meaningfulness. Calling us 'Dasein' thus names us as entities who essentially make things intelligible or who dwell in a meaningful world. Dasein is the entity that understands being. The story that we tell about Dasein is thus not a story about agency, consciousness, animality, or divinity, but a story about sense-making.

Further, Heidegger uses the term 'Dasein' in a way that makes it importantly unlike terms such as 'person' or 'human being.' First, Heidegger almost never pluralizes 'Dasein,' and the few occasions when he does are sufficiently rare to seem like mistakes. This suggests that 'Dasein' is not a count noun, such that we cannot speak of 'one Dasein, two Daseins.' Similarly, Heidegger does not often use the indefinite article ('a Dasein')—unless he also appends the particle *'je,'* which is translated as 'in each case.' (Macquarrie and Robinson, however, do not always translate this particle.) Noting these peculiarities, John Haugeland argues that 'cases of Dasein' refers to people, and he offers tuberculosis as a helpful analogy: "We neither count 'tuberculoses' nor measure amounts of it; it comes, rather, in distinct occurrences or cases (which can, of course, be counted). A person is like an occurrence or 'case' of *Dasein*—except that one doesn't catch it, let alone get over it. *Dasein* is not a species of which we are specimens, a type of which we are tokens, a feature which we have, a spirit which is in us, a condition which we are in, or even a whole of which we are parts (though that's closest). People are to *Dasein* as baseball games are to baseball, as utterances are to language, as works are to literature. *Dasein* is the overall phenomenon, consisting entirely of its individual 'occurrences.'"[29] So rather than having a Dasein here and a Dasein there for a total of two Daseins, we have a case of Dasein and another case of Dasein, giving us two cases of Dasein.

'Dasein,' then, does not refer to a person, although I depart from Haugeland a little in the kind of thing to which I think it does refer. I suggest that we hear the term 'Dasein' verbally. Dasein is *being (Sein)* the there *(da)*. It is a doing, a happening, or an event. Since Dasein is the entity that understands being, it must be the event in which the understanding of being happens: the event of sense-making. (Compare: the entity that determines the winner of a race is the event of the race itself—or, more specifically, the event of the first person crossing the finish line in accordance with the rules.) 'Dasein' thus refers to *making sense of things*,

---

[29] John Haugeland, "Heidegger on Being a Person," *Noûs* 16 (1982): 19–20.

and it picks us out as such events.[30] Each of us is a case of this sense-making; I *am* an ongoing exercise of making intelligible. This reading seems odd only insofar as we are not accustomed to thinking of ourselves as happenings or to thinking of events as entities. The former will be addressed as we go, but the latter is easy to remedy immediately. Events *are*, and they are just insofar as they *happen*. Thus a festival *is* if it takes place. Further, notice that it takes place only if there are festivities—if there are people doing festive things. Similarly, we can say that sense-making or Dasein *is* insofar as it happens, and it happens if there are people making sense of things: cases of Dasein. This is why *Dasein je* is important for Heidegger's picture. Sense-making or Dasein *is* only if it takes place in each case, through people and their sense-making endeavors.

Note that Heidegger does not often use event language to talk about Dasein (although he does, of course, interpret Dasein in terms of temporality). Particularly after SZ, he tends to employ spatial metaphors, especially that of 'the site.' I will say more about this in Chapter 3. In the meantime, I acknowledge this spatial metaphor by employing Thomas Sheehan's translation-interpretation of 'Dasein': openness or open*ed*ness. The insight here is that Dasein, as the entity that understands being, is open to being or is the open *(da)*, where 'the open' implies a space or a clearing.[31]

Heidegger's goal in the existential analytic is to understand what it takes to be Dasein—that is, how sense-making happens. Part of the story of this happening will cover how it takes place in each case, through individuals engaged in sense-making. Thus Heidegger spends time in Division I of SZ explaining how we make sense of entities through our everyday practices. But this is not what he is primarily interested in. "It never occurred to me," he says later, "to try and claim or prove with this interpretation that the essence of man consists in the fact that he knows how to handle knives and forks or use the tram" (FCM177). Heidegger wants to reveal something more fundamental: how sense-making

---

[30] Although this interpretation is not standard, it picks up on widely recognized features of Dasein. Consider comments by Taylor Carman and Richard Polt, both of whom take 'Dasein' to refer to people: "Dasein is therefore more eventlike than objectlike, its 'being' more like a gerund than a substantive." Taylor Carman, *Heidegger's Analytic: Interpretation, Discourse and Authenticity in* Being and Time (Cambridge: Cambridge University Press, 2003), 41. "Heidegger would like us to think of ourselves as an event of opening, rather than as a thing inside a closed sphere." Richard Polt, *Heidegger: An Introduction* (Ithaca, NY: Cornell University Press, 1999), 57. Thomas Sheehan understands Dasein in terms of Aristotle's *energeia atelēs*, which suggests an alternative to 'event' which is similarly dynamic: 'movement.' Thomas Sheehan, "Dasein," in *A Companion to Heidegger*, ed. Hubert L. Dreyfus and Mark A. Wrathall (Malden, MA: Blackwell Publishing, 2007).

[31] Thomas Sheehan, "A Paradigm Shift in Heidegger Research," *Continental Philosophy Review* 34 (2001): 193.

happens at all, in and through us, rather than not. This is why he needs angst, the experience that tunes us into the sense-making taking place in us. What does angst reveal about the event of sense-making?

Angst reveals that sense-making is thrown: "Angst is anxious about naked Dasein as something that has been thrown into uncanniness" (SZ343). Angst reveals thrownness in a direct way (SZ343), although all moods reveal thrownness in one way or another (SZ134). When Heidegger speaks of 'thrownness,' he does not mean that Dasein is thrown *by* something in the sense that it is knocked off balance, tripped up, or sent off-kilter. Heidegger defines thrownness thus: "This characteristic of Dasein's being—this 'that it is'—is veiled in its 'whence' and 'whither', yet disclosed in itself all the more unveiledly; we call it the *'thrownness'* of this entity into its 'there'" (SZ135). Thrownness is the 'that it is' of Dasein: the fact that it is as it is. Heidegger usually adds to this formulation a 'has to be' (in the sense that it *must* be what it is, since nothing else is available). Thus thrownness is the 'that it is and has to be' of Dasein (e.g., SZ134): the fact *that it is* Dasein and that it *has* itself *to be*. Heidegger also puts the point by saying that Dasein is 'delivered over' to itself (e.g., SZ134–135), given over to itself to be itself.

The thought is that to be thrown is to have a starting point—something that we already have or are, and so something with which we are stuck. As always thrown, sense-making is never neutral or undetermined. We have many kinds of starting points and so are thrown into all sorts of things—various situations, our lives, our culture, and so on. While the concept of 'thrownness' can be used to illuminate these dimensions of human life, this is not the level at which Heidegger uses the term.[32] When Heidegger identifies what we are thrown *into,* he almost always describes this as some version of 'being a sense-maker.' We are thrown into or delivered over to our own being (SZ42, 189), ourselves (in our being) (SZ144, 192, 383), the entity that we are (SZ284), the there *(da)* (SZ135, 148, 284, 297), existence (SZ251, 276), our ability to be (SZ383), projection (SZ145), or being-guilty (SZ291). (And since we are the kinds of entities that are *thrown,* we are even delivered over to or thrown into our thrownness (SZ148, 396).) There are two ways to read these claims, corresponding to the two ways in which angst individuates, or (on at least one reading of this distinction) to the two dimensions of thrownness as the *that it is* and the *has to be.* These readings together generate

---

[32] For a full exploration of the potential dimensions of thrownness and a detailed argument for the claim that Heidegger uses the term at its most abstract level, see Katherine Withy, "Situation and Limitation: Making Sense of Heidegger on Thrownness," *European Journal of Philosophy* 22:1 (2014): 61–81.

two levels at which thrownness may be understood or two 'kinds' of thrownness. I shall call these 'thrownness in each case' and 'thrownness itself.' Thrownness in each case is the fact that Dasein is thrown to me to be it and is a burden or a responsibility that is mine. Thrownness itself is the fact that Dasein is at all rather than not. Since Dasein only happens through cases of Dasein, the two ways of talking say the same thing, although in different ways and from different directions. I begin with thrownness in each case.

From the perspective of a case of Dasein, thrownness (in each case) is the fact that I am and have to be a case of Dasein.[33] Dasein is thrown to me to be a case of it, or I am thrown into being a case of it. These two expressions are equivalent because if Dasein is thrown to me to be, then 'catching' it is not optional (even if the throw "does not authentically get 'caught'" (SZ348)). We do not *choose* to be the kind of entity that we are. As Heidegger asks, in italics: "Has Dasein in each case as itself ever decided freely whether it wants to come into 'Dasein' or not, and will it ever be able to make such a decision?" (SZ228, translation modified, original italicized). In the revelation of the Dasein in me in angst, it is revealed that I did not choose to be the kind of entity that I am. Nevertheless, I must be it. That it even matters to me that I did not choose this shows that I have no choice but to be a case of Dasein, since I must already be a case of Dasein in order to be able to choose or in order for my own being to be an issue for me at all. Dasein is thus thrown to me; I am stuck with it. I have to be a sense-maker. It is in this sense that, as we saw earlier, thrownness is a 'burden' for Dasein in each case (SZ135, SZ284). In revealing this burden to me—in individuating me as responsible for being a case of Dasein—angst reveals me as thrown.

Heidegger develops this picture of thrownness later in SZ, using the vocabulary of guilt or responsibility *(Schuld)*. He says of a case of Dasein: "[t]o this entity it has been delivered over, and as such it can exist solely as the entity which it is; and *as this entity* to which it has been thus delivered over, it *is, in its existing,* the ground of its ability-to-be. Although it has *not* laid this ground *itself,* it reposes in the weight of it" (SZ284, translation modified). That I am guilty means, first, that I am not self-made. I did not lay my own ground. Dasein in each case "has been brought into its 'there', but *not* of its own accord" (SZ284). Thus there is a negativity, a 'not,' at my ground. This is thrownness in each case. Yet I

[33] Heidegger occasionally calls this 'factical thrownness' (e.g., SZ413). Compare also EM31/22: "The qualification 'in each case mine' signifies: Dasein is thrown to me so that my self may be Dasein."

must still *be* a self, must *be* something. Existence, Dasein's way of being, must always *be* as a human being's definite possibilities and concerns. Existence is factically determined in this way only in my self-projection onto particular possibilities. Put differently, I *am* a self only by 'making something of myself'—by self-disclosing in a particular way. I must be or become a teacher, parent, lover, mathematician. (This is the Heideggerian source of Sartre's dictum 'existence precedes essence').[34] In taking up definite possibilities, a case of Dasein grounds itself as a self.

So I did not choose to be a case of Dasein and in this sense did not create myself. But as a case of Dasein, I make sense of things—including myself—and I do so by discovering things in light of my inherited world. Thus I take up a project of self-creation by projecting myself onto worldly possibilities. But in thus 'making something of myself,' grounding myself as a self, I do not remedy the negativity of my thrown ground. The negativity is preserved, in two ways. First, even in existential self-creation, a case of Dasein "never comes back behind its thrownness" (SZ284, 383). Even in taking up possibilities from my tradition and grounding myself in these, I am still not the author of my existence as a case of Dasein. I have not chosen to be in the business of making things meaningful, or I am not the cause of the fact of this. As we saw, any effort to take it back or to take my existence over as my own already presupposes that I am the kind of entity that makes sense of things. I must start from the fact that I am a case of Dasein and I can never escape, undo, or fully take over this fact.

Second, my self-grounding has its own characteristic negativity. When I ground myself as a self, I do so by projecting upon one of the many possibilities that my life and tradition offer. This choice of one possibility requires choosing against other possibilities, which I am *not*. My "not having chosen others and [. . .] not being able to choose them" renders my self-projection "essentially null" (SZ285). There is a negativity built into the very structure of choice, which is always a choosing of one thing and not the others.

The negativity of choice is of little consequence; the most basic dimension of guilt is thrownness. Here, the point is that I did not choose to be a case of Dasein but must always start from this. As I noted, the thought that I *could* have chosen to be Dasein is incoherent, since to choose I must already be a case of Dasein. It follows that I cannot appeal to my capacity to choose in order to explain how I first come to be a chooser. This is not a point about the limitation of choice. It is a point about our own self-authorship and our ability to grasp or otherwise take over our

---

[34] Jean-Paul Sartre, *Existentialism Is a Humanism*, trans. Carol Macomber (New Haven, NJ: Yale University Press, 2007), 20.

own ground. If I did not choose to be a case of Dasein then I am not self-made or not the author of my own being. Dasein shares this in common with all entities; no thing authors its own essence (contra Sartre), just as no child names herself. Essences, like names, are always given. Specific to Dasein—the sense-maker—is that it tries to make sense of its own ground: why am I, or how did I come to be, a case of Dasein? But there is something deeply incoherent about the question. Heidegger does not for that reason reject the question; he holds onto the fact that we ask this question—that we attempt to understand our own ground as cases of Dasein—and he locates the difficulty in the fact that there is no answer to it. It seems to Heidegger that I do not have an explanation of the fact that I am a sense-maker. This suggests that thrownness names not so much a finitude in my agency as a finitude in my ability to grasp my own ground.

Heidegger puts this by saying that the 'whence' of thrownness is obscure. The 'whence' of thrownness is that *from which* Dasein is thrown, by analogy with the original location of an object that is thrown through space. Since Dasein is not something spatial, its throw did not originate from a point in space. But it does have an origin or home in the sense of a ground or basis. To ask after that *from which* we are thrown into Dasein is to ask how we come to be this way or where we come from *qua* sense-makers. This question is not asking for a natural, psychological, or social explanation, since sense-making is not a natural, psychological, or social phenomenon for Heidegger. We are not seeking an origin or source that is temporally prior or physically more basic, but instead one that is ontologically prior—a transcendental condition. What makes sense-making possible? Answering this amounts to spelling out what it takes for there to be sense-making—the most basic terms in which sense-making makes sense. But according to Heidegger, this whence is veiled or in darkness (SZ134). Being a case of Dasein is "obscure and hidden as regards the '*why*' of it" (SZ276).

So, in sum, thrownness in each case is the fact that I did not choose to be a case of Dasein but am stuck with it. One important element of this thrownness is that its whence is obscure: I cannot (ultimately) make sense of the fact that I am thus. Such darkness at the end of sense-making is revealed when angst discloses thrownness. We can begin to see why there may be an uncanniness in this: "for the unknown is not that of which we simply know nothing. Rather, it is what pushes against us as something disquieting in what is known."[35] But to properly identify uncanniness, we need to take the interpretation of thrownness up a level.

---

[35] Martin Heidegger, *Kant and the Problem of Metaphysics,* 5th ed., trans. Richard Taft (Bloomington: Indiana University Press, 1997), 112.

My thrownness into being a case of Dasein must be distinguished from Dasein's thrownness into being rather than not. This latter is the second way of reading the claim that thrownness is thrownness into 'being a sense-maker.' Although Heidegger is not very clear about it, I think that it is at this level that we should read his talk of thrownness. This 'pure' or 'naked' thrownness (SZ134, 343) is what I will call 'thrownness itself.' On this interpretation, when Heidegger says (for instance) that "'Dasein' is thrown in such a way that, as being-in-the-world, it is the 'there'" (SZ135), he is talking about the fact that Dasein is the 'there' rather than not—which is to say, is the 'there' rather than not being at all. As we saw, the 'there' or the *da* is the clearing or space within which entities can show up in their being—a space or site of intelligibility. In each case, the *da* will be a particular world: a particular understanding of being. But in itself, the *da* is disclosedness itself, the understanding of being itself. In temporal rather than spatial language, it is the event of the happening of intelligibility, considered in itself rather than in any specificity. (In more familiar vocabulary: "When we talk in an ontically figurative way of the *lumen naturale* in man, we have in mind nothing other than the existential-ontological structure of this entity, that it *is* in such a way as to be its 'there'" (SZ133).) To say that Dasein is *thrown* into being the 'there' is to say that it is thrown into there being Dasein at all: thrown into the fact of making intelligible rather than not.

That this is the level at which Heidegger intends his talk of thrownness to be heard is clear from the fact that after noting that I did not choose to be, he goes on to express the take-home point at this more abstract level. The take-home point is precisely that the whence of thrownness itself is obscure: "[i]n itself it is quite incomprehensible why entities are to be *uncovered,* why *truth* and *Dasein* must be" (SZ228). At this level, thrownness is not that *I must be a case of Dasein* but that *Dasein must be.* To say that Dasein *must* be is not to say that sense-making entities necessarily exist in the universe. Rather, it is to say that for sense-making, the fact *that it is* is a necessary starting point. For sense-making, the fact *that it is* is fundamental and so has the force of necessity.

Similarly, in his introduction of the obscure whence, Heidegger explains: "the 'that-it-is' of its 'there' [. . .] stares [Dasein] in the face with the inexorability of an enigma" (SZ136). He adds that this is so because it is "obscure and hidden as regards the 'why' of it" (SZ276). The question that meets only darkness here is not 'why am I a case of Dasein?' but 'why is there Dasein at all?' What grounds the fact that the *da* or space of intelligibility is at all? Why is there an understanding of being, rather than not? Why must truth and Dasein be? The suggestion is that these unanswered questions are in fact unanswerable; they stand not merely at the contingent limits of our knowledge but at the brink of an essential finitude.

So to say that the whence of pure throwness is obscure is to say that the very fact of sense-making lacks an identifiable ground. This makes it incomprehensible to itself: throwness is sense-making's inability to grasp its own ground. The understanding of being is thus reflexively finite. As thrown, then, Dasein is in some sense alienated or expelled from itself. I shall explain why this is so in Chapter 3. First, we need to understand more fully how this is revealed in angst. For this finitude requires a revelation; such finitude must be encountered in order to be. Just as a question lacks an answer only if the question is posed, so too a ground is obscure or in darkness only if it resists attempted illumination. The whence of throwness must be experienced as withheld, as an absence that is present. This will obtain when Dasein attempts to grasp its own ground or to make itself intelligible to itself. In this reflexive act, Dasein will encounter something that resists intelligibility. This encounter with its own finitude occurs in angst. What must angst be if it reveals the obscure whence of throwness itself?

Originary Angst

Dasein is thrown into being rather than not. The point of this locution is primarily to flag that Dasein is not its own ground and that, in fact, its ground is withheld from it. The 'whence' or *from which* of throwness is obscure to Dasein; sense-making is reflexively finite. Sense-making 'comes to be' thus finite when it attempts to grasp itself but fails. Dasein is thus thrown from an obscure whence only insofar as it encounters its whence as obscure. If to be thus thrown is an existentiale (a structural feature of Dasein) and if Dasein is always making sense of things (and so always implicitly attempting to grasp itself), then it must be the case that this encounter with finitude is happening all the time—and further, that it is an existentiale. (Compare: we are always structurally self-conscious even when we are not explicitly thinking of ourselves.) The revelation of the obscure whence is not only constant but is so because it necessarily belongs to Dasein's sense-making. Being always already open to throwness must be part of being Dasein.

We can reach the same point from three further directions. First, all moods disclose throwness, but most do so in the mode of turning away: "The way in which mood discloses is not one in which we look at thrownness, but one in which we turn towards or turn away" (SZ135). This turning is falling—Dasein's overlooking, looking through, or fleeing from itself (i.e., the backgrounding of Dasein's being). Turning *towards* our thrownness is owned or authentic falling, while turning away from it is unowned or inauthentic.[36] Heidegger often uses the metaphors of forgetting and remembering to describe these two turnings. Both forgetting and remembering presuppose prior knowing. Similarly, both turning towards and turning away from thrownness presuppose a prior 'looking at' thrownness—a pure, positive manifestness from which or towards which the mood turns us. This manifestness of thrownness must be prior to all particular turnings and so prior to all moods—not necessarily temporally but ontologically. Heidegger confirms this picture, if somewhat obliquely: "In an *ontologico*-existential sense," the ontico-existentiell evasion of Dasein's thrown being in moods "means that even in that to which such a mood does not turn"—that is, in Dasein's thrown being—"Dasein is unveiled in its being-delivered-over to the 'there,'" that is, unveiled in its thrownness (SZ135, translation modified). That means: thrownness is unveiled in Dasein's being.

Second: the 'closing off' of Dasein's being that belongs to falling "is merely the *privation* of a disclosedness" and this "manifests itself phenomenally in the fact that Dasein's fleeing is a fleeing *in the face of* itself." Thus falling is possible "[o]nly to the extent that Dasein has been brought before itself in an ontologically essential manner" (SZ184). An original, positive disclosure of thrownness belongs to Dasein's existential constitution.

Third: the call of conscience discloses guilt (and so thrownness). It comes to me *from* an original manifestness, which it presupposes. This is the caller or from-which of the call, which "comes *from* me and yet *from beyond and over me*" (SZ275). It is Dasein who calls, but not me as a case of Dasein, in my concrete existence (SZ276). Heidegger explains this by reminding us that Dasein, as factical and fallen, is always open to its thrownness: "*That* it is factically, may be obscure and hidden as regards the '*why*' of it; but the '*that-it-is*' has *itself* been disclosed to Dasein" (SZ276). This serves as an explanation because the call comes from this original manifestness and the caller is Dasein itself in its naked

---

[36] Heidegger is not consistent in using this distinction between turning (falling), on the one hand, and turning towards (ownedness) and away (unownedness), on the other. Sometimes he implies that falling is always a turning away and so that it is always unowned (e.g., SZ184). This is part of Heidegger's more general tendency to collapse falling into unownedness.

that-it-is—its pure thrownness. So the from-which of the call of conscience is an original manifestness of thrownness itself.

Heidegger's accounts of the whence of thrownness, moods, falling, and the call of conscience all suggest that Dasein must be open to its thrownness in its very being. I will argue that Dasein's fundamental, structural encounter with its own thrownness occurs in angst. But it does not occur in the mood of angst, which is a crisis experience or a mood that irrupts into our lives at particular times. Instead, it occurs in 'originary angst' (WM93). Originary angst is Dasein's most primordial self-revelation and it is a self-exposure that belongs to Dasein as an existentiale. Heidegger himself describes angst as an existentiale when he says that "angst, as a basic findingness [*Grundbefindlichkeit*] belongs to Dasein's essential constitution of being-in-the-world" (SZ189, translation modified). As he puts it in his Kant book, angst is "an event which underlies all instances of finding oneself in the midst of entities which already are."[37] As such, originary angst is not a lived breakdown but is "always latent in being-in-the-world" (SZ189).[38]

We might even go so far as to say that this basic self-exposure is not only latent and not only a structural feature of Dasein's being but in fact coincides with Dasein's being. This would mean that our ground-level openness to the fact that we are and have to be is our openness itself. We see a hint of this when Heidegger describes angst's peculiar self-revelation: "That *about which* angst is anxious reveals itself as that *in the face of which* it is anxious—namely being-in-the-world. The selfsameness of that in the face of which and that about which one has angst, extends even to anxiousness itself. For, as findingness, anxiousness is a basic kind of being-in-the-world. *Here the disclosure and the disclosed are existentially selfsame*" (SZ188, translation modified). Heidegger analyzes moods according to a tripartite

---

[37] Heidegger, *Kant and the Problem of Metaphysics*, 167. I have altered the translation to read 'entities' instead of 'beings' for '*das Seiendes*.'

[38] An alternative reading of the latency of angst—or its "repressed" and "concealed" character (WM93)—takes it to be a mood that we have but do not feel. It would be something like an unconscious mood: an affective basis for our lives that permeates all disclosure but which we are not aware of in the way that we are aware of other moods. However, I do not see that angst, as Heidegger analyzes it, can be experienced without our awareness. Were 'angst' to have its usual sense of an objectless fear, then it could certainly be unconscious. But if angst is the mood in which the entities, tasks, and projects of my everyday life suspend their hold on me, then angst must render impotent anything that might mask or conceal it. Angst is the impossibility of precisely that immersion in everyday life that would cover over or repress a feeling or mood. So angst cannot be at Dasein's ground in the sense of being (unconsciously) experienced but not (consciously) felt. But such latency can certainly characterize other 'moods'; see, for instance, Matthew Ratcliffe, "Depression, Guilt and Emotional Depth," *Inquiry* 53 (2010): 602–626.

schema: he identifies the mood itself (e.g., fear), its *about which* (e.g., one's safety), and its *in the face of which* (e.g., a bear). In the case of angst, the three coincide: Dasein's basic structure as being-in-the-world. What readers do not always notice, however, is that it follows from this coincidence that the disclosing itself—angst—must coincide with being-in-the-world. Being-in-the-world *is* angst. This is a clue, perhaps, as to why angst must be latent: angst's latency is the backgrounding of Dasein's being in falling. Further, it gives us a straightforward way of explaining why Heidegger says not that Dasein is anxious or that I am anxious but that *angst* is anxious. He ascribes anxiousness to Dasein only once in SZ, and only in order to make this very point: "Dasein is anxious in the very ground of its being" (SZ190, translation modified).

We might notice also that talk of 'ground' runs throughout the analysis of angst, and that angst is a "ground-findingness" *(Grundbefindlichkeit)* (e.g., SZ188, 189, 190) or a "ground-mood" *(Grundstimmung)* (e.g., WM88, 89). Original angst can be said to be a mood of the ground in the sense that it is a manifestness at the very ground of Dasein, belonging to it essentially. The manifestness of the fact *that it is and has to be* determines Dasein at the ground rather than 'at the surface' as an existentiell possibility. Further, the ground of the fact *that it is and has to be*—the obscurity of the whence of thrownness—which is revealed in originary angst concerns Dasein's very ground. Finally, since it is only in this encounter with its ground that its ground is obscure to Dasein, it is only in and out of originary angst that Dasein 'comes to be,' or is grounded, as finite in the way that it is. Indeed, as we will see, in WM Heidegger understands originary angst as 'of the ground' in the sense that it is itself the ground from which Dasein in each case first emerges (WM91).

So positing an originary angst makes sense of some of the features of the analysis of angst in SZ. I will argue that there are more substantive reasons to posit an originary angst: the mood of angst cannot do the kind of work that Heidegger needs it to do. If this is right, then we will have to distinguish two phenomena called 'angst.' 'Angst' names both (i) a mood, in which world and self become manifest (as withdrawn) in a life, and (ii) the original manifestness of Dasein to itself, which lies at its ground and somehow grounds Dasein. The former is a disclosure within a life and the latter is a foundational self-openness that constitutes Dasein's openness to being. This distinction is clear in WM but not in SZ. One might argue that the distinction is operative in SZ but obscure to the reader because the term '*Angst*' is used for both phenomena. As with 'truth' in §44, Heidegger would be using the same term for a phenomenon and its condition of possibility but in this case does not make this clear. More likely is that

Heidegger did not realize that he was confusing distinct phenomena—or rather, that he was asking the mood of angst to do more than it can.

The distinction becomes clear in WM, where Heidegger explicitly asks angst to do something that a mood cannot accomplish. Accordingly, Heidegger discusses at length an angst that must be an existentiale and cannot be a mood. It turns out that, just as moods presuppose an original disclosure of thrownness, falling presupposes an original world-disclosure. These revelations are like those in the mood of angst, and so Heidegger posits an originary angst to accomplish them. He claims that angst provides the original manifestness of the nothing that makes it possible for entities to show up *as* entities at all (and not nothing). This is to say that angst grounds falling.

In SZ, Heidegger emphasizes that since in angst entities are indifferent and everyday activity is suspended, angst must be about—and so reveal—*nothing,* no particular thing. Angst lacks an ontic object. "[I]t was really nothing," we say (SZ187). But this nothing is "the most primordial 'something'": the world itself (SZ187). The world is not some *thing;* it is that which makes it possible that there are intelligible entities at all—that things can show up as meaningful or mattering. Thus, as we saw, "[b]eing-anxious discloses, primordially and directly, the world as world" (SZ187). In this sense, angst is about (i.e., discloses) the nothing.

In WM, Heidegger takes this idea further. The world must in some way be manifest all the time, or else we could not make sense of things and ourselves in terms of it. As Heidegger puts it, the manifest nothing or world

> makes possible in advance the manifestness of entities in general. The essence of the originally nihilating nothing lies in this, that it brings Da-sein for the first time before entities as such.
>
> Only on the ground of the original manifestness of the nothing can human Dasein approach and penetrate entities. But since Dasein in its essence adopts a stance toward entities—those which it is not and that which it is—it emerges as such existence in each case from the nothing already manifest. (WM90–91)

The claim is that there must be a prior, fundamental disclosure of the nothing. This disclosure makes it possible for Dasein to comport towards entities. Thus this disclosure first allows Dasein to *be* as Dasein. Heidegger calls this prior disclosure of the nothing or world 'angst.' 'Originary angst' names the fact that "the nothing [i.e., the world] is manifest in the ground of Dasein" (WM95).

The argument is this. We know that Dasein falls into the midst of entities and, in this, 'flees' the nothing or overlooks the world. I have called this flight the backgrounding of Dasein's being and the world. Heidegger now wants to say that falling is the work of the nothing or the world: we are amidst entities (i.e., fall) *because* the world is self-backgrounding (i.e., because we 'flee' it). To express the point that such self-effacing is what the nothing properly *does*—that the world is inherently backgrounded—Heidegger coins a verb from the noun: the nothing *nothings* or *nihilates (das Nichts nichtet)*. We need not hear anything dangerous or dire in this term; it is simply the word for the proper activity of the nothing or world: withdrawing itself. The nothing or the world withdraws (nihilates) so that we turn towards entities and not the nothing which makes this possible: "In its nihilation the nothing directs us precisely toward entities" (WM92).

It follows that "[t]he nothing nihilates incessantly without our properly knowing of this occurrence in the manner of our everyday knowledge" (WM92), as we might, for example, know of what is disclosed in our mood. The manifestness of the nothing is overlooked or looked through, and it shows up in our everyday lives only in the way we deal with entities, for instance in negating them (the 'not') (WM92).

Let me try to put these first two steps more clearly by expressing them in the vocabulary of SZ. We have seen that the world first allows entities to show up insofar as it is that in terms of which entities *are* at all and *are* what they are. We have also seen that the world essentially withdraws or backgrounds itself. In order to be that in terms of which entities show up, the world must get out of the way, as it were (in the same way that the screen that makes possible the projection of a film must itself not be salient if the projected images are to be seen). Because the world allows entities to show up but does not itself show up directly, Dasein gets swept up in entities and absorbed in the world of concern. It does not 'see' what makes this possible. We can express this actively as Dasein's 'looking past' or 'through' the world, or Dasein 'fleeing' its own being. We can also acknowledge that the world is essentially transparent in this way by saying that it is self-backgrounding or self-withdrawing (i.e., the nothing itself nihilates). This is the hidden condition of Dasein's falling *qua* being in the midst of entities and comporting itself towards them.

We know that the mood of angst is important for Heidegger because it reverses this trajectory, disrupting falling and displaying the world in its worldhood. However, the picture just sketched presupposes a different way for the world to be manifest—one that does not disrupt falling but that makes it possible. There must be an ontologically prior manifestness of the world that is looked past in falling. For the world is not simply *there;* it is not the planet Earth or the totality of independently existing objects. The world is the meaningful context in terms of which entities *are,* and to be a meaningful context it must be meaningful *to* Dasein. The world must show up *to* Dasein—it must be had, shared, or lived—in order to *be.* Put differently, there is no world apart from Dasein's *having* a world, and *having* a world means *disclosing* the world (i.e., *being-in-*the-world). In terms of my analogy: the projector screen must be back-grounded, but it must still be visible.

In the terminology of WM, the point is that if the nothing is the hidden condition of possibility of Dasein's engagement with entities, then Dasein must have some kind of openness to the nothing that is ontologically prior to that engagement. Thus Heidegger says that we can use the 'not' in negating something, for example, "only when its origin, the nihilation of the nothing in general, and therewith the nothing itself, is disengaged from concealment" (WM92). There is nothing special about the 'not' or the negative here; Heidegger could just as well have made his point with 'is.' We can see and say *that* and *what* things are and are not only on the basis of a prior manifestness of the nothing—a primordial disclosure of the world. There must be a "manifestness of the nothing belonging es-sentially to Dasein" (WM92).

Heidegger has called the manifestness of the nothing in experience 'angst.' He now calls the essential and original manifestness of the noth-ing 'angst.' Originary angst belongs essentially to Dasein. It is what guar-antees that Dasein is 'held out into the nothing'—that the nothing or world is manifest to Dasein, at its ground. This manifestness is a pri-mordial act of transcendence: a moving out beyond entities as a whole to world or being. And it reveals Dasein's "most proper and deepest fini-tude": the nothing at its ground (WM93).

If we still understand angst as a mood, a problem immediately arises: "must not we hover in this angst constantly in order to be able to exist at all? And have we not ourselves confessed that this original angst is rare?" (WM91). Angst must be constant and latent in order to be the primordial disclosure of the world, and yet the mood of angst seems to be fleeting and rare. There is a conflict between taking angst as a mood and positioning it at the ground of falling.

Heidegger goes on to explain that the experience of angst is rare *be-cause* Dasein falls—and that must mean because originary angst is constantly operative (WM91–92). The solution, it seems, is just to dis-tinguish the mood of angst from originary angst. Insofar as the mood of angst disrupts falling and fleeing, suspending our engagement with entities and bringing the background to the fore, angst is a rare experience. But insofar as angst is the *ground* of falling and flight, it must belong to Dasein's being—not as an experience but as an existentiale. If angst is the manifestness of the nothing that grounds the possibility of comporting towards entities, it cannot itself be a way of comporting towards entities. It cannot be an experience within a life. By positing angst as the ground of falling, Heidegger introduces an 'originary' angst that must be distinguished from the experienced mood of angst.

Retrospectively, we can see the same problem and the same argument in SZ's discussion of falling and angst. Both analyses of angst proceed in the same way and so would seem to require the same distinction between the mood of angst and originary angst. Both take the mood as an onticoexistentiell basis from which to work towards a more primordial or original disclosure. Further, the SZ analysis also seems to posit an original manifestness at the ground of falling. I quoted earlier a passage saying that the 'closing off' that constitutes falling (i.e., backgrounding or nihilation) is "the *privation* of a disclosedness" or manifestness (SZ184), and so presupposes a more primordial manifestness. And when Heidegger claims that angst is an existentiale, it is also because of a feature of falling. He says, "the everydayness of this fleeing shows phenomenally that angst, as a basic findingness, belongs to Dasein's essential constitution of being-in-the-world" (SZ189, translation modified). To belong to Dasein's essential constitution is to be an existentiale, and the claim is that falling reveals this. The 'everydayness' of fleeing can here only mean that falling determines us no matter what—that it is an existentiale. So the claim is that the backgrounding of Dasein as being-in-the-world shows that angst is an existentiale, just as in WM the flight to entities testifies to the original manifestness of the nothing. This argument holds only if something like originary angst is implied by falling. And indeed, just as our direction towards entities is grounded in the nihilating of the nothing, so too "*falling is grounded* [. . .] *in angst*" (SZ186).

As in WM, these claims produce a problem. Heidegger seems to be saying that angst belongs to Dasein's being and grounds or explains why Dasein is amidst entities. But we know also that Heidegger is analyzing angst because it is a mood that disrupts our being amidst entities and exposes us to our being. How can angst both ground and disrupt falling? The problem is not merely that angst is supposed to operate in two directions simultaneously. If angst is a mood that grounds falling then the claim is that we are absorbed in that to which we are open and do not see our openness itself *because* of the mood in which this relationship of salience and non-salience is reversed. The difficulty is that a disruption or reversal like angst presupposes that which it disrupts or reverses and cannot be its condition of possibility. This is not simply a matter of getting the temporal order of explanation backwards, for falling and angst belong to different ontological levels. Falling is an existentiale, a basic structure of human openness. Angst is a mood and so a specific mode of human openness. It is already fallen—where this means it is not an untethered receptivity but a way of being open *to entities*. To say that angst grounds or makes possible falling is to go the wrong way up the ontological ladder. Angst is not the kind of thing that falling *could* be grounded in.

In short: we cannot simultaneously hold that (i) angst is a mood, (ii) falling is an existentiale, and (iii) angst grounds falling. We must reject one of these claims. Dreyfus rejects (ii) by doubling the phenomenon of falling: falling *qua* being-amidst-entities is an existentiale and angst disrupts it, but the falling that angst grounds is something different: the unowned or inauthentic flight from our being. This psychological phenomenon can certainly be motivated by an experienced mood.[39] Ciaramelli rejects (i), but does so by doubling uncanniness rather than angst.[40] This works because what holds falling and angst together is uncanniness. Uncanniness is that from which falling flees: "When in falling we flee *into* the 'at-home' of publicness, we flee *in the face of* the 'not-at-home'; that is, we flee in the face of the uncanniness which lies in Dasein—in Dasein as thrown being-in-the-world, which has been delivered over to itself in

---

[39] Dreyfus approaches the problem from a slightly different direction. He argues that Heidegger makes a mistake in describing falling as a flight from Dasein's own being, if falling is understood as Dasein's structural tendency to become absorbed in the tools and projects of its day-to-day concern. This being-amidst-entities cannot be grounded in a motivated flight; Dreyfus argues that this picture makes ownedness (authenticity) impossible and unownedness (inauthenticity) incoherent. Falling *qua* being-amidst-entities is necessary for going about in the world; both owned and unowned Dasein must be so absorbed. If this absorption is grounded in a flight, then even owned Dasein must flee its being. But it is precisely this flight that is supposed to distinguish owned and unowned Dasein: only unowned Dasein flees. So if falling *qua* absorbed being-amidst-entities belongs to both owned and unowned Dasein and yet depends on falling *qua* flight (which distinguishes unowned Dasein), then unownedness is inevitable and ownedness is impossible. There must be two distinct phenomena of falling: falling *qua* absorption (a structural feature of Dasein) and falling *qua* flight (the ground of unownedness). Angst disrupts the former and grounds the latter. Dreyfus, *Being-in-the-World*; see especially Chapter 13, "Falling," and "Appendix, Kierkegaard, Division II and Later Heidegger" (co-authored with Jane Rubin). Dreyfus is of course right to distinguish the structural phenomenon of falling from unowned falling, but I see no need to follow him in restricting falling *qua* flight to unownedness. The flight from our being is not by itself ownedness but is the structural phenomenon of backgrounding.

[40] Fabio Ciaramelli, "The Loss of Origin and Heidegger's Question of *Unheimlichkeit*," *Epoché* 2:1 (1994): 13–33.

its being" (SZ189). So what grounds falling is not angst *per se* but the uncanniness it reveals. Now the problem is how something revealed in a mood can ground a structural feature of our being. Ciaramelli solves the problem by making a Jentschian move: "there is a doubling of uncanniness [*Unheimlichkeit*]: the *Unheimlichkeit* before *Verfallen* (ensnarement) [i.e., falling] and the *Unheimlichkeit* to which Dasein comes back because of anxiety."[41] The uncanniness prior to falling is the existential condition of possibility of falling, or that from which falling flees. The uncanniness posterior to falling is revealed in angst, and it is the strangeness felt when falling being-amidst-entities is disrupted. There is thus a chain of ontological dependence: a primordial uncanniness motivates falling; falling allows for familiarity and a sense of being-at-home, but angst makes us unhomely or uncanny. Although this does solve the problem (and although Ciaramelli's picture is ultimately not unlike my own), I see no reason that the two uncanninesses must be different. Ciaramelli seems to think that the difference is required because the revelation of uncanniness in angst depends on falling. What depends on falling must be distinct from what grounds it. Yet this shows only that the *revelation* of uncanniness depends on falling and not that there is a second uncanniness that does so.

Indeed, Ciaramelli's argument suggests to me that there is in fact a doubling of the revelation: a revelation of uncanniness that grounds falling and a revelation of uncanniness that depends on and disrupts falling. This is my solution: the doubling of angst. Originary angst grounds falling and the mood of angst disrupts falling. They differ in their ontological 'location,' since one is an experienced mood and the other an existentiale, but they share the characteristic of making the world manifest. They are thus analogous disclosures.

'Originary' angst (WM93) is not a mood but is the ground of all experience and all moods—including the mood of angst. As such, it belongs to Dasein in a way that mostly eludes its ordinary, fallen experience—it is "repressed" or "concealed" (WM93). This is another way of putting the backgrounding of the world or Dasein's being (i.e., the nihilating of the nothing), for what is backgrounded here is precisely the manifestness or revelation of angst. (Compare: what it is for the screen to be backgrounded is for it to be *visible but in the background,* which we can express by saying that its *visibility is backgrounded.* Similarly, the world is manifest (angst) and backgrounded (withdrawn), which is to say that its manifestness is backgrounded (angst is latent or concealed).

---

[41] Ibid., 27.

Further, if Dasein's being is what is backgrounded, and Dasein's being is an openness-to-world, and this is in turn angst, then originary angst must be what is backgrounded.)

How then (if at all) do we experience originary angst? We cannot access the original manifestness of the nothing "through our own decision and will" (WM93), since we cannot simply will the background into the foreground. As with various optical illusions and ambiguous images like the duck-rabbit, we more or less have to wait for the gestalt switch to occur. We see what is otherwise backgrounded only when the mood of angst comes over us; thus originary angst is revealed to us only in the mood of angst. The mood of angst is, in a sense, originary angst bringing itself to the fore—it *unbackgrounds* itself. Thus Heidegger says that originary angst "is always ready" to bring about the mood of angst, "though it only seldom springs" (WM93).

Bringing about the experience of angst, however, is the least of what originary angst does. Originary angst is originary not only because it is the ground of falling but also because it is the origin of Dasein. It lies at the 'origin' of Dasein's openness, which "emerges" "from the nothing already manifest" (WM91). In one sense, this simply repeats the claim that angst grounds falling and so grounds Dasein as amidst entities. Thus angst is an origin or ground in the sense that it is a condition of possibility: it "makes possible in advance the manifestness of entities in general" (WM90). In a deeper sense, angst is originary in that it is Dasein's being. Being open in an angsty way is what it takes to be Dasein. We will have the resources to understand Dasein's origin fully only when we get to Heidegger's origin story in EM and in *Hölderlin's Hymn "The Ister"* in Chapter 3. In the meantime, I need to say something about why we should describe the original manifestness of the world, or Dasein's openness itself, as like the mood of angst.

I have argued that if entities show up intelligibly—if Dasein falls—then there must be an ontologically prior, *a priori* manifestness of the world. That is, the meaningful network of relationships, in terms of which we make sense of entities (including ourselves), must already be lit up for us. Since this is the being-lit-up of that in terms of which entities are at all and are what they are, this is the manifestness of being. In plainer language: we already *have* a background framework of intelligibility in terms of which we understand ourselves and the entities with which we deal. We are always already in a world and so have a way of making sense of things; we know the rules of the game, as it were. Falling is grounded in this since it is only on the basis of such a prior manifestness or having that we can play the game, make sense of things, or be amidst entities.

Accordingly, the world must be *given* to Dasein—and this is to say, Dasein as being-in-the-world must 'come to be.' This giving must 'take place' 'before' any experience of meaningful entities. But the priority here cannot be a temporal priority. Consider: we do not first grasp (whether thematically or not) the meaningful relationships in terms of which things make sense and then proceed to make sense of things and allow entities to show up. Rather, we are always already playing the game of sense-making and always already have some grasp of the rules. It is the prior of this 'always already' that Heidegger is interested in. He is not interested in the personal, historical, or cultural phenomenon of how an individual acquires a world but in the ontological and transcendental problem of how a human being must *have* or possess a world in order to be already making sense of things in terms of it. This ontologically prior manifestness of the world is the condition of possibility of things showing up meaningfully—the ground of being amidst entities (falling).

To call this original manifestness of the world 'angst' is to imply that this manifestness makes sense in angst-like terms. Dasein's foundational openness is analogous to the mood of angst, such that we can understand the former in terms of the latter. Heidegger says little to help us go forward in working out the analogy, but its basic contours are fairly straightforward.

First, like the mood of angst, Dasein's foundational openness can be understood as an event. It is an event of opening, or the becoming manifest of the world. Recall that I suggested that Dasein itself can be understood as an event—the event of sense-making, which takes place in us. Originary angst would then be the inaugural and *inaugurating* episode of this event. It is the curtain rising on the stage, the floodlights illuminating the field, or the conductor raising her baton. This event is not only the first but that which makes all subsequent events possible. The opening of openness, or the becoming manifest of the world, is what first allows any happening of sense-making at all.

This event, of course, does not happen in time—or if it does, this is not what Heidegger is interested in. To call it the 'first' is to say that it is the most basic or most foundational. The event language is thus in a sense metaphorical since it implies a temporal ordering that does not apply here. But this metaphor is at least familiar: in philosophy, we often use temporal and dynamic metaphors to lay out relationships of ontological dependence and grounding. In any case, just as we can tell the story of the experience of angst in time, so too we can tell the story of the becoming-manifest of the world (the happening of originary angst) in the time of the *a priori*. This is the story of what it takes for there to be openness to being rather than not—an origin myth, if you will.

The key event in this story of the becoming manifest of the world is the sudden flaring up of ontological insight. As we have seen, the mood of angst provides ontological insight into what it takes to be an understander of being, specifically by revealing what it takes to be and to have a world. The original becoming manifest of the world is Dasein's coming to *have* a world, or the world coming to *be* (because, recall, the world is not apart from its manifestness). Originary angst is thus Dasein's opening onto being—its opening to the fact that things are and to what they are. So there is not some particular ontological insight at stake here; it is the bursting forth of ontological insight *per se:* the understanding of being. This 'moment of clarity' is the granting of being, which Heidegger will later call '*Ereignis.*'

(We can put the same point differently by replacing talk of the illumination of the world with talk of its 'coming together.' Recall that the metaphor of illumination is a way of capturing the fact that the world is always *for* Dasein and is not apart from Dasein. (So the metaphor cashes out (one of) the hyphens in 'being-in-the-world'). Notwithstanding the importance of this connection, we could also say that in originary angst the world comes to be in the sense that the totality of involvements and the context of significance are respectively and together jointed or articulated. For if the world is how things hang together, then this comes to be when things are thus hung up (always, of course, *for Dasein*). The risk of this way of talking is that it seems to lend itself to an ontic explanation of the sort that we might find in anthropology or cultural studies: how do things and practices come to be arrayed in meaningful ways? It is too easy to leave Dasein and the ontological dimension—that is, the important parts—out of the story.)

The ontological insight in originary angst is our becoming open to being, just as the ontological insight in the mood of angst is or can be (depending on our interpretation) our becoming ownedly open to being. Put differently, the mood of angst individualizes us in the sense of *individuating* us as Dasein: as the open entities that we are and that we have to be. The *a priori* becoming manifest of the world also individuates us, since in it Dasein first comes to be, and so openness first comes to be as a distinct way of being. With the flaring up of ontological insight, there first comes to be openness to entities as the entities that they are. So while the mood of angst is the experience in which we come to *see* what we are (and so become ownedly or authentically open), originary angst is the 'event' in which we (do or can) come to *be* what we are (and so be open at all). It is the birth of the understanding of being.

With this ignition of ontological insight, entities "break open and show what they are and how they are" (WM83). Heidegger thus calls the becoming-manifest of the world or originary angst "an irruption that breaks open" (WM83). Where 'before' (that is, otherwise) there was mute non-intelligibility, entities are 'now' meaningful. So just as the mood of angst is a crisis or rupture in our everyday lives, the becoming-manifest of the world is an irruption into things. In this angst-like event of ontological insight, openness bursts into being and breaks into entities, making them meaningful.

Finally, what makes the mood of angst distinctive as a mood is that it lacks any ontic catalyst. Although any event can precede the mood of angst, nothing causes it. Angst "can awaken [. . .] at any moment. It needs no unusual event to rouse it" (WM93). We cannot say what sets angst off; *nothing* does. Angst just arises, abruptly. We cannot say what sets the event going. So too, the becoming manifest of the world, or the birth of openness, must happen suddenly and without precedent. Like the mood of angst, it has no identifiable origin or ground. Just as we find ourselves thrown into angst, so too Dasein finds itself thrown open. We can only say, 'it happened.'

What accounts for or grounds the original becoming-manifest of the world? What is the ground of our openness to intelligibility or meaningful relationships—the reason that we have a meaningful world at all or the reason that we are sense-making entities? Notice that the unprecedented character of originary angst is the same as thrownness itself, which is revealed in the mood of angst. To say that originary angst is not set off by any precipitating event or efficient cause is to say that the whence of thrownness itself is obscure. Its own origin or ground escapes sense-making. The angst in which Dasein constantly and primordially encounters the obscure whence of thrownness itself is thus originary angst.

How does this originary angst belong to Dasein? We know that it is not a mood but instead makes moods (*qua* disclosures of thrownness) possible. Indeed, originary angst does not seem to be any kind of mode of the existentiale, findingness *(Befindlichkeit)*.[42] Findingness is the

---

[42] '*Befindlichkeit*' is most literally translated as 'findingness' but has also been translated as 'sofindingness' or 'so-foundness' (Haugeland); 'findedness' (Smith), 'attunement' (Stambaugh), 'affectedness' (Dreyfus), 'disposition' (Dreyfus, Emad, Kisiel), 'disposedness' (Blattner, Carman, Kisiel, Wrathall), 'situatedness' (Guignon), 'where-you're-at-ness' (Dreyfus), and (notoriously and misleadingly) 'state-of-mind' (Macquarrie and Robinson). Full references in order of mention: John Haugeland, "Truth and Finitude: Heidegger's Transcendental Existentialism," in *Heidegger, Authenticity, and Modernity: Essays in Honor of Hubert L. Dreyfus,* Vol. 1., ed. Mark Wrathall and Jeff Malpas (Cambridge, MA: The MIT Press, 2000), 52; John Haugeland, "Dasein's Disclosedness," *The Southern Journal of Philosophy* 28, Suppl. (1989): 63; Quentin Smith, "On Heidegger's Theory of Moods," *The Modern Schoolman* 58 (1981): 212; Joan Stambaugh, trans., Martin Heidegger, *Being and*

receptive and reflexive aspect of Dasein, in which it is open to what, how, and where it already is. This reflexive receptivity is manifest in feelings, perception, and similar phenomena, although the paradigmatic mode of findingness for Heidegger is mood. Originary angst belongs to Dasein as an aspect of its findingness.

Consider what it means to be the kind of entity that finds itself. To find myself *(sich befinden)* is to come across or encounter myself as already in a situation or condition—as having already been given to myself in a certain way. I always find myself, that is, as thrown (see SZ135). It is only possible to find myself if I am thrown. Conversely, "[e]xistentially, '*being*-thrown' means finding oneself in some way or other" (SZ340, translation modified). As I noted in the previous section, I only count as thrown (from an obscure whence and whither) if I find myself as such. So an entity that does not find itself as thrown does not count as thrown, even if it is not self-created. Findingness and thrownness mutually imply each other.

So findingness as a reflexive, receptive structure must essentially be a receptivity to thrownness. This is, indeed, its most basic characteristic: "The *first* essential ontological characteristic of findingness that we obtain is: *findingness discloses Dasein in its thrownness and—proximally and for the most part—in the manner of evasive turning away*" (SZ136, translation modified). This does not say that modes of findingness always reveal thrownness in one way or another. It says that findingness itself, as an existential structure, is a disclosure of thrownness—that the prior manifestness of thrownness belongs to the existentiale, findingness, as a structural moment. To say that the manifestness of thrownness belongs structurally to findingness is to say that finding is such that it has always already found the throw of thrownness. This is a kind of reflexivity internal to finding itself, in which finding unveils the thrownness that it

---

Time: A Translation of Sein und Zeit (Albany: State University of New York Press, 1996); Dreyfus, *Being-in-the-World,* 168; Parvis Emad, "Boredom as Limit and Disposition," *Heidegger Studies* 1 (1985): 63; Theodore Kisiel, *The Genesis of Heidegger's* Being and Time (Berkeley: University of California Press, 1993), 492; Blattner, *Heidegger's Being and Time,* 79; Carman, *Heidegger's Analytic,* 192 and throughout; Kisiel, *The Genesis of Heidegger's* Being and Time, 492; Mark Wrathall, *How to Read Heidegger* (New York: Granta Books, 2005), 32; Charles Guignon, *Heidegger and the Problem of Knowledge* (Indianapolis, IN: Hackett Publishing, 1983), 89; Dreyfus, *Being-in-the-World,* 168; Macquarrie and Robinson, trans., Martin Heidegger, *Being and Time* (SZ134). Note that 'findingness' was the term eventually settled on by John Haugeland for use in his posthumously published *Dasein Disclosed.* John Haugeland, *Dasein Disclosed: John Haugeland's Heidegger,* ed. Joseph Rouse (Cambridge, MA: Harvard University Press, 2013).

implies. This is something like a Heideggerian version of the story of self-consciousness.

Since the prior manifestness of thrownness is originary angst, it follows that originary angst belongs to findingness. It is the openness to thrownness that belongs to being finding. The concept of originary angst thus captures the mutual implication of findingness and thrownness, and so can be thought of as the joint or hinge between them. It is a finding that is not a mode of finding—"an event which underlies all instances of finding oneself in the midst of entities which already are," and so an event that does not take place in the ordinary sense.[43] Unlike the mood of angst, originary angst is not something that happens to a person in the course of a life. It is something that happens to or in Dasein—a structural feature of sense-making. At the collision of findingness and thrownness, openness first opens up, the world first becomes manifest. Dasein comes to be as open to being. It is in this primal event that we will find Dasein's uncanniness.

Uncanniness

Originary angst is the birth of Dasein. Ontically, generation operates on a pre-existing material and has an external efficient cause. But if openness comes to be in originary angst, and if originary angst arises without precedent or antecedent, then the coming to be of openness involves no independent ground or origin, whether material or efficient. It has no further reason to be—no material substratum, no theological ground. The flaring up of the manifestness of the world is the end of the explanatory line. Like the mood of angst, it comes out of nowhere and nothing. But the nothing is the world, so to say that nothing set angst off is to say that the world set it off and so that the world brings about its own manifestness. Openness opens itself; the world worlds. The ungroundedness of this event is marked by saying that it is self-grounding.

If the coming-to-be or (less metaphorically) ground of openness cannot be explained by appeal to something prior to or outside of it, then by most norms of explanation this amounts to saying that it cannot be explained. We cannot say how openness arises, in the sense that we cannot identify what it is grounded in. We cannot explain why there is a world for us rather than not. There are of course things to say about

---

[43] Martin Heidegger, *Kant and the Problem of Metaphysics*, 167. I have altered the translation to read 'entities' instead of 'beings' for '*das Seiendes.*'

how we come to have *this* world rather than another; why it is that *these* background practices and values grip us rather than a different set. And there are things to say about why there *is* this world rather than another. Heidegger will base this on a world-founding individual—a thinker, poet, or statesman who opens up a new set of meanings for us. But the issue at stake here is different. It is a question of why we have a world—any world—*rather than not*. By virtue of what do we *have* a world? By virtue of what does the flash of ontological insight occur in us? The picture seems to be that we cannot answer this question since the world becomes manifest in an angst-like—and so ungrounded, self-grounding—way.

The story of originary angst thus reveals that we are finitely open to the ground of our openness. It reveals a finitude in our self-disclosure. This finitude is not contingent. It is not that *we* cannot explain how the world comes to be lit up; it is that *it* cannot be explained. Compare the mood of angst: if there were an ontic ground for this mood (even if we could not identify it) then the mood in question would not be angst. It would be some version of fear (perhaps dread [*Grauen*] (SZ142)).[44] What is distinctive about the mood of angst is that it has no ontic ground. So too with originary angst: it belongs to the becoming-manifest of the world that it cannot be grounded or explained. Thus it is the same to describe this ground as absent and to describe it as obscure. There is no ideal explainer who could have a world in the way that we do and be able to say why or how. This suggests that it is constitutive for having a world that we cannot grasp how we get it, beyond the fact that we do. I will explore this further in Chapters 3 and 5.

Put differently, we are such that we cannot grasp the origin or condition of possibility of our own essence. This is a familiar claim about human nature: the human seeks to explain itself, desires to know, but can never achieve this and so is always charged with the task of self-knowledge.

Such absence or closedness of grounds or origins belongs to thrownness. Thrownness is the 'that it is and has to be' of Dasein (SZ135), which "stares it in the face with the inexorability of an enigma" (SZ136) because it is "closed off" in its "'whence' and 'how'" (SZ348). The closedness of the 'whence' or *from which* of openness is the inexplicable or ungrounded character of the becoming-manifest of the world. It is expressed dynamically in the angst story as a sudden, unprecedented arising. This, I suggest, is the uncanniness in originary angst. Uncanniness belongs to Dasein's thrownness (SZ189, 280) and is a threat *to* Dasein

---

[44] Note that appeals to biochemical grounds (for example) change the explanandum and so would not provide the right kind of ontic ground for the mood of angst.

that comes *from* Dasein itself (SZ189). Dasein is a threat to itself in that it is not, and cannot be, fully open to its own ground. Sense-making cannot make sense of its own happening or arising. As finite in this way, openness is closed off from itself. Thus uncanniness is "primordial, thrown being-in-the-world as the 'un-at-home'—the bare 'that-it-is' in the 'nothing' of the world" (SZ276–277, translation modified).

But uncanniness is, most properly, that in originary angst which grounds falling: falling "flee[s] in the face of the uncanniness which lies [. . .] in Dasein as thrown" (SZ189). Falling as this flight is the withdrawing or backgrounding of being-in-the-world (the nihilating of the nothing). How does the obscure whence of thrownness explain the concealing of the ontological? Falling is also our being-amidst-entities, and this means that uncanniness accounts for the fact that entities show up for us. How does the obscure whence of thrownness make Dasein onticoontological? The full answer to this will not come until Chapter 5. But we can anticipate the answer almost in its entirety if we start with the idea that the finitude at its ground somehow draws Dasein out into its falling openness to entities. Uncanniness, then, is a finitude that *gives* even as it takes; a withholding and closedness that grants an opening.

We have seen this structure of simultaneous giving and taking before. We have seen it in the paired revelation and withdrawal in moods (including in angst, which reveals the ontological while suspending the ontic). We have also seen it in the way that meaningful things show up for us (falling *qua* absorption) when (our) being is backgrounded or overlooked (falling *qua* flight). Heidegger calls this falling absorption in entities 'captivation.'[45] 'Captivation' is a most appropriate term for this correlated giving and taking. If I am captivated or fascinated with the raindrops on my window, then we say that I am 'taken with' them. In this, I am *given* an engaged and attentive relation to those raindrops and also possibilities of various natural scientific and aesthetic discoveries. But I am also *taken from* other entities in my world and my other possibilities—all the other things that I might be doing or paying attention to. Similarly for falling *qua* captivation with the world: Dasein is taken with innerworldly entities and given the possibility of comportment towards them, while that which makes this possible is taken from its view. The term 'captivation' thus captures the logic of revelation and withdrawal

---

[45] For example: "Being-in-the-world, as concern, is *captivated* [*benommen*] *with* the world with which it is concerned" (SZ61, translation modified); "'Unownedness' [. . . amounts to] a quite distinctive kind of being-in-the-world—the kind which is completely captivated [*benommen*] with the 'world' and the *Mitda-sein* [Dasein-with] of Others in *das Man*" (SZ176, translation modified). See also SZ113, 271.

that characterizes falling (the backgrounding of the world, the nihilation of the nothing) as well as the mood of angst, which disrupts falling with a counter-captivation.

We now need to understand how this structure is a captivation *with uncanniness:* a giving that is correlated with the obscurity of the whence of thrownness. That is, we need to understand how the obscurity of the whence of thrownness (uncanniness) is a finitude that does not merely take away but also gives or opens (captivation). This is relatively easy to grasp in the case of ordinary moods, for in these we directly experience the whence as obscure only in the sense that the mood comes over us in a way that escapes our control and full explanation. So it is our thrownness into moods that makes them possible and so that makes possible the openness to entities that any such findingness allows. It is in being finite in relation to moods that we come to be open in and to them. Thus all moods disclose thrownness in one way or another; all moods are grounded in uncanniness (the obscure whence), and all moods have the structure of captivation: a taking that grants, or a withdrawal and revelation.

The argument will be slightly different for ground moods like angst. These are distinctive because they involve a direct revelation of the obscure whence of thrownness. Heidegger draws our attention to the logic of giving and taking in the mood of angst specifically, and associates this with uncanniness: "in this peculiar temporality [of angst] is demonstrated the possibility of that power which is distinctive for the mood of angst. In this, Dasein is taken back [*zurückgenommen*] fully to its naked uncanniness, and captivated [*benommen*] with it. This captivation [*Benommenheit*], however, not only *takes* [*nimmt*] Dasein back from its '*worldly*' possibilities, but at the same time *gives* it the possibility of an *owned* ability-to-be" (SZ344, translation modified). The mood of angst discloses 'naked uncanniness'—it leads Dasein to encounter directly the obscure whence of thrownness in each case. Dasein is captivated by this, where this means that in being thus withheld from itself it is given something: in this case, it is given the possibility of ownedly appropriating its own thrown being.

It is harder to understand how falling is grounded in uncanniness. We know already that falling has the structure of captivation, but why should we think that the *taking* in question is uncanniness, the obscure whence of thrownness? Why should we ground falling in sense-making's reflexive finitude? First, it will have to be thrownness itself that is in question and not thrownness into a mood or thrownness in each case. Second, notice that the obscure whence of thrownness itself need not be addressed only in the language of 'ground,' 'origin,' or 'source.' I argued earlier that the whence of thrownness or 'from which' of Dasein is that which makes Dasein possible, where this means 'the most basic terms in which sense-making makes sense.' That in terms of which entities make sense is their being. The 'whence' is thus the source *qua* the ground of intelligibility. To say that the whence of thrownness is obscure is thus to say that Dasein does not have full access to itself as being-in-the-world—and so does not have access to its being as care. This is withheld from it.

But in this withholding, as we know, everything is given. For it is precisely when the world withdraws that entities can show up in terms of it. And since being is withdrawn, entities can show up in their being only if Dasein comports towards them by projecting them onto their possibilities. In terms of the whence and whither, this is to say that it is because Dasein's whence is obscure (being withdraws) that its whither (disclosure) is also obscure. Here, the obscurity of the whither is the fact that entities (including Dasein itself) do not wear their being on their sleeves, as it were, and so must be allowed to show up in their being ('let be') by being projected onto their possibilities. Dasein must *make* entities intelligible—it must comport towards them. In short: Dasein must comport towards entities (including itself) or discover them in their being because their being is not simply given but is given in the mode of withdrawal, given as uncanny. Thus falling is *given* if Dasein is *taken* from itself in uncanniness. (In Chapter 4 I will put this point by saying that falling is the first consequence of Dasein's uncanniness.)

So falling *is* captivation with uncanniness, which is to say that it is grounded in uncanniness or flees from it. It is the giving that comes out of the withholding of Dasein's being. In being taken from itself in this way (uncanniness), or in being subject to the withdrawal of being (uncanniness), Dasein is given the possibility and necessity of comporting towards entities (falling). Thus we see how "[i]n the clear night of the nothing of angst the original openness of entities as such arises" (WM90).

Krell is thus in some sense right when he says that "what is uncanny is the need of existence to flee from itself," although perhaps not in the sense that he intended.[46] Dasein is not uncanny because it must flee; rather, it must flee because it is uncanny. This is because uncanniness and falling are paired givings and takings. Falling (comporting towards entities, as an ontological concept of motion) is the flight from (i.e., Dasein's movement that is correlate to ('captivation')) uncanniness (the withdrawal of the world or being, the obscurity of the whence of thrownness). And

---

[46] David Farrell Krell, *Archeticture: Ecstasies of Space, Time, and the Human Body* (Albany: State University of New York Press, 1997), 102.

when falling is disrupted in the mood of angst, comportment suspended, being is revealed in an ontological insight: Dasein's being shows up—but only ever as withdrawn, as uncanny. (The mood of angst does not *reverse* falling (and so does not undo the withdrawal of being) but only ever disrupts it.)

Two notes of caution about this story. First, although falling is in some sense the same phenomenon as uncanniness, it is helpful to keep them distinct. We distinguish the two when we think falling as an existential consequence or 'flipside' of uncanniness. We do the same with ordinary cases of captivation: the giving of an attentive relationship to a particular entity is the same movement as the taking of other possibilities from me, but since 'giving' and 'taking' express this movement from different sides or directions we can analyze each separately and even posit one as ontologically (but not temporally) prior to the other. So too with falling and uncanniness.

Second, the story about falling and its grounding in uncanniness is a story about existential-ontological relationships. We are here working at the level of thrownness itself and originary angst, which are *a priori* 'happenings' in Dasein. Uncanniness thus belongs to what it takes to *be* Dasein. It is, namely, to be open to being only as withheld and so to be essentially finite. The story is thus not about what happens in a life or to a particular case of Dasein; it is neither psychological-motivational nor historical.

In particular, Dasein's flight from uncanniness is not an active fleeing but its being subject to the withdrawal of being. I will have more to say about this in the next chapter. For the moment, I want to note that it follows that Heidegger's vocabulary of flight in SZ is deeply misleading. This way of speaking can imply that uncanniness is covered over in falling in the way that it is in unownedness. That is: Dasein in each case attempts to deny its finitude *qua* the withdrawal of the world or the obscurity of its whence. This is why the question of Dasein's reasons for flight arises and why it would seem that only unowned Dasein in each case flees uncanniness (as on Dreyfus's reading). But, as I have argued, the story of falling is not a psychological-motivational story and the story of uncanniness is not a story about unownedness. If we grasp both as existential phenomena, then we can make good sense of the picture as given in SZ. It remains the case, however, that Heidegger's WM talk of withdrawal and nihilation is significantly less misleading.

However, that the vocabulary of flight is misleading does not mean that we should follow Dreyfus and jettison talk of flight altogether. We need to retain the notion of flight in addition to that of falling *qua* absorption because without it Heidegger will not have provided any explanation of falling at all. Flight and absorption together characterize the relationship between uncanniness and falling. Talk of flight emphasizes the taking movement, and so the identity of falling and uncanniness, while talk of absorption emphasizes the giving moment and so falling as distinct from uncanniness. Falling is thus a withdrawing or taking (uncanniness, falling *qua* flight) that gives comportment towards entities (falling *qua* absorption). Without the former, we can never really understand the latter. To leave out the withdrawing moment is to miss the explanation entirely.

But we may yet push for an account of this very withdrawing. Why does being withdraw? It is clear *that* this must be so in order for absorption in entities to be possible. But it is not clear why the logic of captivation must apply here at all rather than some other logic. Why must being withdraw itself in order for entities to show up? As a question about Dasein, this asks, why must Dasein be ontico-ontological? Or why is Dasein's reflexive finitude a *giving* finitude? In Chapter 5 we will see that even the question of *how* this uncanny logic of captivation works cannot be adequately answered, let alone the question of why it applies here. This will turn out to be a positive—and very telling—feature both of uncanniness and of us as entities who understand our own being. But Heidegger does not give us the resources in SZ to pursue the issue to this point, so I will turn to his later texts shortly. It is not until WM that Heidegger begins to think what it means to say that being is intrinsically self-concealing (nihilating), and the first serious treatment of this self-concealing follows shortly after in 1930.[47] The problem of uncanniness pursues Heidegger in his later thought and becomes the question, what is the *lēthē* at the heart of *alētheia* (truth) and whence its deprivation *(a-)*? But although Heidegger follows the SZ analysis of angst with a discussion of truth, he ultimately changes the topic. Instead of explaining why being must be concealed, he explains why being is sometimes concealed in an aggravated way: the psychological-motivational ground of unownedness. Thus he confuses the structural phenomenon of falling with its unowned form. This leads many readers to an interpretation of uncanniness as an unwelcome feeling rather than a feature of our being.

If we keep our sights on falling as an existentiale and uncanniness as the obscure whence of thrownness, the withholding of being, or the nihilation of the nothing, then we need only one final step to complete the picture: we need to situate all of this in originary angst. To say that

---

[47] Martin Heidegger, "On the Essence of Truth," trans. John Sallis, *Pathmarks*.

Dasein is uncanny in originary angst is to say that even as being or open-ness is given to Dasein (originary angst) it is taken away (uncanniness). Thus there is intelligibility only if it is withheld, or given as finite. This is the most fundamental giving and taking, and it underlies that of falling. We can represent this chain of givings and takings thus:

Angst	Being	Dasein
Originary angst, Dasein's 'birth'	Being / openness / world is given; the ontological opens	Dasein is open *qua* ontological
	↓	
Uncanniness / the obscure whence of thrownness / falling as flight	Being is taken / withheld; the world / Dasein's being backgrounds itself; the nothing nihilates	Dasein is finite
	↓	
Falling as absorption	Comportment to entities is given: Dasein irrupts into the ontic	Dasein is open *qua* ontic
	↓	
The mood of angst	Comportment to entities is taken: falling is disrupted (withdrawal); ontological insight is given (revelation), and so the possibility of ownedness is also given	Dasein is philosophical / metaphysical

We thus have a story about how openness 'comes to be' on which it comes to be as finite, and so as falling, as capable of disruption in a mood like angst and so as capable of ownedness or unownedness. The key part of this story is the very first finitude: uncanniness, as the withholding of (Dasein's) being even as it is granted—the obscure whence of thrownness itself. It is this taking that sparks the subsequent givings. Uncanniness is the negativity or finitude at the ground of human being and this is the most primordial mode of being-in (SZ189) or the most basic way in which Dasein is open.

It will turn out that the story is significantly more complicated, especially in its first two steps. This is because Dasein's openness is always finite (there is no pure openness to the ontological) and its finitude is always disclosed (the whence of thrownness is obscure *to a finding*). Recall that I situated uncanniness in findingness as a structural feature belonging to the reflexivity of openness. Because of this reflexivity, uncanniness is not merely a limitation in Dasein but "the most elemental way in which thrown Dasein is disclosed" (SZ276). Understanding uncanniness as a disclosed feature of Dasein will make it more difficult for us to work out the logic of the interplay of openness and closedness, giving and taking. Ultimately, we will see that and why the story cannot be expressed in a linear way.

To anticipate the kind of problem that we will run into, consider Drey-fus's description of Dasein as essentially *wrong,* which is a good way of getting at its essential uncanniness: "Existential guilt reveals not inau-thentic Dasein's moral lapses, or its essential failure to choose; it reveals an essentially unsatisfactory structure definitive of even authentic Dasein. Even if Dasein has done nothing wrong there is something wrong with Dasein—its being is not under its own power."[48] What is wrong with Dasein is not a lack of control, choice, or freedom (in the usual senses of those terms). But something is indeed wrong with Dasein, and it is the disclosure of this that makes angst specifically 'angsty' and uncanniness count as a threat. We cannot understand this threat in psychological-mo-tivational terms; it is not that I feel that something is wrong or that I have reasons to want to reject some aspect of myself as 'wrong.' Rather, there is something *inherently* wrong with Dasein: a finitude internal to it. This is a finitude internal to the granting of being: being and so the 'ground' of Dasein's own being is not directly manifest to Dasein but shows up to it only as obscure or withdrawn. What is wrong with Dasein is that it is reflexively finite. Why is this a wrongness?

Dreyfus takes this kind of finitude in intelligibility to be 'wrong' in-sofar as Dasein seeks secure meaning and finds itself unsatisfied or dis-appointed. But this is still too psychological and it posits a standard of rightness that is unnecessary. First, Dasein does not *seek* meaning (se-cure or otherwise); it *is* the entity that understands being. It is an entity that is 'out for' meaning, always and no matter what. If there is a limit or finitude internal and essential to such sense-making, then this is not merely a disappointing limitation. Such a finitude means that Dasein can be what it is (the entity that understands being) only insofar as it is not fully what it is (does not fully understand (its own) being). Dasein is es-sentially unable to realize its own essence. This is why uncanniness is a threat that "reaches Dasein itself and which comes from Dasein itself" (SZ189)—where 'Dasein itself' means something like 'the very project of sense-making.'

Second, we do not need to posit a contrasting rightness in order to grasp Dasein's situation as wrong. Heidegger puts this by saying that the negativity at Dasein's ground, its uncanniness, is not a lack or shortcom-ing (SZ285). Dasein's grounding in a negativity does not mean that it is

---

[48] Dreyfus, *Being-in-the-World,* 306.

"lacking in comparison with an ideal" (SZ285). This is because Dasein's finitude is *essential* to it: in being uncanny it is not failing to be what it is. What Dasein *is*, in fact, is essentially *un-at-home* (*un-heimlich* or *un-zuhause* (SZ189)). It is negatively or finitely related to its own home or essence. It is not fully coincident with itself. This means that Dasein is *supposed* to be wrong. Its wrongness is a kind of rightness.

But if this is right, then uncanniness must belong to Dasein's essence. Dasein is not essentially the entity that understands being but the entity that *finitely* understands being. What makes Dasein what it *is* is thus not its openness to being so much as the withdrawal of being from it. This would suggest that the obscurity of the whence of thrownness is the whence itself—that Dasein's uncanniness is its essence rather than a blemish on its essence. But how are we to understand this?

Clearly, we are in the territory of a peculiar kind of finitude and a peculiar kind of essence. We will find this peculiarity inscribed in the very word 'uncanniness,' and specifically in the distinctive way in which the *un-* of *Unheimlichkeit* negates. I will discuss this in Chapter 5. What we need to do now is to carefully spell out the full story of original angst. Heidegger finds a retelling of this story in the first choral ode from Sophocles's *Antigone*, which poetically projects Dasein's uncanniness. By following the ode, we will be able to tell the story sketched in the chart in full detail. The next chapter tackles the first two steps.

3

Being Uncanny

I N THE *SYMPOSIUM,* Plato's character Aristophanes tells a story about the origin of love.[1] This fantastical story follows originally spherical creatures who, having threatened the gods, were split in two as punishment. Human life as we now know it is the quest for our respective 'other halves.' This quest is love or *eros.* In describing human life in this way, Aristophanes's story gives us a set of basic concepts in terms of which to understand life and love: transcendence, impiety, punishment, and insufficiency. It is an origin story not in the sense that it goes back to the beginning of a historical timeline but in the sense that it goes deep into our ways of making sense of things to articulate and to reinforce our foundational concepts.

Heidegger takes the first choral ode (the "Ode to Man") from Sophocles's *Antigone* to be doing something similar. Like the play from which it comes, the ode has received much philosophical and literary attention.[2] It reads as a narrative of human development, describing characteristic human activities and skills through a progressive historical development from the time of the 'primitive' hunter-gatherer to that of the 'civilized' city-dweller. But as Heidegger reads it, the ode is not an account of what prior generations have accomplished, which we might check against our knowledge of history and social evolution. The ode is indeed an origin

---

[1] Plato, *Symposium,* trans. Alexander Nehamas and Paul Woodruff (Indianapolis, IN: Hackett Publishing, 1989).

[2] For an exhaustive discussion of how *Antigone* has been appropriated by Western philosophy (and German philosophers in particular), see George Steiner, *Antigones: How the Antigone Legend Has Endured in Western Literature, Art, and Thought* (New Haven, CT: Yale University Press, 1996). Steiner memorably notes the privileged role of tragic conflict or confrontation in *Antigone:* "It has, I believe, been given to only one literary text to express all the principal constants of conflict in the condition of man. These constants are fivefold: the confrontation of men and of women; of age and of youth; of society and of the individual; of the living and the dead; of men and of god(s)" (231).

story, but the origin it tells is not a historical origin. The story is not ontic but ontological: it is an account of the human essence or what it means to be human. Like Aristophanes's story, the ode gives us the basic conceptual framework within which to make sense of human being. It is the later Heidegger's retelling of the story of original angst.

In a sense, the ode not only *tells* the origin of the human being, it *is* the origin of the human being. It is in the choral ode specifically, and in the *Antigone* play and Greek tragedy more generally, that "Greek [b]eing and Dasein [. . .] were authentically founded" (EM154/110). This is to say that the ode establishes or founds the Greek—and by extension, Western—understanding of what it is to be human and of what it is to be at all. What Heidegger calls 'poetry' or 'art' accomplishes for a community this founding of intelligibility, laying out what things *are*—how they hang together, how they make sense, how they matter. "Poetry is the saying of the unconcealment of [entities]."[3] Heidegger calls this saying or founding work 'poetizing' or 'poetic projection.' The choral ode is "a poetic projection of human being [*Seins [des Menschen]*]] on the basis of its extreme possibilities and limits" (EM165/119). It lays out for the Greeks how the human being is to be understood; it "provides the authentic *Greek* definition of humanity [*Mensch*]" (EM161/116).

So by interpreting the ode, Heidegger can uncover those basic concepts and categories in terms of which human being makes sense—both those in terms of which we ourselves are intelligible and those that we use in making everything else intelligible. In following Heidegger's project, we must thus follow at least two interpretive guidelines. First, we must not read the ode's timeline as a historical timeline, and second, we must not read the ode's characters ontically.

First, the timeline. In telling an intelligible origin rather than a historical origin, a poetizing like the ode gives us a pre-history or "primal history" of the sort that Heidegger calls "mythology" (EM166/119). Such a myth is true not if the events recounted actually happened in the past but if the narrative lays out the phenomenon in an intelligible way. Thus there is a sense in which the ordinary timeline of events recounted is fictional. If we are to speak of time here, then the time that the story traverses is the essential time of the 'prior' in the *a priori*. That is to say that what gets laid out on the timeline is not a series of events but the structure of an essence. In following the story from one event to another, we grasp

[3] Martin Heidegger, "The Origin of the Work of Art," trans. Albert Hofstadter, *Basic Writings: From* Being and Time *(1927) to* The Task of Thinking *(1964),* ed. David Farrell Krell, 2nd ed. (New York: Harper Collins, 1993), 199.

relations of *ontological* priority and posteriority. Heidegger himself uses such a mythical timeline to understand essences by treating an essence not as a static thing (a spatial fiction) but as something that happens (a temporal fiction). Thus he turns 'essence' *(Wesen)* into a verb, saying that human being *essences (west)*. He does this because he uses the same temporal fiction to make sense of being. Being essences (EM173/124) in that it is coming-into-appearing. I will return to this later. The point for now is that the ontic timeline of the story, while fictional, is nonetheless ontologically significant.

Second, the characters. It will be impossible to understand the ode as a poetic projection of human being if we persist in taking the ode's characters at face value, as the natural entities and human phenomena that are most significant for human existence. It is by reading the entities mentioned as figures for ontological phenomena that Heidegger can take the ode as a story about being and Dasein even though it mentions only nature and the human being. Thus words like 'sea,' 'earth,' and 'living things'—each of the 'characters' in the ode—refer not to natural entities but to ontological phenomena. Holding fast to this is the major interpretive challenge in reading the ode. It requires that we translate the ode's ontic vocabulary into appropriate ontological vocabulary. This is difficult because Heidegger only intimates the direction of this translation,: "The first strophe and antistrophe name the sea, the earth, the animal as the overwhelming" (EM166/119). 'The overwhelming' is one of Heidegger's words for being. The ode needs to talk about being by speaking of entities because being is never accessed directly. As Derrida puts it: "Being, which is nothing, is not a being, cannot be said, cannot say itself, except in the ontic metaphor. And the choice of one or another group of metaphors is necessarily significant."[4]

The basic 'metaphor' used in the choral ode is nature, *phusis*. The natural entities in the ode are all figures of being. This is because, according to Heidegger, the Greeks understood being as *phusis*. I shall return to this. For now, start with the idea that the ode makes an ontological rather than an ontic claim. Thus its talk of nature articulates and founds what it is *to be* a natural entity. But for the Greeks (according to Heidegger), *phusis* refers beyond those entities that we are inclined to call 'natural'; it refers to entities as a whole and as such (EM14/10). Combining these ideas, we see that the ode, in its talk of natural entities, is speaking of being.

---

[4] Jacques Derrida, "The Ends of Man," *Margins of Philosophy,* trans. Alan Bass (Chicago: University of Chicago Press, 1982), 131.

Further, "just as little as the first strophe and antistrophe speak only of nature in the narrower sense does the second strophe speak only of the human being" (EM166/119). Just as the natural entities in the ode are ways of addressing being, so too 'human being' in the ode refers neither to individual human beings nor to the human race but to Dasein. Like 'Dasein' (SZ12, 42), '(the) human being' picks out the human with regard to its being. As Heidegger later says, 'the human being' names "the essence of Western humankind [*Menschentum*]": our (Western) Dasein.[5]

Accordingly, the ode is not telling us what the human being *is* by telling us how it interacts with entities in its environment. This is how Heidegger's interpretation of the ode is typically read.[6] Instead, the ode is telling us what the human being *is* by explaining the human relationship to *being*. It is the story of Dasein. And on this story, Dasein is *deinon,* uncanny.

As he often does, Heidegger acknowledges that his reading of the ode goes beyond what is said on the surface of the text. This is quite deliberate, and it stems from Heidegger's understanding of what it means to engage in interpretation and translation (see, for instance, HI61/74).

[5] Martin Heidegger, *Hölderlin's Hymn "The Ister,"* trans. William McNeill and Julia Davis (Bloomington: Indiana University Press, 1996), 43/51, translation modified. Hereafter HI. Page references in the text will be given in the form (HIxx/xx), where the first page number refers to the English translation and the second to the *Gesamtausgabe* edition—Martin Heidegger, *Hölderlins Hymne "Der Ister," Gesamtausgabe,* Vol. 53 (Frankfurt am Main: Vittorio Klostermann, 1984). Heidegger says, "When we speak of '*der Mensch*' here and throughout these remarks, we always mean the essence of the historical *Mensch* of that history to which we ourselves belong: the essence of Western *Menschentums.* '*Der Mensch*' means neither '*der Mensch* in general', 'universal *Menschheit*', nor indeed mere 'individual' *Menschen,* nor even some form or other in which several or many are united" (HI43/51, translation modified). Let me take 'Western' as understood, since although it is significant for the text's discussion of the unhomeliness of the German people, it is not particularly relevant to my more general discussion of uncanniness. In EM, the translators render '*der Mensch*' variously as 'humanity,' 'the human,' 'the human being,' 'human beings,' and 'humans.' To preserve the ontological dimension of Heidegger's discussion, I usually amend the translation to read 'the human being' (although not when quoting the translation of Sophocles's ode). (Similarly for HI). I transliterate Heidegger's Greek (which is not transliterated in the English translation) and alter the translation to read 'entities' instead of 'beings' for '*das Seiendes*'.

[6] For example, Richardson takes the first strophe and antistrophe to describe "those beings which are completely external to There-being and surround it, v.g. [sic] the sea, the earth, the animal kingdom." William Richardson, *Through Phenomenology to Thought* (New York: Fordham University Press, 2003), 270. Haar has the ode describing the human being as the entity who "can raze and subjugate the earth, capture and tame wild animals, invent sciences, arts and techniques, institute political life" in a "conflicting encounter with natural forces, other human beings, the gods." Michel Haar, *Heidegger and the Essence of Man,* trans. William McNeill (Albany: State University of New York Press, 1993), 153 and 152.

He holds that "[t]he authentic interpretation must show what does not stand there in the words and which is nevertheless said" (EM173/124). Rather than limiting itself to explicating the propositional content of a text, authentic interpretation reveals what the text allows to show up or make sense—even if the text accomplishes this indirectly or despite itself. But while Heidegger's vocabulary and translations are unfamiliar and his interpretation extreme and novel (he would say, *violent*), the picture of the human being that he finds in the ode is not too far removed from what a thoughtful reader of the ode might herself come to. It presents a familiar picture of the human being.[7] Let us read it in full (in Heidegger's translation):

> Manifold is the uncanny, yet nothing
> more uncanny looms or stirs beyond the human being.
> He ventures forth on the foaming tide
> amid the southern storm of winter
> and crosses the surge
> of the cavernous waves.
> And the most sublime of the gods, the Earth,
> indestructible and untiring, he wears out,
> turning the soil from year to year,
> working the ploughs to and fro
> with his horses.
>
> And the flock of birds that rise into the air
> he ensnares, and pursues
> the animals of the wilderness
> and of the ocean's surging waves,
> most ingenious man.
> He overpowers with cunning the animal
> that roams in the mountains at night,
> the wild-maned neck of the steed,
> and the never-tamed bull,
> fitting them with wood,
> he forces under the yoke.
>
> And into the sounding of the word
> and swift understanding of all
> he has found his way, even into courageous
> governance of the towns.
> And he has pondered how to flee

[7] For more on the plausibility of Heidegger's reading as a reading of Sophocles's ode, see Haar's discussion in *Heidegger and the Essence of Man*, 151–155.

exposure to the arrows
of unpropitious weather and its frosts.
Everywhere venturing forth underway, experienceless without any way
    out,
he comes to nothing.
The singular onslaught of death he can
by no flight ever prevent,
even if in the face of dire infirmity he achieves
most skillful avoidance.

Craftiness too, as the work
of his ability, he masters beyond expectation,
and if he falls on bad times
other valiant things succeed for him.
Between the ordinance of the earth and the
order ordained by the gods he ventures:
Towering high above the site, forfeiting the site
is he for whom non-entities always are
for the sake of risk.
Such shall not be entrusted to my hearth,
nor share their delusion with my knowing,
who put such a thing to work. (HI58–59/72)[8]

A thoughtful reader of the ode might take the surface story to be that the human being leaves its natural habitat to brave the foreign environment of the sea; it depends on and is rooted in the earth and its cycles, yet through agriculture tries to control the earth and exploit its cycles; the human being is a predator who does not merely kill to survive but makes slaves of animals, relying on their natural order and instincts at the same time as it disrupts them; it builds walls and invents technologies like medicine to ward off the inevitable effects of its natural environment and condition. In short, the human being is the entity for whom it is natural to be unnatural. The human being is naturally unnatural or unnaturally natural. The human being is such, we may suppose, because it is dissatisfied with its given condition or is born inadequate to its environment and so is moved to reach beyond itself: to explore, control, and learn. The finitude of the human being sparks transcendence. The ode's claim, on this kind of reading, is that it is precisely this reaching-out-from-poverty, this erotic gesture, that makes the human being what it is.

---

[8] Martin Heidegger, *Hölderlin's Hymn "The Ister,"* trans. William McNeill and Julia Davis (Bloomington: Indiana University Press, 1996), 58–59. Reprinted with permission of Indiana University Press.

It is something with precisely this shape that Heidegger finds expressed in the ode and that he calls 'uncanniness.' The difference is that he understands the human being as Dasein. So while the ode is typically read as an account of the origin of the human being, Heidegger reads the origin in question as the ground of the understanding of being—the 'first' coming-into-appearing of being and human being. The ode tells this origin as a story about the human being's audacity and perseverance in the face of overwhelming difficulty, which Heidegger reflects by telling the story of Dasein's struggle to bring being to appearing. This is the remarkable and mysterious happening by which the human being first attains that which makes it what it is and so in which it comes to itself—not as builder of civilization but as openness to being. According to Heidegger, this achievement consists in the human being's essential expulsion from its essence, or the productive play of its essence and non-essence. This mirrors the ode's picture of the human as both natural and unnatural. To say that the human being is uncanny, then, is to say that the openness to being is grounded in a play of appearing and concealment, essence and non-essence. So while Heidegger's reading will go well beyond the surface text of the ode, and while it is certainly violent in some sense, it does not obviously abuse or usurp the text for its own purposes. It is plausibly a reading *of* the ode and its claim that the human being is the uncanniest entity.

To Deinon

πολλὰ τὰ δεινὰ κοὐδὲν ἀνθρώπου δεινότερον πέλει
polla ta deina kouden anthrōpou deinoteron pelei. (line 332)[9]

Vielfältig das Unheimliche, nichts doch
über den Menschen hinaus Unheimlicheres ragend sich recht.

Manifold is the uncanny, yet nothing
uncannier than man bestirs itself, rising up beyond him. (EM156/112)

The human being is *deinoteron*—more uncanny—than other entities. '*Deinon*' is usually translated into English as 'terrible,' 'fearsome,' 'mighty,' 'powerful,' 'wondrous,' or 'strange.' Heidegger translates (and so interprets) it in German as '*unheimlich*' (uncanny). He explains this translation in EM by hyphenating: *das 'Un-heimliche'* (the un-canny). This draws our

---

[9] Sophocles, *Sophocles: Plays: Antigone,* ed. P. E. Easterling and R. C. Jebb, trans. R. C. Jebb (London: Bristol Classical Press, 2004).

attention to the element of the *-heim-* or home. What is *un*-homely or *un*-canny is "that which throws one out of the 'canny', that is, the homely, the accustomed, the usual, the unendangered" (EM161/115). Being thrown out of the homely—being un-homely or un-canny—is "the basic trait of the human essence [*des Menschenwesens*]" (EM161/116), the "essential trait of the human being [*Wesenszug des Menschen*]" (HI73/89).

On the face of it, the claim is that the human being is unique because it is uncannier than other entities. Since Heidegger goes on to identify the happening of uncanniness with the happening of unconcealment (EM178/127), human uncanniness must be the strangeness of its openness to being. This is the most *deinon,* the most strange, because it is unique. Open to being, the human being is radically unlike other entities. And yet it dwells amidst them. This makes the human being unhomely—and unhomely precisely where it makes its home. This is how William Richardson interprets the claim in both EM and SZ: Dasein is uncanny because its openness to being makes it a stranger in the ontic.[10] To be uncanny is to be unique, and Dasein is the most unique because it is ontico-ontological. The home with respect to which it is uncanny or unhomely is the ontic realm, the realm of entities.

I have interpreted Dasein's uncanniness in SZ quite differently, primarily in that I have understood the 'home' from which Dasein is estranged as its own ground rather than the ontic realm. It remains to be seen which reading best fits Heidegger's interpretation of the ode. Initially, we can worry about whether Richardson's interpretation can accommodate the EM claim that not only the human being but also being is *deinon* (EM159/114). We should also notice that the HI interpretation of uncanniness breaks out of the terms of Richardson's reading. Here, Heidegger does not understand '*deinon*' simply in terms of the strange, estrangement, and the stranger. According to Heidegger, calling the human being more *deinon* than other entities brings into play the unity and multiplicity of the full range of resonances of the Greek term. When Sophocles says that the human being is *more deinon* than other entities, and so implies that the human being is the *most deinon* entity, the claim is not about the quantity or extent of human uncanniness (e.g., HI90/112, EM173/124). The uncanniest is not "the augmentation of the uncanny to the highest degree" (EM173/124). Rather, the human being is *deinon* in a special kind of way.

The opening lines of the ode tell us that the *deinon* is manifold *(polla).* The human being is the most *deinon* because it is characterized by the

---

[10] "The There [i.e., Dasein] is the most awesome and strange [i.e., *deinotaton*] of beings because, open to Being, it is constitutionally es-tranged from the beings amid which it dwells." Richardson, *Through Phenomenology to Thought,* 275; see also ibid., 74: "the dwelling places of the ontic are not There-being's true abode [*Unheimlichkeit*]."

unifying and unified ground of this manifold. According to Heidegger, to say that the *deinon* is manifold is not to say that many things are uncanny (as the standard translation of the ode has it). It is to say that the *deinon* itself is internally folded and multiple in kind (HI68/83). Such internal folding belongs to the essence of the *deinon,* and it is manifest in the multiple senses of the term. Heidegger puts this by saying that *deinon,* "as a genuine word, names what it tells of in such a way that, as a word, it itself is of such a kind as that which it names" (HI68/83). To be *deinon* is to be manifold and *deinon* is the kind of word that is *itself deinon:* manifold as a word. It has several different meanings. The character of this manifold tells us something about what it is to be *deinon.*

Heidegger collects the senses of *deinon* into three groups: the fearsome, the powerful *(Gewaltige),* and the un-habitual *(Ungewöhnliche)* (HI67/82). Each of these in turn contains two inner possibilities. The *fearsome* can be (i) that which is frightening and motivates flight (e.g., a snake) or (ii) that which is worthy of honor, towards which one turns in awe and reverence (e.g., the gods). The *powerful* can be (i) actively violent (e.g., a boxer) or (ii) that which prevails over everything, governing and determining it (e.g., a queen). The *un-habitual* may (i) be extraordinary in a way that is outside the habitual (e.g., a genius) or it can (ii) remain within the habitual as an intensification of it: a being skilled in everything (e.g., a polymath) (HI63–64/77, HI67/82). The senses listed under (i) tend towards the threatening and disruptive, while those under (ii) approach the sublime. But what Heidegger wants us to notice is the structure. The internal complexity of the *deinon* is a structured multiplicity: each of the three primary meanings branches into two senses that are both opposed and related. This is less a forking than a folding. If I fold a piece of paper, I produce two opposite edges that are united at the crease. They are simultaneously opposed and united. The *deinon* is not only manifold or multiple; it is mani*folding* in this way.[11]

[11] In the manifold of the '*deinon*' we can see something of the shape of Heidegger's own manifold discussions of uncanniness: (A) In SZ, Heidegger thinks uncanniness primarily in terms of the first sense of '*deinon*'—as that which occasions the flight of falling (the *fearsome,* the threat of which motivates avoidance and flight) and as that which opens the possibility of ownedness—which is a *turning-towards* (uncanniness) in *heed* and *respect.* (B) In EM, he uses the vocabulary of the powerful *(Gewaltige)* and so focuses on the second sense of '*deinon*'. We will see that the human being's uncanniness here consists in the reciprocity between (ii) being as uncanny in the violence *(Gewalt)* of its overwhelming *(überwaltigen)* sway *(Walten)* (its *prevailing* over everything) and (i) the human being as uncanny *qua* the entity that is violence-doing *(gewalt-tätig)* in disclosively struggling against concealment *(active violence).* (C) In HI, Heidegger speaks most often of the third sense, the un-habitual (e.g., HI74/91), most likely because it resonates with the vocabulary of the foreign used in his reading of Hölderlin's poem. Overall, however, the HI analysis is less concerned with the un-habitual *per se* than with the unity of all three senses of '*deinon*'. Thus this text can be read as unifying Heidegger's three primary discussions of uncanniness.

But the *deinon* is nonetheless singular. There is an essential unity hidden behind its manifold and folding senses. This unified essence must account for the internally folded character of the *deinon*. Heidegger calls this internal folding 'counterturning': "something counterturning prevails in what the Greeks name *deinon*" (HI63/77). So the question is, what unifies and grounds the counterturning in the *deinon*? Heidegger answers: the counterturning itself. The reason that the *deinon* is manifold is that it is intrinsically, essentially counterturning. The multiplicity of meanings of '*deinon*' implicitly points towards this essence and unity but does not directly manifest it. The counterturning essence of the *deinon* must be brought out in an interpretive translation of *deinon* as *unheimlich*. This in turn requires that the *Unheimliche* be grasped "more decisively as the unhomely [*das Unheimische*]" (HI73/89)—a term that Heidegger has used earlier in HI to interpret Hölderlin's poem, "The Ister." So 'the uncanny' grasps the concealed and unified essence of the *deinon* only when it is understood as 'the unhomely.' 'Unhomeliness' is the human being's singular essence (HI68/83) as excessively uncanny: "[u]ncanniness in the sense of unhomeliness thus exceeds infinitely, that is, in essence, all other forms of the uncanny. Strictly speaking, unhomeliness is not at all one form of the uncanny among others, but is essentially 'beyond' these" (HI76/94).

So the claim that the human being is *more deinon* than other entities or the *most deinon* entity is not the claim that the human being is especially determined by one or another senses of the *deinon*. It is also not the claim that it is all three heaped together (as if the human being were the most fearsome *and* powerful *and* un-habitual entity). That the human being is the most *deinon* entity means that in it the unifying ground of these meanings is displayed. The opening lines of the ode now say that the *deinon* is manifold or counterturning but nothing is counterturning in the way that the human being is. Determined by the singular essence of the *deinon*, uncanny human being must be unhomely or uncanny in the sense of counterturning.

EM also understands the uncanny human being as a counterturning or unified folding: the human being is "doubly *deinon* in an originally united sense" (EM160/115). The difference is that while EM tends to emphasize the multiplicity (the two poles between which the counterturning turns), HI tends to stress unity and singularity (the counterturning itself, as a single movement). But the point remains the same: to be singularly *deinon* (HI) is to manifest the essence of the *deinon*, which is a counterturning or internal doubling—a being doubly *deinon* (EM). This suggests that in both HI and EM, uncanniness is to be understood in terms of counterturning. I will argue that there is a single account of uncanniness behind both texts and that it is one in which the home in relation to which the human being is unhomely—that from and towards which it turns—is the human being's own essence.

There are, of course, significant differences between EM and HI and the readings of the choral ode in each.[12] Most of these differences lie in Heidegger's interpretive and exegetical strategies. In particular, the HI discussion is longer and broader than EM, covering more pages and more of the *Antigone* play. Considering Antigone herself in HI leads Heidegger to make the only significant substantive change in his reading: a reversal in his interpretation of the ode's closing lines (HI97/121, 105/130–131). But in another sense, Heidegger's HI reading of the ode is narrower than that in EM, because he has accomplished much of the conceptual work on uncanniness indirectly in his interpretation of Hölderlin's poem in the first part of the lecture. Heidegger can then focus on the three explicitly counterturning moments in the ode (plus the closing lines), whereas in EM he does the conceptual work by reading the ode's strophe-by-strophe narrative. Let me begin by following the latter strategy: I will work through the story of being and human being, determining what it means to describe the human being as essentially uncanny or counterturning.

The Story of Being

The "saga" (*Sage*) of being (EM76/55) is told in the ode as the story of the human relationship to nature, *phusis*.[13] For Heidegger, *phusis* names

---

[12] For further discussion of the similarities and differences between the two analyses, see Miguel de Beistegui, *Heidegger and the Political: Dystopias* (New York: Routledge, 1998), especially Chapter 5, "Before Politics"; Richard Capobianco, "Heidegger's Turn toward Home: On Dasein's Primordial Relation to Being," *Epoché: A Journal for the History of Philosophy* 10:1 (2005): 155–173, and *Engaging Heidegger* (Toronto: University of Toronto Press, 2010), especially Chapter 3, "The Turn towards Home"; Véronique M. Fóti, "Heidegger, Hölderlin, and Sophoclean Tragedy," in *Heidegger toward the Turn: Essays on the Work of the 1930s*, ed. James Risser (Albany: State University of New York Press, 1999); Clare Pearson Geiman, "Heidegger's *Antigones*," in *A Companion to Heidegger's Introduction to Metaphysics*, ed. Richard Polt and Gregory Fried (New Haven, CT: Yale University Press, 2001); and Jacques Taminiaux, "Plato's Legacy in Heidegger's Two Readings of *Antigone*," in *Heidegger and Plato: Toward Dialogue*, ed. Catalin Partenie and Tom Rockmore (Evanston, IL: Northwestern University Press, 2005).

[13] Even though Heidegger is here attempting to think being without the human being—as "the overwhelming coming-to-presence *that has not yet been surmounted in thinking*" (EM64/47, my italics), the human being is still part of the story of being. Thus in an interview with Richard Wisser, Heidegger says, "[T]he question of Being and the development of this question needs, as a prior condition, an interpretation of *Dasein*, i.e., a definition

'nature' in a very specific way: "Precisely what prevails as all-powerful for immediate experience claims the name *phusis* for itself. Yet such is the vault of the heavens, the stars, the ocean, the earth, that which constantly threatens man, yet at the same time protects him too, that which supports, sustains and nourishes him; that which, in thus threatening and sustaining him, prevails of its own accord without the assistance of man" (FCM30). Or again: "We translate ['*phusis*'] with 'nature' and think little enough about it. For the Greeks, *physis* is the first and essential name for entities themselves and as a whole. For them the entity is what flourishes on its own, in no way compelled, what rises and comes forward, and what goes back into itself and passes away. It is the rule that rises and resides in itself."[14]

From one perspective, '*phusis*' refers to a specific set of entities distinguished from the human being and its creations. But in a broader sense, it refers to everything—all that is, in its coming-to-pass. Thus '*phusis*' is a name for being (HI108/135); it names what it takes to *be* rather than not. And this is an overwhelming, sustaining and threatening, prevailing. Heidegger calls it the emerging, abiding sway: "*phusis* means the emergent, self-upraising, the self-unfolding that abides in itself. [. . .] This sway is the overwhelming coming-to-presence that has not yet been surmounted in thinking" (EM64/47). By looking at what this is and how it works we can thus address the question with which Heidegger opens EM: how does it stand with being? ("*Wie steht es um das Sein?*") (EM35/25). One way to do this is to look at the way that *phusis* is poetized in the choral ode, which speaks of sea, earth, and living thing. Each is a way of naming being—as that which emerges (sea) and that which holds sway (earth) in entities (the living thing).

Being is that by virtue of which entities are (and are as they are) rather than not (SZ6). Crudely, being is what makes entities *be*. This is expressed in the ode's passage about the earth:

---

of the essence of man. And the fundamental idea of my thinking is exactly that Being, relative to the manifestation of Being, *needs* man and, conversely, man is only man insofar as he stands within the manifestation of Being. Thus, the question as to what extent I am concerned only with Being, and have forgotten man, ought to be settled. One cannot pose a question about Being without posing a question about the essence of man." *Martin Heidegger in Conversation,* ed. Richard Wisser, trans. B. Srinivasa Murthy (New Delhi: Arnold-Heinemann Publishers, 1977), 40.

[14] Martin Heidegger, *Nietzsche,* Vol. I: *The Will to Power as Art,* trans. David Farrell Krell (New York: Harper Collins, 1991), 81. 'Entity' and 'entities' have been substituted for 'the being' and 'beings' as translations of '*das Seiendes.*'

> The noblest of gods, as well, the earth,
> the indestructibly untiring, he wearies,
> overturning her from year to year
> driving the plows this way and that
> with his steeds. (EM156/112)

The earth is described as a god, indestructible and untiring. Earth is not merely soil or dirt but what we might call 'Mother Earth' or 'capital-N Nature.' Nature in this sense governs all life—it presides over the birth, growth, and death of natural entities. It is an all-encompassing life force or spirit—or, in a less pagan and more scientific vein, an all-encompassing, life-enabling system. What does this tell us about being? Just as the earth governs all life and death, so too being governs all that is and is not. It is what makes the difference between what is and what is not. In determining this, being 'holds sway' over entities just as nature 'holds sway' over natural entities. Heidegger thus calls being 'the sway' *(Walten)*.

As thus governing, being *is* not apart from entities. It is not an entity itself but is always *of* entities (SZ6). This is particularly clear if we understand being as intelligibility, which must always be the intelligibility *of* something. So to understand what it takes for entities to be (intelligible), we need to understand how being or intelligibility comes to be *of* entities. Entities are intelligible only if we make sense of them. Heidegger puts this by saying that the human being "draw[s] [or tears] [*reißen*] being into entities" (EM171/123). He uses the same word when he describes the domestication of the animal: the human being "tear[s] [*reißen*] this life away from its own order" (EM165/118). This is expressed in the second stanza of the ode:

> Even the lightly gliding flock of birds
> he snares, and he hunts
> the beast folk of the wilderness
> and the brood whose home is the sea,
> the man who studies wherever he goes.
> With ruses he overwhelms the beast
> that spends its nights on mountains and roams,
> and clasping with wood
> the rough-maned neck of the steed
> and the unvanquished bull
> he forces them into the yoke. (EM156–157/112)

The horse is 'captured and subjugated' (EM165/118) by the human being, who encloses it in a paddock and harnesses it under bridle and bit.

So too, being is 'captured and subjugated' by the human being. Intelligibility is harnessed to entities, such that it becomes the intelligibility *of* something.[15] This is what Heidegger calls 'discovery' and it means that the human act of *making* intelligible is an essential part of the story about how entities come to be. (More on this later.)

Before turning to the human being's role in this story, we must ask how it stands with being. What must being be like such that all this is possible? The opening stanza of the ode tells us that we can grasp being as like the sea:

> He fares forth upon the foaming tide
> amid winter's southerly tempest
> and cruises through the summits
> of the raging, clefted swells. (EM156/112)

Notice that the sea is not described as a large body of water—as the placid, untiring source of intelligibility. This is a different characterization of being than that which we find in the invocation of the earth, and it is a more primordial characterization. The sea is a "foaming tide"—raging, stormy waves. The human being ventures out into this tempest—but only on the summits of the waves. It does not venture into the depths of the sea. As Heidegger reads it, the ode says of the sea that it "constantly drags up its own depths and drags itself down into them" (EM164/118). This surfacing and submerging, to summits and depths, characterizes being. Being is that which forcefully and violently emerges. It struggles to come into appearing, emerging into unconcealment in a struggle with concealment.

This is a very dynamic way of talking about being. The word 'being' is a gerund, and so it can be heard statically, like a noun, or dynamically, like a verb. Thus far, we have seen being characterized statically: being is the intelligibility that entities have. Both the earth and the animal passages express being statically. But the opening lines about the sea address being as dynamic, as something that happens or is in process. Being is still what makes the difference between entities being (intelligible) and not, but instead of describing this as something that entities have or are governed by, a dynamic approach grasps what makes this difference as an activity or event. If an entity *is* (intelligible), then it *shows up* (as intelligible). Being is this event of showing up. As Heidegger puts it: being is presencing,

---

[15] Heidegger considers this to happen primarily in the work of art. See, e.g., EM170/122 and "The Origin of the Work of Art" (in *Basic Writings*).

coming-into-presence, appearing, unconcealing. To grasp being, we must grasp how this showing up, presencing, or unconcealing happens.

'Unconcealing' is an important term for Heidegger because it suggests that the showing up of entities is grounded in an ontologically prior concealment. This is not merely a linguistic claim or game about the form of the word '*un*concealment,' although Heidegger often gives this impression—particularly when addressing unconcealment as the Greek *a-lētheia* (conventionally, 'truth'), which pairs the alpha privative (*a-*) with *lēthē* (forgetfulness or concealment). The insight is that the appearing or presencing of entities (being) is not simply given or there but is (i) a happening ('essencing') which has articulable moments and which (ii) does not itself come to presence.

To understand this, compare the showing up of entities to the performing of a play. The characters and story of the play show up to us only if something does not show up—namely, the way that the characters and story are brought into view, through the acting of the actors, the stage management, and so on. The mechanics of the production, in the broad sense, must withdraw or conceal themselves for the dramatic action to be manifest. Similarly for the showing up, or being, of entities. For an entity to *be*, to show up intelligibly, what allows this to happen must be concealed. What allows it to happen is the event of showing up (being) itself. So being must be self-concealing or self-withdrawing. We have encountered this before: the self-veiling of (our) being. Here, however, what veils itself is not the world *qua* a meaningful context but the event of meaning or showing up itself, and this veils itself essentially and constantly, not just in everyday life. Expressed statically: for entities to be intelligible, we must encounter intelligible *entities* and not intelligibility itself. We see the *things* that make sense and not *how* they make sense. Or again: entities show up intelligibly only if *they* show up and their showing up does not itself show up. Like acting, being must withdraw or conceal itself.

As in a play, this concealing is prior to showing up or unconcealment. It does not happen beforehand (i.e., temporal priority), but it is a prerequisite (i.e., ontological priority). It is a condition of an entity *being* that its *being* withdraw. As Heidegger says elsewhere, "The concealment of entities as a whole, un-truth proper, is older than every openedness of this or that entity. It is older even than letting-be itself, which in disclosing already holds concealed and comports itself toward concealing."[16]

[16] Martin Heidegger, "On the Essence of Truth," trans. John Sallis, *Pathmarks*, ed. William McNeill (Cambridge: Cambridge University Press, 1998), 148. I have modified the translation to read 'entities' or 'entity' instead of 'beings' or 'being' for '*das Seiendes*'.

This ontological priority means that concealment lies at the 'origin' of all unconcealment.

Further, to say that concealment is older than letting-be itself is to say that it is not effected by Dasein. Dasein's comportment presupposes withdrawing, and this withdrawing is something that happens to Dasein or something to which it is subject. It is not that *we* conceal being; rather, being conceals itself. It is the metaphorical agent of its own withdrawal: self-withdrawing, self-concealing.[17] Another way to put this is to say that concealing is a positive phenomenon of being or belongs to it. Heidegger calls it the "un-truth that is most proper to the essence of truth."[18] Heraclitus, he thinks, says the same thing when he says, *"phusis kruptesthai philei"* (conventionally: nature loves to hide). As Heidegger reads him, Heraclitus here says, "being [*phusis*] intrinsically inclines toward self-concealment" (EM121/87). So, in sum: "Being means: to appear in emerging, to step forth out of concealment—and for this very reason, concealment and the provenance from concealment essentially belong to being. Such provenance lies in the essence of being, of what appears as such" (EM121/87).

As self-concealing presencing, the happening of being is a struggle. There is a struggle within being between its tendency towards unconcealment and its tendency towards concealment. This is a peculiar kind of struggle. The happening of being is presencing, but presencing is not the vanquishing or overcoming of concealment. As we have seen, presencing requires concealment. Thus it cannot struggle against concealment for the sake of obliterating it. The presencing of entities takes place only in being's self-concealment, and this concealment takes place only in the presencing of entities. So being's two opposed tendencies struggle against each other not for the sake of negating one another but precisely in order to allow one another to take place. Their struggle must be conceived as a productive tension or reciprocal interplay between the opposed yet symbiotic forces of concealing and unconcealing.[19] Presencing arises out of,

---

[17] Some scholars distinguish being *qua* unconcealment from being *qua* unconcealing-concealing by using a capital 'B' for the latter (Being) and a lower case 'b' for the former (being). I do not follow this convention because I consider it to be unnecessary (since the context of the discussion usually serves just as well to indicate what is meant) and misleading (insofar as a capital letter implies a reification of being). However, I have retained the capital 'B' in all quotations, unless otherwise noted.

[18] Heidegger, "On the Essence of Truth," 148.

[19] Since the struggle produces not a third term but the two original terms, this interplay cannot be understood as a Hegelian dialectic. Heidegger is consistently critical of Hegel's dialectic, and he claims that it is inconsistent with true finitude (FCM209). Just how different the two are will emerge as we proceed, and it will be especially clear in Chapter 5.

or takes place in, this tension. Thus Heidegger follows Heraclitus again in interpreting being's internal struggle as a productive or originary *polemos* or confrontation *(Auseinandersetzung)*: "Confrontation [*polemos*] is indeed for all (that comes to presence) the sire (who lets emerge)" (EM65/47) (conventionally: War is the father of all).

Since it confronts itself and struggles against itself in this way, being is violent. But here, 'violence' *(Gewalt)* does not mean 'brutality and arbitrariness,' 'disturbance and offense' (EM160/115). Rather, violence is the 'tenseness' in the tension between concealing and unconcealing, "the strife of the striving" between them (EM120/87). Thus Heidegger's talk of violence, struggle, and confrontation in EM is not a glorification of aggression or strength over pacifism or quietism. It is instead a way of expressing the tense opposition within being between its powers of concealing and unconcealing. Being is essentially violent because it maintains itself in the internal tension of its struggle with itself.

The ode poetically expresses this *polemos* in the figure of the sea. The inherent conflict between concealing and unconcealing is "the winter storm" of the sea. The tempest is the tension and interplay between being's two opposed tendencies. Thus the sea "constantly drags up its own depths and drags itself down into them" (EM164/118). This restless dragging up to the surface and dragging down into oblivion is the double movement of concealing and unconcealing. Being, as the sea, drags up its own depths in allowing entities to show up and drags itself down into those depths in concealing itself. The human being rides only on the crests of the waves and does not venture into the depths of the sea. This is to say that we encounter only the intelligibility of entities and not (except perhaps in special circumstances) being itself as concealing and unconcealing. Described thus, the sea names being in its *emerging*—as dynamic coming-into-unconcealment and sinking-into-concealment.

This, then, is the story of being as presencing. It culminates in the presencing or intelligibility of entities and begins with two key characteristics of being. First, as earth, presencing is something continuous and unchanging that underlies all ontic change and becoming ("the concealed presencing of stillness and tranquility amid constant and unconcealed absencing and presencing, that is, amid the appearing of change" (HI72/88)). Second, as sea, presencing is not the static property of bare presence but an event with its own dynamic power. It is to be understood in terms of the tempestuous sea *(pelagos)*, which "stirs itself of its own accord and thus does not flow away but remains and abides within itself in its surging" (HI72/88).

Being is thus both constant (earth, sway) and dynamic (sea, *polemos*). Being is a constant presenc*ing:* a continuous, irruptive happening. To express these two characteristics, the word that Sophocles uses for 'to be' in the ode is not the usual *'einai'* but *'pelein.'* *'Pelein'* is the verb used in the ode's opening lines, usually translated as 'is.' It originally referred to a being-in-motion ('to go,' 'to come,' 'to rise') and came to mean 'to be' in the sense of 'to become.' Heidegger's translation seeks to preserve this motility. He translates *'pelein'* as *"ragend sich regt"* (EM: "bestirs itself, rising up beyond"; HI: "looms or stirs").[20] The one exception is in HI, where he renders it *'walten':* 'prevails' or 'holds sway' (HI52/65). This latter translation makes clear that *pelein* is to be identified with *phusis* (HI108/135): being as coming-into-presence, which in EM is grasped as the overwhelming sway (*überwältigenden Walten*). *'Pelein'* means "to emerge and come forth of its own accord, and thus to presence" (HI71/88).

But *'pelein'* is not just another word for being. In the opening lines of the ode, it is the verb that tells us that the human being *is* uncanny. Thus it expresses what it takes to be uncanny. As Heidegger puts it, the *deinon is* in the manner of *pelein:* "[t]he uncanny 'is' in the manner of a coming forth (looming), and in such a way that in all its stirring it nonetheless abides within the inaccessibility of its essence" (HI74/90). This gives us two important clues for understanding the human essence as *deinon.*

First, as the most *deinon* entity, the human being must be characterized by *pelein* in a distinctive way. The human being's presencing as the entity that it is will not be just another dimension of the 'living things' chapter of the story. If that were the case, then the human being would come to presence in the way that all other entities do. But the human being is related to being, and so to its *polemos* and sway, in a special way. This is clear in the ode: the human being is present throughout the first strophe and antistrophe. It is the human being who captures and subjugates

---

[20] Beistegui argues that *"ragend sich regt"* has slightly different senses for Heidegger in these two texts: "In 1942, *pelein* still 'means' *ragend sich regt*. The translation is left unaltered. *Pelein* means *sich regen,* to be in motion, and this motion is further defined in terms of a *Ragen*. Yet the *Ragen* itself does not refer so much to a rising above and a surpassing, as to a *Hervorkommen,* a coming forth or a bursting out. Into what? Into the Open, into presence. Thus *pelein* points in the direction of the presencing whereby every being breaks into the Open, finds its place and holds its position within presence. *Pelein* is thus synonymous with *einai,* with being in the sense of presencing. [. . .] The move that is enacted in the interpretation of 1942 seems to be from an understanding of *pelein* as a specific kind of motion to that originary motion that is presupposed in every motion. [. . .] *Pelein* points to the constance [*sic*] behind change, to the tranquillity and the motionlessness underneath the storming sea of becoming, of presencing and absencing." Beistegui, *Heidegger and the Political,* 131.

the living thing, drawing being into entities. The human being breaks in *(einbrechen)* to the sway of the earth and breaks it up *(umbrechen)*. The human being breaks forth *(ausbrechen)* and breaks away *(aufbrechen)* into the sea. The human being is constantly implicated in being's struggle to come to appearing; it is enveloped in the sway *(umwalten)* of the over- whelming *(das Überwältigende)* and pervaded by it (EM166/119). The story of being and the story of the human being are thus interwoven. The story of being's happening as *pelein* is also the story of the human being's happening as *pelein* and so as *deinon.*

Second, if what it takes to be *deinon* is to come to presence in the manner of *pelein,* and if the essence of the *deinon* is counterturning, then *pelein* or presencing must manifest the essence of the *deinon.* There must be a counterturning here. Thus Heidegger can describe being itself as *dei- non* (EM159/114); not only the human being but also being is counter- turning. But we can already see this counterturning in being—in the play of concealment and unconcealment. Presencing happens only through a self-concealing; being gives itself by withholding itself from manifest- ness. Presencing *is* or happens only in a corresponding absencing—that is, presencing happens *through* absencing.[21] This is being's counterturn- ing. What, then, of the human being's counterturning? Is the human be- ing *deinon* in the sense that it also presences through a self-absencing?

The Story of Human Being

As uncanny, the human being is counterturning. In what sense? Heidegger claims that what is distinctive about the human being's counterturning is that it is an inward or intrinsic counterturning, in contrast to the extrinsic counterturning of other *deinon* entities (HI84/103–104). At stake here is the way in which the manifoldness of the *deinon* is manifest in the entity. Consider an entity that is *deinon* because it is fearsome in the sense that it is frightening; my example was a snake. This way of being fearsome is opposed to the other way of being fearsomely *deinon,* namely being awe-inspiring, which some other entity may manifest (e.g., the gods). Al- though the *deinon* itself turns between frightening and awe-inspiring, it is

---

[21] Beistegui puts this clearly: "[T]here is an originary movement of presencing which, as such, is never present, a movement whose only mode of being is absencing. In presence, what comes to the fore is not presencing as such, but always this or that being, the essence of which never is present, but always is or rules and unfolds as this constant absence. The law of presence is such that what it presents is only its counter-essence; presence happens only in the covering up of its essence." Beistegui, *Heidegger and the Political,* 132.

not the case that each of these entities do. The counterturning is external to the snake and to the gods and to their respective *deinon*-characters. So these entities are *deinon* in an extrinsically counterturning way. The human being's character as *deinon* is different: an inward counterturning. The human being turns counter not to something else but to itself. This is what makes it unhomely (HI84/104).

If the uncanny human being turns counter to itself, then we need to determine what the human being is. The human being, as Dasein, is the entity that understands being. It is open to being or is the open 'space' or 'clearing' in which being appears as the being of entities. The human being is the entity to whom entities show up in their being and the entity from whom being withdraws. It is the 'open site' in which being presences and absences—the site (or event) of intelligibility. It is this open site that turns counter to itself, and it does so by itself presencing and absencing *(pelein)*. Heidegger says that this is "the essence of uncanniness itself, namely, presencing in the manner of an absencing, and in such a way that whatever presences and absences [*das An- und Abwesende*] here is itself simultaneously the open realm of all presencing and absencing [*der offene Bereich aller Anwesung und Abwesung*]" (HI75/92). The 'open realm of all presencing and absencing' is the site of openness in which being presences and absences and which the human being *is*. To say that this site presences and absences is to say both that (i) it effects or enables presencing and absencing (both the presencing and absencing of being (i.e., appearing), of which it is the site, and the presencing and absencing of entities (i.e., change and becoming), which takes place in this site) and (ii) the open site *itself* presences and absences, turning counter to itself. The task is to understand in what sense the human being turns counter to itself (ii) and how this is related to its openness to being (i).

A few more preliminaries first. Since the human being's intrinsic counterturning is its uncanniness, the *un-* of uncanniness corresponds to the *counter-* of counterturning. It is crucial to notice that this counterturning is not a mere switching between presencing and absencing but a counterturning within presencing: a presencing that comes to pass *by means of* absencing. Thus when Heidegger says that "[t]he uncanny itself is [. . .] that which presences and at the same time absences" (HI72/89), this 'at the same time' does not mean that the human being presences and also absences. Rather, like being, the human being presences *through* absencing. This is why Heidegger insists that the *un-* of uncanniness does not signal a lack of the *heim* (home, canny). The uncanny human being remains related to the *heim,* and its absencing is not mere not-being but its way of presencing. Thus the *un-* of uncanniness names the human being's absencing *qua* a way of presencing. The *un-* signals an interplay of presencing and absencing, or the turning movement between these that makes presencing possible. (I explore this more fully in Chapter 5.)

We have yet to determine what this presencing and absencing is. The primary difficulty for doing so is that Heidegger uses several different vocabularies to express his point. Not only do EM and HI use different terms but HI itself uses several. There is a severe vocabulary explosion to be managed. Each vocabulary contributes something distinctive to the account or makes some aspect of it easier to see or to say, so none can be left out. But Heidegger does not make clear how—or even that—the various vocabularies work together, and there is no obvious key for translating between them. The following is an outline of how I will put the vocabularies together.

The open site that the human being is can be understood dynamically as a happening: a *seeking* of the homely. This seeking presences in the manner of absencing, and the absencing is a *failure* to attain the homely. So the human being seeks the homely *by* failing to attain it. The homely is the human essence, so such failure is a "reversal that turns [the human being] away from [its] own essence" (HI77/94). We can put the point, then, by saying that the human being turns between its essence and the counter of that essence: the non-essence. The thought is that the human essence contains its non-essence in a distinctive way. Thus we can also say that the human being's absencing is a deprivation of, or exclusion from, its essence. It is in this self-loss that the human being comes to be or comes to presence, and so it is by not being in its essence that the human being is in its essence. We will see that this picture coincides with the SZ account of uncanniness: that the human being comes to be in its self-disclosure of its essential origin as concealed. That is, the disclosure of original concealment (the obscure whence of thrownness) is the absencing in which the human being comes to presence. It is the origin of openness or, expressed dynamically, the happening of unconcealment. This is uncanniness (EM178/127). As intrinsically counterturning between self-possession and self-loss, openness and finitude, the human being is the most *deinon*—the uncanniest—entity.

The Human Essence

> Into the sounding of the word, as well,
> and into wind-swift all-understanding
> he found his way, and into the mettle
> to rule over cities.

He has considered, too, how he might flee
exposure to the arrows
of unpropitious weather and its frosts. (EM157/113)

Since the open site presences *in the manner of* absencing, we can understand this presencing only by determining how it absences. But first,
we need some grasp of the presencing to which the human being comes.
What is it to be the open site? The answer is given in the second strophe
of the ode. The human being is open to being in "language, understanding, mood, passion, and building" (EM166/119). These are 'powers' of
openness or disclosure. It is through these powers that the human being draws being into entities or brings it into appearing—that is, makes
things intelligible. In accordance with the following strophe, Heidegger
names these disclosive powers, as a whole, *'technē'* or 'knowing' (usually translated as 'art,' 'skill,' 'craft,' 'cunning'). *'Technē'* is making-
intelligible or bringing into appearing through language, understanding,
mood, and so on.

So in asking how the open site presences by means of absencing, or
how it turns counter to itself, we are asking how the disclosive powers
(the open site) come to be (presence) as the essence of an entity. By what
absencing does this occur? How do the disclosive powers come to be?
Questions in this vicinity are traditionally expressed as questions about
how language or (self-)consciousness arises. Heidegger rejects one kind
of answer immediately: the disclosive powers are not tools or inventions
that humanity has created for itself (EM167/120). The reason is that it is
the disclosive powers that make the human being what it is and one cannot precede—and so cannot invent—one's own essence. The human being is not self-made. Accordingly, Heidegger does not translate the Greek
'edidaxato' as the traditional 'learned' or 'taught himself' but as 'found
his way into': "Into the sounding of the word, as well, / and into wind-
swift all-understanding / he found his way."

Finding its way to the disclosive powers is the human being's finding its way into being, the overwhelming. The human being "found its
way into the overwhelming and therein first found itself—the violence of
that which acts this way" (EM167/120, translation modified). Like sea,
earth, and living thing, the disclosive powers are names for being as the
overwhelming. They are being's own powers of unconcealing or coming-
into-appearing. Thus Heidegger describes them as "the violent forces by
virtue of which entities disclose themselves as such"—but only "insofar
as the human being enters into them" (EM167/120). Since the disclosive
powers belong to being and make the human being what it is, they name

being insofar as it *pervades* the human being in its sway or holds sway *through* it *(durchwalten)* (EM166/119). The human being is not only open to being and so enveloped by it *(umwalten)* but pervaded by it.

It follows that the human being is a contestant in being's *polemos*. Recall that the *polemos* is being's internal struggle between concealing and unconcealing. Since being grants the human being the power to bring it into appearing (the disclosive powers), its internal *polemos* takes place as the struggle between the human being (*qua* disclosing) and being (*qua* concealing). Being struggles against itself *through* the human being, who thus struggles against being. The strife of this struggle is what Heidegger calls 'violence.' Since the human being takes part in this struggle, it is the violence-doer: "violence-doing in the midst of the overwhelming" (EM160/115).

This is not a new thought for Heidegger. The claim is that making-intelligible is to be conceived as an assault (EM178/127). As he puts it in FCM, "entities are torn from concealment. Truth [or unconcealment . . . is] something stolen, something that must be torn from concealment in a confrontation [*Auseinandersetzung*] in which precisely *phusis* strives to conceal itself" (FCM29, Greek transliterated). In SZ: "[t]ruth (uncoveredness) is something that must always first be wrested from entities. Entities get snatched out of their hiddenness" (SZ222). The hiddenness of entities is not an ontic hiddenness, as when the door is hidden by boxes. It is an ontological hiddenness—the hiddenness of entities *in their being,* which is the withdrawal of being in presencing. The human being must snatch or steal entities from such hiddenness in the sense that it must bring them to appear in their being, even as their being recedes from appearing. The human being must make things intelligible, even as intelligibility itself recedes from view. This is the struggle with concealment: the *polemos*. In this sense, making-intelligible is a violent struggle with being. Since the human essence is to make intelligible, to be open, it follows that the human being or Dasein *is* the struggle with being.[22] It *is* the violence-doing of *technē:* "[v]iolence, the violent, within which the doing of the violence-doer moves, is the whole circuit of machination, *to machanoen,* that is delivered over to him" (EM169/121).[23]

---

[22] For an excellent exploration of Dasein as *polemos*—although one which departs from my reading in significant respects—see Gregory Fried, *Heidegger's* Polemos: *From Being to Politics* (New Haven, CT: Yale University Press, 2000), particularly Chapter 2, "Polemos as Da-sein."

[23] Thus Heidegger: "[O]ne might think that the *deinotaton* means that the human being is the most actively violent entity in the sense of that animal full of cunning that Nietzsche calls the 'blond beast' and 'the predator'. Such predatory uncanniness of the human being as historical, however, is an extreme derivative and consequence of a concealed uncanniness that is grounded in unhomeliness, an unhomeliness that in turn has its concealed ground

As disclosive, the human being is essentially implicated in being's *polemos*. But how did the human being find its way into this? How does the human being come to have the disclosive powers? What opens us to intelligibility? This story is told in the opening strophe of the ode, which gives the first episode of the saga and so the origin of the human being:

> He fares forth upon the foaming tide
> amid winter's southerly tempest
> and cruises through the summits
> of the raging, clefted swells. (EM156/112)

The human being's 'faring forth' into the sea does not refer to sea travel or fishing but poetically projects the human being's entry into being's struggle. Heidegger calls this a 'breaking away' (*aufbrechen*, breaking open) into the overwhelming sea (EM164/118), or the 'breakaway' *(Aufbruch)* into being (EM182/131). The human being breaks away into the overwhelming sea, stretching out beyond itself towards being. This openness is the human being's transcendence: its violence-doing *(technē)*. The task is to understand how this comes to pass.

Breaking forth (*ausbrechen,* breaking out or breaking loose) is always a breaking *from* or *out* of somewhere. Seafaring humanity ventures *away from* firm land (EM164/118). It breaks out *(auszubrechen)* from that-which-is-homely *(Einheimische)* (EM174/125).[24] Since the human being gives up or leaves behind that from which it breaks forth (EM164/118), it

---

in the counterturning relation of being to the human being" (HI90/112). Compare my account of the human being's violence as disclosure *(technē)* with the more existentiell interpretation of such violence (and corresponding critiques of Heidegger) in, for example, Fóti, "Heidegger, Hölderlin and Sophoclean Tragedy"; Wendy C. Hamblet, "A Tragic Ethos: The Irresponsibility of the Host in Martin Heidegger's 'The Ister,'" *Journal of the British Society for Phenomenology* 35:2 (2004): 157–167; and in Jacques Derrida's brief analysis in the final few pages of *The Beast and the Sovereign,* Vol. 2, trans. Geoffrey Bennington (Chicago: The University of Chicago Press, 2011). Miguel de Beistegui (whose own reading is much like mine) critiques naïve, existentiell interpretations of Heidegger's talk of 'violence' in his *Heidegger & the Political.* For an intermediate reading, see Fried's *Heidegger's Polemos.* Fried takes Dasein's violence to be an ontological move within the ontic political realm: "Heidegger's ontological violence is done to the 'ordinance and fit' *(Bau und Fug)* of the reigning dispensation of meaning as it stands in the polis"; Dasein that engages in such violence is *"authentically* amoral in that its violence steps beyond *(hupsipolis),* transgresses conventional mores, thereby either renewing them or destroying them in preparation for a new dispensation." Fried, *Heidegger's* Polemos, 143 and 144.

[24] Polt and Fried's translation of '*Einheimische*' as 'familiar' in this passage is misleading since *einheimisch* and its variants are elsewhere translated with versions of 'at home' (e.g., EM161/116). Further, it should be clear that I take the issue of whether the (at-)homely is the same as the familiar (and so whether uncanniness is a breakdown of the familiar) to be a major interpretive question.

enters the *polemos* or acquires the disclosive powers by giving something up. The human being comes to presence as the entity that it is by surrendering something (absencing).

What the human being gives up is not freely given; it is taken from it. The human being does not fare forth into the sea of its own accord. This is again the idea that the human being's coming to its essence is not a matter of choice or self-creation. Heidegger often expresses this by attributing the agency to being rather than to the human being. He says that being *needs* the human being and so *throws* it open. Being needs the human being to be its site or lieutenant (lit. 'place-holder'). The human being must "take over and fulfill the governance of the sway of the overwhelming" (EM183/132). Being needs the human being to break away into it, to enter the *polemos,* in order for being to come into appearing. This is because intelligibility only takes place if something is *made* intelligible—if being is captured and subjugated in entities. Just as a flock needs a shepherd, being needs the human being to draw it into entities and bring it to a determinate stand as the appearing *of* something.[25] What being needs in the human being is an open site in which it can happen— an open 'space' in which it can take place as the coming-into-appearing of entities.[26] Because being needs the human being so profoundly, being posits for itself a site of openness: "the almighty sway of being violates Dasein (in the literal sense), makes Dasein into the site of its appearing" (EM190/136). The word Heidegger uses here (*vergewaltigen,* to violate) is a word used specifically for rape.[27] (This is a somewhat histrionic word choice on Heidegger's part, and I suspect that in choosing this term he was thinking only of the fact that it adds to the dozen or so words based on the stem '*walten*' that are at play in EM.) Dasein is broken open *(aufbrechen)* to be the site in which being can appear. Dasein's breaking away *(aufbrechen)* into being is thus its being thrown open *(aufbrechen)* by being. It is thrown by being so as to be the openness of the *da.* As thrown open, Dasein is not merely openness but open*edness.*[28]

[25] Heidegger calls the human being the "lieutenant of the nothing" in "What Is Metaphysics?" (WM93) and describes the human being as "the shepherd of being" in "Letter on 'Humanism'" (in Martin Heidegger, *Pathmarks,* 252 and 260).

[26] To borrow an image of Heidegger's, we might say that being is like the light by virtue of which things are illuminated. In order to illuminate, the light requires an open space or field. Heidegger uses the image of light extensively in, for example, Martin Heidegger, *The Essence of Truth: On Plato's Cave Allegory and* Theaetetus, trans. Ted Sadler (London: Continuum, 2002).

[27] The translators point this out in footnote 85 (EM190/136).

[28] I take this term from Thomas Sheehan, who explains its force: "[H]uman beings are the *Da* not occasionally or by their own choice, but *of necessity.* We cannot *not* be the

Being violates the human being and opens up its openness by throwing it the disclosive powers. But being is not some super-entity or cosmic force. The task of understanding how the human being comes to the disclosive powers, then, is the task of understanding being's violent creative act in light of the fact that being is not an entity and possesses no agency. We need to take the story out of the metaphor in which Heidegger couches it. To do this, I will return to the ode, which expresses the human being's coming to have the disclosive powers as an act of finding.

Presencing

We have seen that the human being's faring forth into the sea is its entry into being's *polemos,* or its coming to have the disclosive powers. In this, the human being breaks into being. But it also breaks away from firm land: something is taken from it. The human being bears the passivity and negativity of its thrownness, finding itself with the disclosive powers in the way that we might find ourselves with extra burdens. This is the poetic projection of the human being's coming to have disclosive powers, but we have yet to understand it in a way that does not attribute agency, and so entity-status, to being. What does it mean to say that being throws the human being? The alternative vocabulary for the same phenomenon is that of finding: the human being finds itself and so comes to its essence. That is, the human essence as open or disclosive first happens in the human being's self-finding. By thinking through this presencing, we will be able to approach the human being's absencing.

That the human being comes to its essence as disclosive in a self-finding sounds like the idea that the human being attains consciousness in an act of self-consciousness.[29] It does manifest the same self-presupposing structure, since finding is a disclosive act, and Heidegger was well aware

---

open (the possibility of taking-as) just as we cannot not be our own minds. In Heidegger's early language, we are always already *thrown-open (geworfen).* We are not thrown 'into' the open, as if the *Da / Lichtung / Welt* already existed without us; we are not open 'to' the open, as if it were something separate from us; we do not 'transcend to' the open as if we had to cross from here to there; and we do not 'project' the open as if we brought it about as our own personal achievement. Without us, there is no open at all; but with us, the open is always apriori operative. [. . .] To-be-the-open is to be apriori open*ed*.' Thomas Sheehan, "A Paradigm Shift in Heidegger Research," *Continental Philosophy Review* 34 (2001): 194. The *a priori* or always already of this openness is the space of the primal history which the ode narrates.

[29] The picture also echoes Kierkegaard's account of the self in *The Sickness unto Death,* as a "relation which relates to itself." Søren Kierkegaard (as Anti-Climacus), *The Sickness unto Death: A Christian Psychological Exposition for Edification and Awakening,* trans. Alastair Hannay (London: Penguin Books, 1989), 43.

of the various versions of this picture in the history of philosophy. As Heidegger explains it, for the human being to find itself and come to its essence in the disclosive powers is for the human being to "take up this sway itself directly into [its] violence" (EM166/120). That the human being takes up being (*qua* the disclosive powers) as its own is another way of saying that it is pervaded by being. This "happen[s] only insofar as the powers of language, of understanding, of mood, and of building are themselves surmounted in doing violence" (EM167/120). This is the key claim. To 'surmount' *(bewältigen)* is to tame (EM184/132), to discipline and dispose (EM167/120). This is a reference to being *qua* the living thing, which needs to be drawn into entities (captured and subjugated) so that it can be the appearing *of* something. Being, the overwhelming *(Überwältigende)*, is what-is-to-be-surmounted *(Zubewältigende)* (EM166/119). To say that the disclosive powers must be surmounted is to say that they are the essence of the human being only if they are first drawn into this entity. Since the human being performs this drawing or surmounting, this is necessarily a self-disclosure. The human being must disclose itself in its being. And since this is the human being's coming to its essence, it follows that the human being *is* what it is only insofar as it self-discloses as such. To see what is odd about this, consider that being *qua* the disclosive powers is both (i) that which is disclosed *and* (ii) that which performs the disclosing or with which the disclosing is carried out. The human being draws the disclosive powers into itself as its essence *by means of* the disclosive powers. It comes to be disclosive by disclosing itself. This act presupposes itself.

One more time, more slowly: the disclosive powers are that which bring being into appearing in entities, including the human being. Since the human being's self-disclosure brings the disclosive powers into appearing in it, the human being's self-disclosure is the disclosure of the disclosive powers themselves (in both senses of the genitive). The human being's self-finding is the reflexive self-disclosure of the disclosive powers. Yet for the disclosive powers to work at all, they must first come into appearing, or happen, themselves. Since they belong to being and since being always appears as the being of some entity, this means that the disclosive powers must come into appearing as the essence of some entity. But this in turn means that in order to self-disclose as the essence of the human being, the disclosive powers must already be the essence of the human being. In other words: the human being *is* what it is only if it self-discloses or finds itself as such, but what it *is* is disclosive. The human being is disclosive by virtue of the fact that it self-discloses. How can this be an explanation of how the human being comes to be disclosive if it presupposes that the human being is already disclosive?

The human being's coming to be disclosive is a self-constituting event.[30] The disclosive powers bring themselves about; their reflexive self-disclosure is self-constitution. Heidegger would describe this as "attain[ing] itself as ground by leaping an originary leap *(Ur-sprung)*" (EM7/5). This is a kind of self-grounding, in which something "attains its own ground by leaping, performs it in leaping" (EM7/5). In this context, the claim is that openness opens itself up. This is what it means to say that being throws the human being or opens it. In traditional terms: language or (self-)consciousness, as determinative for the human being, is neither an invention nor a faculty. The human being comes to be conscious by grasping itself as such. This self-enabling leap has no antecedent or precedent. (This is why the analogy with angst, which I discussed in Chapter 2, works.) The essential origin of the human being is not to be determined by tracing it back to some prior entity or force. This is "the suddenness and uniqueness of Dasein" (EM174–175/125), which erupts in a self-constituting act of self-finding.

This self-enabling act is the origin of both the human being and being. The self-disclosure of the disclosive powers is the opening up of the site of openness and so is the original coming-into-appearing, which first allows all coming-into-appearing. It is the primal case of surmounting the overwhelming—the 'first' disclosure of being or the first act of making-intelligible. In this self-finding, then, being first 'is' as both the power of coming-into-appearing (unconcealing) and the coming-into-appearing of an entity (unconcealment). This fills out the claim that being *needs* the human being or that it must happen *through* the human being. It also explains why Heidegger describes the *polemos* as an originary struggle. The origin of being and the human being is a self-constituting act, and it is a disclosing act, and disclosing is a struggle. Thus both being and the human being originate in the struggle of unconcealing: "[t]he struggle meant here is originary struggle, for it allows those that struggle to originate as such in the first place" (EM65/47). We can locate no creator or first cause at the origin but can only say that "the violent powers of the released excessive violence of being suddenly emerge and go to work as history" (EM174/125).

---

[30] Compare Heidegger's argument in the *Parmenides* lectures that the human being is the entity that presences by means of its own 'look.' Martin Heidegger, *Parmenides*, trans. André Schuwer and Richard Rojcewicz (Bloomington: Indiana University Press, 1998), e.g., 107.

As such, this origin in self-finding self-disclosure is the "inception in which, from overabundance, everything breaks out at once into what is overwhelming and is to be surmounted" (EM166/119)—that is, in which being breaks out into appearing. While we cannot ground this event in something prior, surely there is something to be said about this 'over-abundance.' That is: what makes self-finding self-constituting? What about it allows it to open up openness? Notice that we have yet to locate the absencing in this story of presencing. Is absencing the 'overabundance'? To determine this, we need to investigate the character of the *polemos,* which is always a struggle with concealment.

Absencing

I have argued that, for Heidegger, the human being and being come to appearing when the human being findingly self-discloses as disclosive. Openness opens itself up when it surmounts (discloses) being (the disclosive powers). But there is a wrinkle. The human being "can never surmount the overwhelming" (EM171–172/123). This does not mean that the human being cannot disclose being or make it intelligible, for it can and does. But in doing so, the human being *shatters* against being because being is insurmountable. Heidegger says that the human being is "posited as the breach into which the excessive violence of being breaks in its appearing"; it is opened as the site of openness but in such a way that "this breach itself shatters against being" (EM174/124). The reason is that being is self-concealing. The result is that openness opens itself finitely—that is, by means of a self-absencing. Let me explain.

Recall that being's self-concealing or self-withdrawal is the non-presencing of presencing itself, which is presupposed by the appearing of entities. This non-presencing belongs to presencing, in the sense that it is the inner condition of possibility of presencing. That which presences (entities) can presence (be) only if presencing itself (being) does not come to presence. It follows that even though being is what-is-to-be-surmounted *(zubewältigende)*—even though it needs to be brought into appearing—it is at the same time that which cannot be surmounted, that which cannot itself directly come into appearing. So against being's self-withdrawal, the disclosive powers 'shatter.' Like the "unvanquished bull" mentioned in the ode, being can be captured and subjugated but it can never be domesticated.

The self-concealing of being adds a crucial element to the story of the human being's origin as the self-disclosure of the disclosive powers. I argued that the disclosive powers constitute themselves by bringing themselves into appearing as the essence of an entity. As with all disclosure, this coming-into-appearing must take place against original concealment or in the self-withdrawal of being. What makes the coming-into-appearing of the human being as disclosive importantly different from the presencing of other entities is not just that the human being brings itself to appearing but that in doing so what comes to appear as the essence of an entity is unconcealing or coming-into-appearing itself. Since the disclosive powers are being's own powers of presencing, when the human being comes to presence as disclosive what presences is presencing itself. In the human being's originary self-finding, unconcealing itself is unconcealed. But being is not just unconcealing; it is also self-concealing. It does not come to presence but absences itself. Being must withdraw so that the entity may appear. It follows that in bringing itself to presence, the human being's being as disclosive must withdraw from it. But this withdrawal too is disclosed. Thus the human being's coming to be, or the unconcealment of unconcealing, is the unconcealment of *concealment*. The human being's originary self-disclosure is the disclosure of (its own) being as withdrawn or concealed.

If this is confusing, it is because we are watching the human being as it is tossed around on the sea of being, exposed to its stormy appearing and concealing. Or again, we are trying to pin down the arising of originary angst. Let me restate the point in different terms. When the disclosive powers constitute themselves by disclosing themselves as the essence of an entity, this self-disclosure discloses the concealment that grounds all appearing and so that grounds the disclosive powers. Thus the disclosive powers disclose concealment as their ground (condition of possibility, origin) and—what is the same—they disclose their origin as concealed. Thus they disclose their own finitude: they encounter a limit to their disclosive power, precisely with respect to their own origin. They shatter against being. Being, that is, shatters against itself.

Being's self-concealment is thus a human finitude. Further, this finitude is productive or generative. Since it is concealment that makes presencing possible (presencing takes place only if it withdraws from itself), it is this finitude, as found, that opens up openness. Put differently, openness opens itself because it is finite. It is because the self-finding discloses finitude (concealment) and discloses finitely (shatters) that it is self-constituting. Thus we see why the *polemos* is originary or originating and why in the inception "everything breaks out" from "overabundance" (EM166/119). This overabundance is the finitude or negativity of concealment. This finitude is not a lack or a privation but a pregnant, enabling finitude. What is crucial to see about this picture is that it is not merely *being* finite that rends openness open but the *disclosure* of this finitude in a self-finding. The finitude that opens openness *is* only when openness is opened to it. Crudely: disclosed finitude 'produces' openness and openness 'produces' disclosed finitude. Openness and finitude make each other possible. They co-produce one another in an originary, reciprocal, mutually constitutive relationship.

Taken out of the narrative of origination, the claim is that Dasein, as disclosive, is grounded in its self-disclosure as finite. Finitude is not merely a limit on the human being's openness but an enabling condition of openness. There is transcendence only if it is finite. (Thus God, who is not finite, is for that reason not transcendent either.) But the finitude that makes transcendence or openness possible is a *found* finitude and so itself presupposes openness. Openness grounds finitude and finitude grounds openness. The choral ode expresses these relationships as an inceptive story. But how does this help us to understand where the disclosive powers like language come from or what makes them possible?

The human essence is to be disclosive, open, unconcealing, violent. But this violence shatters against being because the human being cannot surmount the overwhelming. Concealment renders openness finite. Concealment is the self-withdrawal of presencing, and to say that it cannot be surmounted is to say that the human being's self-finding can disclose it only *as* concealment and so can disclose its origin only as *concealed*. Thus Heidegger says that the origin of language, and of the disclosive powers generally, "remains a mystery [*Geheimnis*]" (EM182/131). This does not mean that we have yet to figure it out. The mystery-character is neither contingent nor the result of some deficiency on the part of the disclosive powers. It is not the result of some lack of "cleverness" (EM182/131) or a "failure of knowledge" (EM166/119). Rather, it is due to the fact that language "can have begun only from the overwhelming and the uncanny, in the breakaway [*Aufbruch*] of humanity into being" (EM182/131)—that is, in the human being's self-constituting self-finding, which essentially discloses concealment. The mystery of the origin or ground of the disclosive powers is not only essential; it is also constitutive. There are disclosive powers, the human being is disclosive, *only if* the ground of these powers—their essential origin—shows up as concealed or mysterious. This is why Heidegger describes both the inception *(Anfang)* (EM166/119) and the essence of being human *(das Wesen des Menschseins)* (EM175/125) as mysteries. These are the same mystery, for they name the same thing. The inception told in the choral ode is the inception of being or presencing, which is at the same time the origin of the disclosive powers and so is the ground of openness, and is thus the origin and ground of the human being. In short: the essence of the human being is the inceptive happening of presencing, and it lies in the mysterious origin of language.

Talk of 'mystery' recalls Heidegger's discussion in "On the Essence of Truth." Here, Heidegger uses 'the mystery' *(das Geheimnis)* to refer to being as self-concealing, and he identifies this self-concealing as the non-essence of truth. This non-essence is not *extrinsic* to the essence but belongs to it as an enabling ground.[31] So too in EM, the mystery-character of the inception or origin marks the original finitude that makes disclosure possible. This finitude, the disclosure of concealment at the origin, can thus be understood as the human being's non-essence. The human being's essence as open or unconcealing is grounded in the non-essence: closedness or concealment. We know that it is this originary mystery that the disclosive powers find in their self-constituting self-disclosure. They find, or disclose, their non-essence. What these powers "yield to the human being immediately is merely the non-essence [*Unwesen*]" (EM166/120, translation modified). Heidegger goes on: "and thus they drive the human being out and keep it out of its own essence" (EM166–167/120, translation modified). We have returned to the idea that the seafaring human being gives something up and in this becomes unhomely. What exactly is this unhomeliness, and what is it that the human being gives up in coming to itself? What exactly is this absencing?

The human being departs from the homeliness of its essence when it finds the non-essence. Since the non-essence is concealment, this departure from the essence occurs in the human being's primary finding of originary concealment.[32] What is thus taken from the human being, or what it gives up, in being open*ed* to being is full openness.[33] We can see

[31] Heidegger, "On the Essence of Truth," 148.

[32] So while Fóti says that "self-estrangement [. . .] renders the origin unfindable," I am arguing that the origin is findable but only as concealed/ment and that such finding-as-concealed *is* self-estrangement. Véronique M. Fóti, *Heidegger and the Poets: Poiēsis / Sophia / Technē* (New York: Humanity Books, 1992), 105.

[33] One difficulty for this reading is that when Heidegger speaks of the disclosive powers as casting the human being out of its essence or yielding the non-essence, he appears to locate this not in a primal self-finding but in the human being's self-misunderstanding: "This pervasive sway becomes no less overwhelming because the human being takes up this sway itself directly into its violence and uses this violence as such. This merely conceals the uncanniness of language, of passions, as that into which the human being as historical is disposed, while it seems to him that it is *he* who has them at his disposal. The uncanniness of these powers lies in their seeming familiarity [*Vertrautheit*] and ordinariness [*Geläufigkeit*]. What they yield to the human being immediately is merely the non-essence [*Unwesen*], and thus they drive the human being out and keep it out of its own essence. In this way, what at bottom is still more distant and more overwhelming than sea and earth becomes something that seems to the human being to be the nearest of all" (EM166–167/120, translation modified). The claim looks

in this the human being's breaking forth into the sea. When the human being breaks forth and enters being's *polemos,* what it gives up is firm land: "it gives up the place [*Ort*], it heads out—and ventures to enter the superior power of the sea's placeless [*ortlosen*] flood" (EM164/118). This place is the *polis:* "the ground [*Grund*] and place [*Ort*] of the Dasein of the human being itself [*des Daseins des Menschen selbst*]"; it is "the site [*Stätte*], the Here [*Da*], within which and as which Being-here [*Da-sein*] is historically" (EM162/117). This is what Dasein surrenders in being thrown open. How we read this surrender depends on how we understand Heidegger's talk of the *polis* and the homely.

The dominant interpretation considers the human being's giving up of the homely *(das Heimischen)* to be the breakdown of familiarity. What is homely is the familiar, ordinary, and usual; the home is the everyday world or the prevailing understanding of being. Accordingly, to give up the homely is to experience the mood of angst. This occurs in an exercise of owned creativity, which is described near the end of the ode in the figure of the *hupsipolis apolis* creator. The creative individual challenges the prevailing understanding of being and opens a new world. Like the sovereign, such a creator remains outside both the order that she creates and the order that she transgresses. This unhomely situation is the creative individual's uncanniness.[34]

---

to be that the disclosive powers are uncanny because they seem to be familiar and ordinary (insofar as the human being takes them up as its own and so seems to have them at its disposal) when they are actually fundamentally unfamiliar (because the human being is thrown into the disclosive powers and so is at *their* disposal). Thus the human being misunderstands its relation to the disclosive powers and this is its uncanniness. But notice that Heidegger goes on to say that this self-misunderstanding does not *constitute* human uncanniness but is instead *evidence* of it: "The extent to which the human being is unhomely [*unheimisch*] in its own essence is *betrayed* by the opinion it cherishes of itself as that which has invented and which could have invented language and understanding, building and poetry" (EM167/120, translation modified, my italics). As we will see in Chapter 4, one of the significant consequences of uncanniness is that the human being is vulnerable to misunderstanding and to mere seeming or semblance. Because it is a consequence of uncanniness, such misunderstanding is good evidence for it. We can also see that the human being is especially prone to misunderstanding the origin of its disclosive powers, since this origin is concealed/ment. This particular self-misunderstanding thus concerns the human being's uncanniness, making it a misunderstanding about uncanniness that confirms uncanniness.

[34] Versions of this reading are offered in, for example, Fóti, *Heidegger and the Poets;* Fried, *Heidegger's* Polemos; Geiman, "Heidegger's *Antigones*"; and Charles Guignon, "Being as Appearing: Retrieving the Greek Experience of *Phusis*," in *A Companion to Heidegger's* Introduction to Metaphysics, ed. Polt and Fried. There is certainly textual support for this reading. Heidegger glosses the homely as "the accustomed, the usual, the unendangered" (EM161/116), "what is most directly nearby and what is usual" (EM179/128), "the usual hustle and bustle" (EM179/129), and "the seeming of the customary, the usual and the trite" (EM180/129).

I say more about the creative individual and being *hupsipolis apolis* in Chapter 4, where I address the second half of the ode. Here in the first half of the ode, the story told is not about the opening of a new world from out of a prior one, or about an experience of a particular case of Dasein. It is instead the story of the birth of Dasein: the primal opening of any world at all. The home that Dasein gives up, then, cannot be the familiar. For the seafaring human being to give up the place (the *Ort*, the *polis*) cannot be for the creative individual to surrender the prevailing understanding of being in her transgression of it. So what is it that the human being gives up? Heidegger makes this clear in the passages I quoted: the *polis* is not first of all the everyday world or the prevailing understanding of being but the *da*. It is openness itself, the site of presencing and absencing. Of course, the *da* always takes place as a particular openness, a particular world. But from the perspective of the story of the opening up of openness, the *da* and the *polis* name openness in abstraction from its particular manifestations. If this is right, then the claim is that what the human being gives up when it is thrown open is its openness, the *da*. Since this openness is the human being's essence, the opening up of openness involves the surrender of the essence.

The home, then, must be Dasein's essence. This is not a 'home' in the sense of that which makes things familiar, usual, or safe (except insofar as these are possible only on the basis of Dasein's openness). It is a home in the sense of that from which something originates, or in which it is grounded.[35] Ontologically, the origin or ground is the essence of an entity. So what is homely for Dasein is what is essential to it. (This does not mean that Dasein must in each case explicitly grasp its own essence or being; this would be again to insist on understanding the homely as the familiar. The home *(heim) qua* the essence may—and perhaps even must—remain somewhat strange or secret *(Geheimnis)*.) In HI, Heidegger makes very clear that the home or homely refers to being (e.g., HI112–113/140, 118/147, 120/150). To understand this, recall that being is not some super-entity standing over and against the human being, who enters into a relation to it. Being is presencing, or the showing up

---

[35] Heidegger uses the vocabulary of 'home' at various times, in various ways. The 'home' or 'homely' for Heidegger can be the familiar (e.g., that in which we dwell, which we understand), the most familiar (e.g., the everyday public world), that from which we start (e.g., the everyday), the source (e.g., being, our essence), the proper (e.g., being, our essence), or the destination of a journey (e.g., being, our essence). For an account of how Heidegger's deployment of the vocabulary of 'home' changes over time, see Capobianco, *Engaging Heidegger* (especially Chapter 3, "The Turn towards Home") or the earlier version of this argument in Capobianco, "Heidegger's Turn toward Home: On Dasein's Primordial Relation to Being."

of entities, in a self-concealing. Insofar as this presencing is gifted to the human being as the disclosive powers, and so as its essence, being takes place in the human being's essence—it is, and happens in, the open site (the human being's disclosedness). So being 'is' nothing apart from the human essence. Both can be said to be the home.

The absencing of the open site is thus to be understood in terms of the non-essence or the unhomely. Dasein's departure from the homely in its being-thrown-open, or taking on the disclosive powers, is its being cast out of its essence. In entering being's *polemos* and becoming pervaded by being, the human being gives up being. In coming to its own essence or home, the human being gives up its essence or home. In coming to presence, the human being absences. What sense does this make? How can absencing or self-surrender be the human being's way of presencing?

Absencing as Presencing

We have seen that the human being's presencing is its coming-to-be as the open site, in the self-disclosure of the disclosive powers. The human being's absencing, in turn, is the finding of being's self-concealment—which here includes the concealment of the origin of the disclosive powers. It remains to think these two together as an essential counterturning between absencing and presencing, the homely and the not homely, the essence and the non-essence. This will be the human being's uncanniness. Heidegger has multiple vocabularies for the human being's essential counterturning, especially in HI: seeking the homely, deprivation, and exclusion from the essence.

1. Seeking the homely: The primary vocabulary is that of the home or *heim,* here understood as being. Heidegger describes the human being as seeking the homely but turning counter to it. In this, he grasps being-the-open-site dynamically, as the event of seeking the homely. To seek the homely is to seek being, and to seek being is to disclose it—to bring being into presencing. The human being is always and essentially this seeking; it is "[c]onstantly on a path toward the homely site" (HI90/111). This seeking turns counter to itself in that it fails to attain that for which it is looking. The homely, being, is not attained because it refuses itself to the human being (HI90/111)—it absences itself or withdraws from the human being's disclosedness. This is being's own counterturning presencing and absencing *(pelein).* Being presences and absences *to* the human being, such that its inner counterturning is always a counterturning relation to the human being (HI90/112). Being gives itself and refuses itself to the human being, who is thus always seeking the homely.

2. Deprivation: Accordingly, "[t]he unhomely one is deprived of the homely" (HI75/92). Heidegger had analyzed deprivation some thirteen years earlier in FCM, where he contrasted deprivation with a lack or absence of something that could or ought to be present (FCM195). Here, too, he is using 'deprivation' as an alternative concept to that of a 'lack' in order to understand how absencing can be a way of presencing—that is, how the *un-* of uncanniness serves to negate it. (More on this in Chapter 5.) The *un-* does not simply negate but preserves a certain relation to the canny or homely: "deprivation is the way in which the unhomely one possesses the homely, or to put it more precisely, the way in which whatever is homely possesses the unhomely one" (HI75/92). As FCM argues, deprivation is not a lack but a certain kind of having and not-having (e.g., FCM195, 210–211). Specifically, it is a way of not having *in* a having (FCM211)—that is, a way of absencing in one's very presencing *(pelein)*. To be deprived of the home or the homely is thus to have, and in this very having not have, the home.

Since the home is being and since being is the presencing of entities to and in the human being, to *have* being cannot here mean simply to *be* (present) rather than not. To have being is to be open to being—that is, to have entities show up in their being. Thus in FCM, the animal's having of 'world' is its openness for . . . (FCM248, 269), and here in HI the human being's "being homely in" or having being is its "'seeing the open'" (HI91/114). To see the open is to understand being, to be the open site of presencing, to seek the homely. Correspondingly, not to have the homely is not to be open. But this is not a simple lack. The human being is deprived of being in the sense that its having of being *is such that* it does not have being. To be deprived of the homely is for the human being to be open in such a way that it is not open in its very openness. Let me explain this in a different vocabulary.

3. Exclusion from the essence: As I have argued, to speak of a counterturning relation between being and the human being is to speak of a counterturning *within* the essence of the human being. Being's refusing itself to the human being is a self-refusal within the human being: the human being's being-deprived of being is a being-deprived of itself. That is why the seeking that fails to attain the homely (being) is a seeking that "seeks *itself*" and one that "does not find *itself*" (HI84/103, my emphasis). So while seeking and deprivation are, on the face of it, relations between the human being and being (the homely), they are ultimately ways of describing the human being's absencing. This absencing is a reflexive phenomenon: a self-absencing. The human being absences to itself. The human being's self-absencing is its not-being-open to itself

or its not having or failing to attain itself, where 'itself' means 'its essence.' Thus EM describes the human being as driven out of its essence (EM166–167/120). In HI, the human being is said to be characterized by an "exclusion from entry into its own essence" (HI76/93, translation modified), such that "within its own essence, [it] finds no entry to this essence, remains excluded from it and without any way out that could allow it to enter the center of its own essence [*die eigene Wesensmitte*]" (HI74–75/91). (Note that Heidegger immediately rephrases this as the human being's seeking-yet-not-attaining the homely, thus confirming my synthesis of the vocabularies.) Or again: the human being is "in a certain manner excluded from the origin of its own essence" (HI130/163). The point is that the human being is "excentric" (HI28/32) to its own essence. As in EM, the uncanny is that which "throws one out of" the homely (EM161/115) in the sense of the essence.

Heidegger is clearly having difficulty with his language: the human being is excluded from *entry* into its essence, from entry into the *center* of its essence, and from the *origin* of its essence. But the problem is not that of unambiguously identifying that *from which* the human being is excluded. The problem is expressing the nature of the exclusion. Talk of *ex*clusion implies a simple negation, just as talk of being *un*canny or *un*homely does. But the human being is not excluded from the essence in the sense that it is entirely outside of its essence, as if it were not invited to a family gathering. The human being remains inside, or in relation to, its essence, but in such a way that it is off-center or out-of-joint in its essence—like a guest in someone else's home or the black sheep of the family. Since the *un*- or *ex*- does not put the human being entirely outside of its essence, the human being's relation to its essence is a peculiar one of inclusion and exclusion, being inside and outside. This is another way of expressing the human being's having and not having—or its seeking and failing to attain the homely, or its presencing and absencing. It is its counterturning: *pelein*, uncanniness. If the nature of this uncanny, counterturning play of inside and outside is unclear, then the rhetorical effort to avoid implying a total exclusion from the essence manifests itself in an ambiguity in that *from which* the human being is excluded. Hence Heidegger's shifting language.

So what is the claim here? As we have seen, the human being finds the origin of its essence only as concealed/ment and so cannot open or uncover its essential origin. This is its absencing. Such absencing amounts to an exclusion from the essence as openness not in the sense that the human being *lacks* openness but in the sense that its openness is reflexively finite with respect to its own origin or ground. The human being does not *have* its essence because, as thrown, it cannot *open* or disclose its ground. Consider that the fullest formulation of the exclusion would be: the human being is excluded from entry into the origin (or center) of its essence. The entry spoken of here can only be the entry afforded by openness. To enter an essence is to disclose it as the essence of an entity. To be excluded from such entry is (given that this is not a total exclusion) for such disclosure to be finite in some way. If we now agree that the center of an essence *(Wesensmitte)* is its origin or ground, then we can say that to be (i) excluded from (ii) entry into the (iii) center of the essence is to (i) finitely (ii) disclose the (iii) origin or ground of that essence. So to say that the human being is excluded from (entry into) the (origin or center of) its essence is to say that it finitely discloses its essential origin. The human being encounters the 'whence' of thrownness as obscure. In this, the human being withdraws or absences from itself.

4. To sum up, let me return to talk of being. We can now see what it means to say that the human being simultaneously has and does not have (i.e., is deprived of) being. Being is the origin or ground of the human being's essence. It is that which throws the human being (origin), makes possible the human being's disclosing (ground), and constitutes the center of its essence.[36] The human being *has* being in the sense that it is open to being, but it does *not* have or is not open to being *qua* the ground or center of its openness (the home, the origin of the throw). This reflexive finitude in the human being is a finitude in the disclosure or presencing of being; it is the self-absencing of being. The human being cannot disclose being as its origin because being, in its very presencing, withdraws from presence. It shows up only as concealed or absent. Being is thus that to which the human being is not open, that from which it is excluded, that which its seeking fails to attain, and that which presences and absences. Thus failing to attain the homely (being), being deprived of the homely (being), exclusion from (the origin of) the essence, and the presencing and absencing of the human essence, *all name the same phenomenon.* That phenomenon is the human being's counterturning or its uncanniness.

But it remains to understand how and why the concealment of being or finite self-disclosure of the human being amounts to the human being's very presencing. Why does the open site presence through absencing?

---

[36] This is why, immediately after identifying deprivation as the way in which the human being possesses the homely or is open to being, Heidegger says that this is strictly the way in which the homely (i.e., being) possesses the human being (HI75/92). The human being has being insofar as being needs the human being and so throws it into being the site of openness. To say that being possesses the human being is to say that it is the essential origin or ground of the human being and so eminently holds sway over it.

Here is the first step. As the ode tells us, for any entity to presence is for the human being to draw being into it or disclose its being. The human being's presencing is thus always a self-disclosing or a drawing being into itself. This presencing must take place within the open site, since all presencing and absencing takes place within this site. Heidegger puts this by saying that the human being "not only 'see[s] the open'" (understands being), "but in seeing it, also stand[s] within it" (HI91/114). To stand within the open site is to come to presence as an entity within it. But as we know, the human being itself is this open site. This puts the human being in a peculiar position: it must bring itself to presence *as* the open site *within* that very open site.[37] This is another way of putting the earlier point that the human being must draw the disclosive powers into itself by means of the disclosive powers. In temporal terms: the human being's presencing both presupposes and first institutes the open site. In spatial terms: the human being must be simultaneously both inside and outside of the open site—both the frame and the picture, the location and what happens in it. This is another way of saying that the human being is the ontico-ontological entity; the open site in which all entities (ontic) come to presence in their being (ontological) takes place as an entity (ontic), so must come to presence within itself or bring itself to presence. Put differently, entities *are* only when they show up to the human being, so for the human being to be an entity it must show up to itself. Thus the human being's presencing must be a self-presencing in the sense of a presencing *to* itself and in the sense of a presencing *enabled* by itself. The human being's self-disclosure is self-constituting. The human being brings itself to presence as an entity.

Now for the second step. Why must this self-instituting self-disclosure involve finding the origin (being) as withdrawn? Why does the human being come to be in finding its origin as concealed/ment and so in an exclusion from the essence or the counterturning presencing and absencing? We know that the human being draws being into itself *qua* entity, taking up the disclosive powers. When the human being draws being into entities, being withdraws or absences so that entities may show up in their being. Being becomes transparent, as it were—like the light in a room. So when the human being self-discloses in its being, being will also withdraw so that the human being may show up to itself as the entity that it is. So the human being presences only in the withdrawal of being.

---

[37] With this characterization, Heidegger's picture of the human being's uncanniness begins to look similar to the empirico-transcendental doublet that Foucault finds in modern accounts of the subject. I will address this in the Conclusion.

Here is the key point: unlike other entities, the human being presences *to* itself (it is the entity that is open to being, to presencing) and this means that (its) being withdraws *from* it. (Being would not withdraw were it not for the human being's openness; there is an obscurity or an absence here only if it is disclosed, made present, as such.) So the human being is *open to* the withdrawal of (its) being in its self-disclosure. What this withdrawal looks like to the human being is not non-being, simple absence, or self-unintelligibility. The human being grasps itself in its being, whether explicitly or not. Since the human being is the open site of being's presencing and absencing, the withdrawal of being to which it is exposed is not merely the withdrawal of its own being but the withdrawal of being in the presencing of all entities. So the withdrawal in question is the withdrawal of being *per se*, not merely of the being of the human. But now recall that, as the open site, the human being has its origin or ground—the whence of thrownness—in being. So the withdrawal of being in the presencing of all entities amounts to the withdrawal of the human being's origin and ground.

It follows that presencing itself, and not just the human being's presencing, requires that the human being presence and self-absence in this way. There can *be* an ontological entity, the site of understanding being, only if it is finitely open to its origin or ground. The human being's presencing—indeed, all presencing—requires the human being's uncanny exclusion from its essence. (That the human being can *be* as the kind of entity that it is only if it self-absences in this way is the point of attributing such absencing to being and naming being as that which throws the human being, needs it, and rends it open.) So the human being presences in the manner of absencing in the sense that it comes to be as the entity that it is only in the withdrawal of being, its essential origin, from the reach of its openness. The open site presences only as absent to itself—and that means, only as finite, with respect to its own origin. To be ontological, to be open, one must be finite. This is the human being's inner counterturning in the way of *pelein* and so the human being's uncanniness.

Uncanny Human Being

We have seen that the human being's presencing and absencing is its self-constituting, finite self-disclosure. This is its expulsion from the essence, its deprivation of the homely, and its seeking but failing to attain the homely. The picture is this: the human being *has* openness insofar as it *is* the open site—the entity that understands being, the *da*. But the human being does *not* have openness insofar as it cannot wield openness perfectly against itself. The human being cannot open the origin of its openness in being. The reason is that being, the human being's origin, absences or withdraws from openness. The whence of thrownness is obscure. This is the human being's inner counterturning *(pelein)*; it is its uncanniness.

Further, we have seen that all presencing requires this absencing. This suggests that the human being is *essentially* uncanny. Uncanniness is required for there to be being, or entities as such, at all. The human being must be uncanny. Put differently, uncanniness "does not first arise as a consequence of humankind [*Menschentum*]" (HI72/89), as if it were a quality present in the world by virtue of human presence. Rather, uncanniness is in a sense the human origin, the essential prerequisite for the human being what it is at all: "humankind emerges from uncanniness and remains within it—looms out of it and stirs within it" (HI72/89). If the human being's self-constituting self-disclosure does not stand under the scope of its volition or agency but instead under the necessity of its essence as an ontological entity, then although the human being's self-disclosure is self-constituting, the human being is not thereby self-made. "[T]he unhomely is nothing that the human being itself makes but rather the converse: something that makes it into what it is and who it can be" (HI103/127–128, translation modified).

The human being's uncanniness is presupposed by any and all presencing; if there is intelligibility, there is uncanniness. So the human being cannot make things intelligible without being uncanny and it cannot make itself intelligible except as uncanny. But what is it to make oneself intelligible as uncanny? It remains to connect all this talk of counterturning presencing and absencing to what Heidegger says explicitly about uncanniness—especially in EM. Let me conclude and summarize by showing how the human being's uncanniness on Heidegger's various characterizations fits with and reinforces the interpretation that I have offered.

In EM, Heidegger identifies the human being's superlative uncanniness in two ways. First, he says that the human being is the uncann*iest* entity because of the way that it is related to being—because of the "unitary, reciprocal relation" (EM169/121) between being and the human being. This relation makes the human being "one of a kind, according to its kind, within the uncanny" (EM173/124)—and so, as HI has it, singularly uncanny. Second, Heidegger locates the human being's superlative uncanniness in the fact that the human being is "doubly *deinon* in an originally united sense" (EM160/115). I said earlier that speaking of being singularly uncanny and being doubly *deinon* amount to the same thing.

One formulation expresses the unity of the counterturning movement and the other emphasizes the two poles between which the counterturning moves. It is time to show how this works.

I begin with being doubly *deinon*. Heidegger distinguishes the two dimensions of uncanniness and indicates their unity: "[T]he human being is the uncanniest, not only because it spends its life essentially in the midst of the un-canny understood in this sense [i.e., being *qua* uncanny], but also because it steps out, moves out of the limits that at first and for the most part are accustomed [*gewohnten*] and homely [*heimischen*], because as that which does violence, it oversteps the limits of the homely [*heimischen*]" (EM161/116, translation modified). This says: the human being is uncanny not only because it is open to being but also because the human being drives itself from what is homely for it. The first dimension of human uncanniness is the human essence as transcendent or open and the second is the non-essence: human finitude. These two dimensions are the same as the two aspects of the human being's faring forth into the sea. By working out this duality in the human essence, we will be able to see how it amounts to the reciprocal relation between being and the human being, which is Heidegger's other way of putting the human being's superlative uncanniness.[38]

The first dimension of the human being's uncanniness consists in the fact that the human being "spends [*verbringt*] its essence [*sein Wesen*] in the midst of the un-canny" *qua* being (EM161/116, translation modified). The human being is the entity that is essentially exposed or open to being, or the entity that makes intelligible. It is 'enveloped' by being. The human being breaks away *(aufbrechen)* into the overwhelming sea or being (EM182/131), entering being's *polemos*. As thus transcendent or open, the human being is not self-contained. Its essence has a dative structure and so points beyond itself. This is the significance of the human being's dwelling "in the midst of" being: it is open *to* being rather than mutely placed in it. Since the human being is open *to* being, it "essentially belongs to being" (EM160/115) and so does not belong entirely to itself (EM32/23).

The second dimension of the human being's uncanniness is its overstepping the limits of the homely or its self-casting out of its own essence. This is tied up with the first dimension of uncanniness in the same way that breaking away *(aufbrechen)* into the overwhelming sea is tied up with breaking

---

[38] My argument will thus in effect cash out Fynsk's claim that "'To deinotaton' names the *finitude* in man, whose occurrence [. . .] marks, and is marked in, the reciprocal confrontation of technē and dikē." Christopher Fynsk, *Heidegger: Thought and Historicity* (Ithaca, NY: Cornell University Press, 1993), 124.

forth *(ausbrechen)* from or out of somewhere. Notice that this vocabulary of into-which and from-which belongs to thrownness. The from-which of breaking forth *(ausbrechen)* is the whence of the throw of thrownness. And just as the seafaring human being gives up firm land, so too Dasein gives something up when it is thrown open. This is the human being's departure from the homeliness of its essence, and it indicates the finitude of openness which 'takes place' when the human being breaks forth into the sea or finds its way into the overwhelming. The finding in question is the originating self-finding of the disclosive powers, which reveals concealment at the origin and so constitutes openness finitely. Precisely in finding and coming to itself, the human being gives itself up.

So the first dimension of the human being's double uncanniness is the human being's openness to being (transcendence), and the second is the finitude of this openness by virtue of concealment. The two are originally united as a double uncanniness or a counterturning. Notice that it is hard to discuss the second dimension without appeal to the first: human finitude is always a *found* finitude; the departure from the homely is always a finding-the-way-into-the-overwhelming and so is a function of the human being's openness. Thus the second dimension leads to the first: "as that which does violence, the human being oversteps the limits of the homely, precisely in the direction of the uncanny in the sense of the overwhelming" (EM161/116, translation modified)—that is, precisely in such a way that it is open to being. This says that it is precisely in the human being's finite self-finding that it comes to be open to being. The two dimensions of uncanniness are originally unified because finitude is always found, and this finding is the opening that produces openness. In short, the human being is doubly uncanny because its non-essence (concealment, finitude) belongs to its essence (openness, transcendence) in such a way that each brings the other about.

This co-enabling relationship is thus an original unity in the sense that from it the two terms of the unity first arise. ("[O]riginary unity first lets that which is unitary spring forth" (HI39/46).) The human being's uncanniness is the originating unity of its finitude and openness—its being finitely open or openly finite. This productive interplay of finitude and openness is an originary, self-grounding leap or self-enabling self-constitution. It is thus the productive or enabling power of finitude, as found, that ensures the unity of the two dimensions of uncanniness. It does so because, as disclosed, the human being's finitude is inceptive or enabling: it opens up openness. (More on this in Chapter 5.)

This opening is the happening of uncanniness—which, as Heidegger says, is thus nothing other than the happening of unconcealment

(EM178/127). The finitude of the human being's self-finding is the inception or essential origin not only of the human being as unconcealing but also of being as unconcealment. It is as such an origin or ground that being uncanny "is the basic trait of the human essence, into which every other trait must always be drawn" (EM161/116). Put differently, the human being "harbors" an inception, which is "most uncanny and mightiest" (EM165/119)—the inception "in which, from overabundance, everything breaks out [*ausbricht*] at once into what is overwhelming and is to be surmounted" (EM166/119). The human being's superlative uncanniness means that all presence and presencing is born in the human being from its finitude.

We can now see in what sense being, the overwhelming, is *deinon*. Being is *deinon* in that it "induces panicked fear, true anxiety, as well as collected, inwardly reverberating, reticent awe" (EM159/114–115). But being is not uncanny because it makes us *feel* a certain way (EM161/115, HI74/90). As the overwhelming, being is presencing itself in all its inherent force, scope, and remarkableness—a mysterious and awe-inspiring event. Being is such because it conceals itself even as it reveals: because it happens in the way of *pelein*, presencing in the manner of absencing. It is being *qua* concealing—and, more specifically, as disclosed as concealing—that is *deinon*. Thus being is "the alienating," which "first discloses itself" "[w]hen one is put out of the home [*heimischen*]" (EM178/127): being first opens up in the human being's finite self-finding, and it opens up as that which alienates the human being by refusing it full disclosure. Put differently, being is *deinon* in the sense that it "does not allow us to be at home" (EM161/116) in our essence, and it does so because, as concealing or absencing, it renders our openness essentially finite. In plain language this means: it is a requirement of intelligibility that its origin cannot be made intelligible, and this entails that making-intelligible occurs finitely. Thus being (intelligibility) does not allow us (making-intelligible) to be at home in our essence (to make (it) fully intelligible). Being is *deinon* because it casts us out of the homely.

This brings us to Heidegger's second way of expressing the human being's superlative uncanniness in EM: the 'unitary reciprocal relation' between being and the human being. This is a relation between the human being *qua* essentially open and that to which and by which it is essentially open(ed) (i.e., being). Naming being as *dikē* (fittingness, justice) in relation to the human being's *technē* (i.e., being disclosive), Heidegger describes the reciprocal relation this way: "the *deinon* as the overwhelming *(dikē)* and the *deinon* as the violence-doing *(technē)* stand over against each other [. . . ;] *technē* breaks out [*aufbrechen*] against *dikē*, which for its part [. . .] has all *technē* at its disposal" (EM171/123). This is a description of the *polemos* and the human being's entry into it as its being thrown open. Note first that *technē*'s breaking out against being *(aufbrechen)* is the human being's breaking away *(aufbrechen)* into the sea *qua* being open to being (the first dimension of the human being's double uncanniness). Second, note that the fact that this openness is at the disposal of being means that the human being is thrown by being or finds its way into openness (the second dimension of the human being's double uncanniness). So the reciprocal relation between being and the human being is the co-enabling relation between the human being's openness and its finitude—its unified double uncanniness. Expressed as a relation between being and the human being, this reciprocal relation is the fact that the human being brings being into appearing (by drawing it into entities—the living thing) and being brings the human being into appearing (by throwing it (into) the disclosive powers). Thus each allows the other to happen, and in doing so each allows itself to happen.[39] In short: the reciprocal relation or the human being's superlative uncanniness is the self-enabling character of finite openness or open finitude.

It follows that when Heidegger glosses the human being's superlative, double uncanniness as the fact that it "uses violence against the overwhelming" (EM160/115), we cannot simply read this as saying that the human being is the uncanniest because it uses the disclosive powers to bring being into appearing. This would amount to Richardson's reading of uncanniness: the human being is the uncanniest because it is the only entity open to being. What makes the human being the uncanniest is not its openness but rather the self-constituting reciprocity between openness and finitude. As I have argued, this reciprocity renders the human being unhomely not in the ontic realm but in its own essence as openness. Thus we must interpret the human being's use of violence against the

---

[39] Alternatively, we can express this as the interface between the human being's belonging to being (i.e., openness to it) and being's need of the human being (the human being's thrownness, finitude). The point of the reciprocity, and so the gist of human uncanniness, is that it is precisely in belonging to being that the human being belongs to itself. Thomas Sheehan explains: "*Das Zugehören* and *das Brauchen*—our 'belonging' to the open, and the open's 'need' of us—are complementary expressions of a single facticity: the interface of *Da-* and *-sein*. There is an unbreakable reciprocity (back-and-forth-ness, *reci-proci-tas*) between our thrown-open essence *(-sein)* and the possibility-of-sense-making *(Da-)*, and this apriori interface constitutes the dynamic structure of *Dasein*. In *Beiträge* Heidegger calls it a *Gegenschwung* (a 'back-and-forth-ness': GA 65, 251.24), or a *kehriger Bezug* (a 'reciprocal relatedness': GA 65, 7.21) or simply *die Kehre*, the reciprocity of openness' ineluctable sense-making and sense-making's grounding in openedness.

"There are not two apriori's [sic] here, but only one: thrown-open-ness-as-ability-to-make-sense-of. The hyphens hold together *Geworfenheit* and *Entwurf*, whose reciprocity is the essence of *Dasein*." Sheehan, "A Paradigm Shift in Heidegger Research," 195.

overwhelming in terms of this reciprocity ('back-and-forth-ness'): the human being turns being's power back against itself. As Fynsk enigmatically and parenthetically puts it: "one of the two meanings of 'deinon' folds or doubles in such a way as to mark the difference between physis and technē and to found the conflictual relation."[40] Fynsk does not elaborate on this folding, but I have described it several times in various vocabularies: the self-constituting self-disclosure of the disclosive powers, the opening of openness in the self-finding of its finitude, the self-grounding leap of finite openness or of open finitude, the co-enabling interplay of essence and non-essence, the human being's essential self-expulsion from its essence, the originary unity of the human being's double uncanniness, and the reciprocal relation between being and the human being. We have seen that the back-and-forthness involved in this relation is an originary struggle or confrontation (*Auseinandersetzung, polemos*) in which the human being and being burst into openness. As an expression of its uncanniness, the human being's 'use of violence against the overwhelming' thus does not simply name its bringing-being-into-appearing *qua* making entities intelligible in their being. Rather, it names the original bringing-into-appearing in which both the human being and being first happen. This is not the human being's general making-intelligible but the very self-inauguration of making-intelligible and intelligibility.

Thus, as we saw, the human being's superlative uncanniness is "the happening of unconcealment" (EM178/127). The human being's essence as the uncanniest is "the relation that first opens up being to the human being" (EM181/130). In the happening of uncanniness, being and the human being are first granted. This picture of uncanniness has thus filled out Miguel de Beistegui's suggestion that '*deinon*' is "an early word for *Ereignis*."[41] '*Ereignis*' (event, (event of) appropriation, enowning) is a word that Heidegger uses after EM to name the event by virtue of which *there is* being. It is that which gives being or that which opens up openness. By showing 'uncanniness' to name the co-enabling relationship between openness and finitude, I have shown that the concept of uncanniness is an attempt on Heidegger's part to think this phenomenon.

Uncanniness is the essential finitude of human openness, which first opens up openness. It is the exclusion from the essence in which the human being first comes to its essence as open. This uncanniness happens

---

[40] Fynsk, *Heidegger: Thought and Historicity,* 120.

[41] "This confrontation between man and nature Heidegger designates further as the opposition between technē and *dikē*, which is the twofold essence of the *deinon*. Could the *deinon* be an early word for *Ereignis*, for the event through which man and being are brought together and reciprocally ap-propriated?" Beistegui, *Heidegger and the Political,* 123.

in a primal, counterturning self-finding—the assault of *technē* against *dikē,* the human being's faring forth into the sea, its finding its way into the disclosive powers. In this opening, being withdraws or conceals itself and the whence of thrownness—the origin, the home—is accordingly disclosed as concealed. Uncanniness is thus also this obscurity, as found and as constitutive for openness. It is in the human being's uncanniness that being is given, or openness opened up. Thus the human being is *essentially* uncanny—it has to encounter obscurity at its ground in order to be what it is at all. Uncanniness is not an accident that befalls the human being or its essence but is constitutive for that essence. This makes the human being superlatively uncanny.

I argued at the outset that this picture, while not on the surface text of the ode, is nonetheless anchored in it. But does the picture make sense? On a surface reading, the ode can be interpreted as saying that the natural condition of the human being is to be *un*natural. How can this be? There is a structural question here about the coherence of the origin story. Recall that the unity of the human being's double uncanniness means that being cast out of the essence belongs to the human essence. When being throws the human being out of the homely, when the human essence expels itself from itself by yielding the non-essence (concealment), this is not simply the human being's departure from what is essential to it. Rather, it *is* what is essential to it. The claim is that the human being first *has* an essence or is what it is only because it departs from its essence or is not what it is. Does this mean that the human being has a dual essence—that from which it departs (i.e., to be open) and that which it attains in this departure (i.e., to be uncanny)? How else can we make sense of the idea that it is in its departure from its essence that the human being first comes to its essence, such that it belongs to its essence (its 'home') that it is not at home in it? Put differently, the question asks whether it makes sense to claim, as I take Heidegger to do, that the human being is uncanny with respect to itself (rather than, for example, with respect to other entities). Or again, given that the account of uncanniness is an account of the human being's ground or origin: how can we read Heidegger's account as the story of the human being's essential origin if the essence he describes is doubled and so the origin self-originating and non-linear? How can openness produce itself in opening up to its own finitude? How can an entity *be* in the manner of *pelein?* How are we to make sense of uncanniness?

This question is even more important than it first appears to be. I will return to it in Chapter 5. First, I need to finish reading the choral ode, and in particular to draw the existential consequences of uncanniness.

4

Being the Uncanny Entity

THE OPENING STROPHES of Sophocles's choral ode tell the inception
of the human being: the opening up of openness. This is the
story of uncanniness. In outline, it holds that the human being is a self-
constituting and polemic turning between openness and finitude, transcendence and thrownness. Such turning is a consequence of the fact that
being withdraws or conceals itself when an entity shows up in its being,
and so of the fact that Dasein's being withdraws or conceals itself when
Dasein first presences to itself. So the human being "stems from the uncanny [*ungeheure*] district of withdrawing concealment and in the 'here'
traverses a mortal course through entities in the midst of entities as a
whole."[1] In this chapter, I follow the story to its later stages: to Dasein's
dwelling amidst entities and its owned and unowned ways of being the
uncanny entity. The human being is the play between presencing and absencing, opening and concealing, transcendence and finitude; how does
this play play itself out in the entity?

Heidegger works out what it is to be the uncanny entity using the vocabulary of the *polis*. 'The *polis*' is another term for the clearing, which—
as uncanny—presences and absences. Heidegger captures the uncanny
motion of the *polis* with the image of a central core or pole which itself
swirls or whirls: "The *polis* is *polos,* that is, the pole, the swirl [*Wirbel*]
in which and around which everything turns. These two words name
that essential moment that the verb *pelein* says in the second line of the
choral ode: that which is constant, and change" (HI81/100). '*Pelein*,'
recall, is the verb used in the ode (instead of '*einai*') to name the uncanny

[1] Martin Heidegger, *Parmenides,* trans. André Schuwer and Richard Rojcewicz (Bloomington: Indiana University Press, 1998), 129. In quoting from this text, I substitute 'entities'
for 'beings' as a translation of '*das Seiendes,*' and I substitute 'the human being' (and 'it')
for the translator's 'man' (and 'him'). I also transliterate all Greek terms.

way of being: counterturning presencing and absencing. As we saw in Chapter 3, '*pelein*' names a constancy of motion, which we understood as constant presencing (as absencing). This constancy reappears here in the character of the *polis* as a pole: a locus, center of gravity, or a fixed point of reference for all discovery of entities. At the same time, the *polis* swirls or turns in that it presences by way of absencing and so happens as a swirling giving-and-refusing.

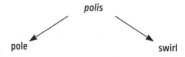

To say that the *polis* swirls or whirls is to say that Dasein is essentially uncanny or *is* in the way of *pelein*. Its openness is given in such a way that it is withheld from it. The uncanny entity oscillates within this presencing and absencing, exposed to the absencing of (its) being and so to the presencing of (its) being. As we have seen, this makes the human being ontico-ontological. As ontological or open to presencing, the human being is transcendent in the sense that it is metaphysical: it moves beyond entities to being. This has several consequences, including that the human being is capable of experiencing the mood of angst. The ode notes these by describing the human being as both *hupsipolis* and *apolis:* rising high in the *polis* and yet forfeiting the *polis* (HI59/72).[2] In this description we see "the inner contour of the essence of the uncanniest" (EM163/117): a counterturning between a positive moment *(hupsipolis)* and a negative moment *(apolis)*. This counterturning is a local counterturning within the uncanny entity's counterturning essence, like the rotation of a planet in orbit. As we will see, the human being turns between being *hupsipolis* and being *apolis* insofar as it goes beyond entities to being but always recoils from being's uncanniness.

---

[2] Heidegger interprets the Greek '*pantoporos aporos*' and '*hupsipolis apolis*' as each naming a single, counterturning phenomenon. This interpretation is violent and implausible. Usually, each word of the two pairs is taken to belong to a separate (but juxtaposed) phrase, so a punctuation mark is inserted between them when presenting the originally unpunctuated Greek text. Thus Jebb translates: "yea, he hath resource for all; without resource he meets nothing that must come" (lines 360–361) and "When he honours the laws of the land, and that justice which he hath sworn by the gods to uphold, proudly stands his city: no city hath he who, for his rashness, dwells with sin" (lines 369–371). Sophocles, *Plays: Antigone*, ed. P. E. Easterling and R. C. Jebb, trans. R. C. Jebb (London: Bristol Classical Press, 2004).

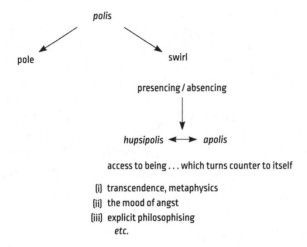

As ontic or open to being's absencing, the human being *falls*. We have already seen (in Chapter 2) that falling is the first or nearest consequence of Dasein's uncanniness. We find the same inward, local counterturning structure in the structure of the falling entity that we do in the transcending entity: as falling, the human being is *pantoporos aporos*, "[e]verywhere venturing forth underway, experienceless without any way out" (HI59/72). To be *pantoporos* is to discover entities in their being and to be *aporos* is to fall prey to seeming, mistakes, and idle talk. To be the uncanny entity is to turn between these two.

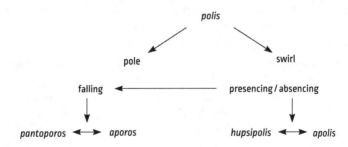

As falling and relating to entities, the human being is open to the *polis* understood not as a swirl but as a pole. Let me pause a moment to

explain this. To think the *polis* as a pole is to think the *da* or open site
not as a pure space of intelligibility but as the site in which a particular
world or understanding of being transpires: "From this site and stead
there springs forth whatever is granted stead and whatever is not, what is
order [*Fug*] and what is disorder, what is fitting [*Schickliche*] and what is
unfitting" (HI82/101). Thus the *polis* is the site of *dikē* and of history as
well as the ground of the political. '*Dikē*' is another of Heidegger's words
for being. Whereas '*phusis*' names being itself as emerging-concealing,
'*dikē*' names being as structuring and articulating—that is, being *qua* the
being of entities.

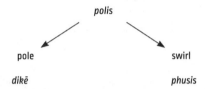

'*Dikē*' is usually translated as 'justice' but Heidegger understands it as
'fittingness' *(Fug)* (EM171/123). We might gloss it as 'how things hang
together': the world as a set of meaningful relations.[3] In a difficult passage from the *Parmenides* lectures (which were delivered a semester after
HI) Heidegger explains: "[i]n the *polis* as the abode of the essence of the
historical human being, the abode that discloses and conceals entities as
such, the human being is encompassed by everything that, in the strict
sense of the word, is ordered to it but is thereby also withdrawn from it.
We do not understand 'ordered' here in the extrinsic sense of 'added to'
or 'put on', but in the sense of 'assigned', as that which is ordained to
the human being, in such a way that the human being is delivered over
to this and is ordered into it, and must abide in it, if its essence is to be

---

[3] Fried explains this well: "[J]ustice allows the Dasein that assembles around the pole
of the polis to recognize and appropriate as its own the various interlocking, if confronta-
tional, tasks given to it as a historical Volk; justice and polemos are equally primordial. In
Introduction to Metaphysics, Heidegger discusses dikē (justice) as *Fug (EM,123).* Justice
as Fug is 'jointure', an articulation of an interpretive whole within which Dasein uncovers the dispensation of its Being-in-the-world. The way in which beings gain articulation
as a whole, within the full horizon of practices that unite beings and Dasein around the
pole of the polis, is through a justice that polemically articulates the joints and seams *(Fugen)* of meaning among disparate beings. The same articulation, through the 'mutual self-
recognition' of strife, must orient Dasein in the polis as well. Justice arranges the world of
the polis into the joints and harmonies of its structure *(Bau),* a structure that necessarily
stands, like a stone archway, through the dispensation of stress and opposition." Gregory
Fried, *Heidegger's* Polemos: *From Being to Politics* (New Haven, CT: Yale University Press,
2000), 142.

in order. What is ordered to the human being in this way, what befits the human being and orders it, we name with the single word *order*, in Greek: *dikē*."[4] A world orders all things in relation to each other, thereby making them what they are. This is '*dikē*,' the 'law' of being. Because '*dikē*' first means order and so ordering, it can come to mean justice in the sense of putting things back in order and setting them aright.

Strictly, the *polis* is not the same as, but is the *site* of, *dikē*, world. It is the clearing in which a world takes place. However, as with any site, it can be addressed by speaking of what takes place in it. It is as addressed as such that the *polis* can be understood as a pole, around which all entities turn. Heidegger says, "The essentially 'polar' character of the *polis* concerns entities as a whole. The polar concerns entities in that around it entities, as manifest, themselves turn" (HI81/100, translation modified). Entities turn around the *polis* in the sense that they only *are* (and are not) by virtue of their relation to it. Thus entities presence and absence in relation to the *polis*. The *polis* "is the site in which all entities and all relational comportment toward entities is gathered. It is the 'pole' among all entities and for all entities in their being" (HI86/106). The *polis qua* world is that in terms of which we discover entities.

The *polis* is thus also that in terms of which we disclose *ourselves* as the entities that we are. This is to say that the ordering of *dikē* is not something that we merely view or (insofar as we are understanders of being) enforce; it is first of all something to which we are subject. The human being is "delivered over to this and is ordered into it, and must abide in it, if its essence is to be in order."[5] We are ordered *by* this 'world order' *(dikē)*—which is to say, there is a place in it in which we fit. There is something that we *are*, some way in which we *make sense* or are intelligible, and we must conform to this if we are to be in accordance with what we are. The history of a people will be the process of engaging in such self-becoming and so coming into their own—coming to properly inhabit the order into which they are destined and so coming to properly inhabit their historical essence. "The *polis* is the 'where', as which and in which order is revealed and concealed. The *polis* is the way the revealing and concealing of order occur such that in these occurrences the historical human being comes into its essence and especially into its counter-essence."[6]

---

[4] Heidegger, *Parmenides*, 92.
[5] Ibid., 92.
[6] Ibid., 95–96.

So we have two ways of thinking the *polis:* (i) in terms of its happening in presencing and absencing, and (ii) as what takes place within this: the *dikē* that governs the intelligibility of entities. Corresponding to these, there are two ways of describing the uncanny entity in its relation to the *polis.* As exposed to the *polis* in its presencing and absencing, the uncanny entity is *hupsipolis apolis.* As a consequence of this, the human being falls and is *pantoporos aporos,* where this means that it comports towards entities and the *polis* as a pole.

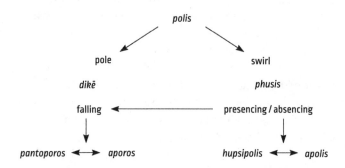

Explaining these two main features of the uncanny entity amounts to explicating the various senses of transcendence and finitude, insofar as they follow from what it is to be uncanny. We will see that there are various ways to cash out what it is to be *hupsipolis apolis* and *pantoporos aporos,* characterizing the uncanny entity at various levels or depths.

Finally, if to be the uncanny entity is to be *hupsipolis apolis* and *pantoporos aporos,* then to be ownedly or authentically uncanny is to be ownedly *hupsipolis apolis* and ownedly *pantoporos aporos.* To see how to be the uncanny entity ownedly, we will have to leave the choral ode and consider Sophocles's character Antigone, whom Heidegger takes to exemplify owned uncanniness. Working out how she does so will show in what sense *Antigone* remains a 'political' drama for Heidegger and Antigone a 'political' heroine.

Being *Pantoporos Aporos:* Falling and Seeming

The first consequence of the human being's uncanniness is that we are tuned into the entities that turn around the pole of the *polis* rather than the *polis* itself. Put differently, the human being's openness to being always takes place within the ontic realm, amidst entities. (Thus William Richardson's interpretation of uncanniness turns out to capture its first consequence: "[t]he There is the most awesome and strange [i.e., *deino-taton*] of beings because, open to Being, it is constitutionally es-tranged from the beings amid which it dwells.")[7] Accordingly, when Heidegger describes the human being as seeking to become homely in the midst of entities (HI84/104), this does not mean that it is seeking to be *at home* in the midst of entities. (Indeed, we already consider ourselves to be at home there (HI76/93).) Rather, our seeking of the homely is the seeking of being and it *takes place in the midst of* entities, in the ontic. We are open to being only as the being of entities. Heidegger expands on this: "For it belongs to this kind of uncanniness, that is, unhomeliness, that whatever is of this essence knows of entities themselves and knows of them as entities, addressing them and enunciating them. This is something of which no thing of nature and no other living entity is capable. The human being alone stands in the midst of entities in such a way as to comport itself toward entities as such. For this reason, it is left to entities of this essence alone to forget being in their relation to entities" (HI76/93). This last sentence addresses our openness to entities in their being negatively, describing it as a forgetting of being. We are familiar with this phenomenon in both its positive and negative forms from SZ, where it is called 'falling.' Falling is the necessity of being amidst entities: we can relate to being only by comporting towards entities. I have argued that in SZ falling (the 'flight' from uncanniness) is a near consequence of uncanniness. Because being is withdrawn from it, Dasein falls and comports towards entities. In the other direction: entities show up as entities (falling) only because their being or presencing does not show up (being's withdrawal). When being is thus *taken* from it, Dasein is *given* its being-amidst-entities. I discussed this in Chapter 2 as 'captivation.' I explored it in Chapter 3 as the struggle to bring being into appearing in entities, which is described in the choral ode as the capturing and subjugating of the living thing: Dasein must 'capture' being as it withdraws and draw it into entities. This is the first consequence of uncanniness: being withdraws and entities show up.

Even as it falls, Dasein turns. There is an uncanny counterturning internal to falling. We see this in the choral ode in the description of the human being as *pantoporos aporos*:

---

[7] William Richardson, *Through Phenomenology to Thought* (New York: Fordham University Press, 2003), 275. Richardson gives a similar reading of uncanniness in SZ: "the dwelling places of the ontic are not There-being's true abode." Ibid., 74. So Dasein is uncanny in that its openness to being makes it a stranger in the ontic.

> Everywhere venturing forth underway, experienceless without any way
> out
> he comes to nothing.
> The singular onslaught of death he can
> by no flight ever prevent,
> even if in the face of dire infirmity he achieves
> most skillful avoidance. (HI59/72)

The human being is *pantoporos,* 'everywhere venturing forth underway,' and yet at the same time *aporos,* 'experienceless without any way out.' '*Poros*' means a "passage through" *(Durchgang)* (HI79/97) and here this is understood as a "passageway through entities" (HI76/93). So while the usual translations of the ode have *pantoporos* as being resourceful or having many ways and means *(poroi),* Heidegger takes it to name the human being's making its way through entities in the sense of discovering them and making them intelligible. This takes place *within* the *polis;* it is our "venturing through" the *polis* as a site (HI89/111).

As *pantoporos,* the human being is everywhere able to discover entities. As Thomas Sheehan puts it, we are "pan-hermeneutical": "We necessarily make some sense of everything we meet, and if we cannot make any sense at all of something, not even interrogative sense ('What is this?'), we simply cannot meet it."[8] In this, the human being is also *aporos.* This does not mean that we lack passages through or ways of discovering entities. The relationship here is not simple negation; it is counterturning. The passages that we have through entities turn against us: they lead somewhere other than where we want to go. What we are seeking in our openness is *being,* but discovering entities in their being does not lead *through* to being. We are not taken through the presence of present entities to *presencing* or being itself. Instead, discovering entities leads to the absencing of being (i.e., the nihilation of the nothing) and to entities. Thus we find only "[t]he 'nothing' [. . .] which, turning counter to being, directly excludes the human being altogether from being" (HI76/93, translation modified). We here encounter the self-withdrawal of being, but not in itself. We encounter it as its flipside: the showing up of entities. Thus our passageways lead "to something [i.e., entities] and to nothing" (HI79/97) and we "remain stuck with particular entities in each case" (HI76/93).

Only an entity that is *pantoporos* can be *aporos* and *vice versa.* The negation indicated by the *a-* of *aporos* is not a lack but an uncanny

---

[8] Thomas Sheehan, "Making Sense of Heidegger: A Paradigm Shift," *Heidegger Circle Proceedings* (2012): 224, 226.

counterturning internal to falling. Because being withdraws, the human being seeks being (the homely) amidst entities and this means that "[w]hatever the human being undertakes turns in itself [. . .] counter to what the human being is fundamentally seeking from it" (HI84/104, translation modified). So to be *pantoporos aporos* is to manifest the counterturning structure of uncanniness. *Pantoporos aporos* expresses uncanniness "from the side of *poros*" (HI75/92).

In EM, being *pantoporos aporos* is a different and further consequence of uncanniness. In HI, to be *pantoporos aporos* is to fall and relate to being mediately, through entities (i.e., to be ontico-ontological, as opposed to simply being ontological, which is impossible). In EM, to be *pantoporos aporos* is to discover entities in a way that always involves covering over (as opposed to a pure uncovering without remainder, which is impossible).[9] Here, *poros* is not a passage through entities to being but a path or route *(Bahn)* to entities themselves (EM162/116). As in HI, to be *pantoporos* is to go out to entities in the sense of discovering them and making them intelligible. But the force of this in EM is that we know our way about amidst entities; we know how to deal with them, how to stand with respect to them. The point is not so much that we are ontico-ontological as that, as a consequence of this, we are in the midst of familiar entities and dwell in a familiar world.

The counterturning internal to being *pantoporos* is correspondingly different. As *aporos,* we are without a way out *(Ausweglos).* This does not mean that we are no longer able to comport towards entities but that we get trapped in our usual ways of doing so. Human beings are "continually thrown back on the paths that they themselves have laid out; they get bogged down in their routes, gets stuck in ruts, and by getting stuck they draw in the circle of their world, get enmeshed in seeming, and thus shut themselves out of being" (EM168/121). This is the decline involved in public intelligibility and common sense. Our ways of discovering entities—our routes—become so well traveled that they become ruts. This amounts to having no way, being *a-poros,* because we no longer travel our routes *as* routes to entities. We see only what we expect to see and do not allow entities to show themselves as they are. As such, we do not have genuine access to entities; we are not genuinely amidst them. There is a sense in which we are "flung from every route" (EM162/116). Our

[9] Thus I disagree with Taminiaux, who takes *pantoporos aporos* in EM to mean "the risk involved in being cast out of every relation to the familiar everydayness." Jacques Taminiaux, "Plato's Legacy in Heidegger's Two Readings of *Antigone*," in *Heidegger and Plato: Toward Dialogue,* ed. Catalin Partenie and Tom Rockmore (Evanston, IL: Northwestern University Press, 2005), 39. Taminiaux does not elaborate on or justify his interpretation.

very act of uncovering entities, of making routes to them, turns itself into a covering over and becoming route-less.

Once again, the *a-* in *aporos* does not straightforwardly negate. We still have routes *(poroi)* and can still discover entities (we are *pantoporos*) but we do so in a counterturning way: our routes cease to be genuine routes to the entities themselves (they are *aporoi*). This is an inner counterturning, an inner play of essence and non-essence: "[t]he violence-doing [*technē*], which originally creates the routes, begets in itself its own un-essence [*Unwesen*]" (EM168/121). Such being *pantoporos aporos* is a manifestation and consequence of our essential uncanniness.

One might object that these two readings of being *pantoporos aporos* are too epistemological and insufficiently existential. I have argued that to be *pantoporos aporos* is to be mediately related to being (HI) and/or to get stuck in usual ways of making sense of things (EM). But the ode goes on to speak of death: the human being is *pantoporos aporos* but "no skillfulness, no acts of violence, no artfulness can stave off death" (HI75/92). Why is death relevant? As with the discussion of death in SZ, the key is to understand death as an ontologically significant phenomenon. It is not the end of a life, whether biological or social, but a limit inherent in intelligibility. Thus in HI, Heidegger says of death that it belongs to being and that because we also belong to being we thereby belong to death (HI120/150). Similarly, EM discusses the mention of death in the ode and concludes that because the human being is subject to death, Dasein "is the happening of un-canniness itself" (EM169/121). As a feature of being that is intrinsically tied to uncanniness, death must be withdrawal, concealment, absencing. Thus to say that the human being cannot prevent the onslaught of death is to say that there will always be a fundamental limit to intelligibility that we cannot cross or surmount. There are unintelligibilities, concealments, and obscurities—epistemological 'illnesses'—that we can conquer. But the absencing that is built into being's presencing is a finitude that necessarily cannot be overcome. Intelligibility is essentially finite. So this part of the ode does not discuss mortality but invokes the idea that the overwhelming can never be surmounted (EM171–172/123) and so that *technē* will always shatter against being (EM174/124). There will never be full intelligibility.

We have seen that making-intelligible is finite because being withdraws (death, uncanniness), and so as a consequence we can relate to it only *via* entities (HI: *pantoporos aporos*). We relate to entities by means of ways of making sense of things that can become routines (EM: *pantoporos aporos*). Recall that it is by being stuck in such a discovering rut and seeing only what she expects to see that Jentsch's traveler mistakes the snake for a tree branch. We can tell the same story from the other side, as a story about the tree branch showing up as something that it is not. Seeming, appearing, and untruth are all consequences of Dasein's uncanniness. Thus Heidegger: "We first press forward fully to the happening of un-canniness when we experience the power of seeming together with the struggle against seeming in its essential belonging to Dasein" (EM161–162/116).

In HI, Heidegger discusses seeming by speaking of non-entities and risk. The story is as follows. As Dasein falls, entities show up to it in their being; they "emerge of their own accord and thus come to presence" (HI88/109–110). But they do not always come to presence as the entities that they are. Because being, as uncanny, withdraws, entities do not wear their being on their sleeves (as it were). They thus have the possibility of coming to presence as what they are not—not as nothing but as what Heidegger calls 'non-entities,' 'das Un-seiende.' (This term is Heidegger's translation of the ode's 'mē kalon.') Non-entities appear (i.e., are discovered) but *not* in truth. They 'shine out' but *not* as themselves. Again, this *non-* is not a straightforward negation. It is a counterturning (HI88/110): non-entities are entities insofar as they show up for us and they are non-entities insofar as their appearing or showing up turns in itself to present the entity as it is not. So "[e]ntities themselves as emergent and appearing are, as such, simultaneously self-concealing and mere appearing. Thus entities themselves play out their appearances and hide non-entities within such appearances" (HI89/111).

We find the same idea in SZ in the discussion of the phenomenon (§7a) as well as in the discussion of ontic truth and untruth (§44). For Heidegger, truth in the sense of correspondence is grounded in a more original phenomenon of truth. A correspondence between a judgment and entities requires, first, that entities show up as entities—that they are discovered in their being. This discovering is or produces 'ontic truth,' the uncovering or showing up of entities. Being in ontic truth (discovering) is thus the same as being *pantoporos* (in both the HI and EM senses). It is made possible by ontological truth: the disclosure of being. Only on the basis of the disclosure of being (ontological truth) can entities be discovered as the entities that they are (ontic truth). Only then can a judgment correspond or fail to correspond to the way that entities are (truth as correspondence). By virtue of being disclosing, then, "Dasein is 'in the truth'" (SZ221, original italicized).

But Dasein is also in untruth and it is so because it falls (SZ222). (Thus Heidegger also grounds untruth in thrownness, to which uncanniness belongs (SZ223).) As we know, uncanny Dasein is subject not only to the disclosure of being (ontological truth) but also to its withdrawal—what we might call 'ontological untruth.' It follows that the being of particular entities is never directly manifest to falling Dasein and so that "[t]ruth (uncoveredness) is something that must always first be wrested from entities" (SZ222). (Notice in Heidegger's language an anticipation of the violence metaphor that he employs in EM.) Once an entity has been *discovered* in its being, the discovered entity and its way of being discovered can be passed along and so become subject to the decline of habit and public intelligibility. Thus Dasein's discovering of entities becomes determined by *das Man:* by the standard, usual, and average take on things. Dasein in each case (whether owned or unowned) discovers entities in the way that *everyone* does. Such discovery uncovers entities (ontic truth) but also covers them over or distorts them: "That which has been uncovered and disclosed stands in a mode in which it has been disguised and closed off by idle talk, curiosity and ambiguity" (SZ222). This covering over is ontic untruth. To be in ontic untruth is for discovering to involve covering over.

As with *a-poros,* the *un-* of this untruth is not a lack of truth or a failure of discovery but a modification of truth. Ontic truth is a kind of uncovering that *also* covers over: "Entities have not been completely hidden; they are precisely the sort of thing that has been uncovered, but at the same time they have been disguised. They show themselves, but in the mode of semblance. Likewise what has formerly been uncovered sinks back again, hidden and disguised" (SZ222). The first of these is ontic untruth *qua* seeming, and the second is ontic untruth *qua* distortion by *das Man.* The former anticipates the non-entities of HI, and the latter anticipates the *aporos* of EM. In neither case is the disguising conscious or deliberate. It stems from the fact that everyday discovery tends to take shortcuts and use shorthands rather than taking the lead each time from the entities themselves in genuine discovering. So another way to grasp Dasein's being *pantoporos aporos* is to say that it is counterturningly in ontic truth and untruth.

Heidegger explicitly connects ontic untruth to uncanniness in SZ. In its being in untruth, Dasein in each case is cut off from a genuine relationship to the entities that it discovers and the possibilities onto which it projects them. As thus cut off, Dasein in each case "is constantly uprooting itself" (SZ173), and it "drifts along towards an ever-increasing groundlessness as it floats" (SZ170). Heidegger goes on: "the uncanniness of this floating remains hidden from" Dasein in each case (SZ170). This says: the uprootedness and floating of being in untruth is uncanny. Being in untruth is uncanny because, as we have seen, (i) it is in a counterturning relation to being in truth and so has an uncanny structure, and (ii) this being in truth and untruth is a consequence of Dasein's essential uncanniness.

I have argued that because we are *aporos* in the HI sense—that is, falling or ontico-ontological—we are in untruth (SZ), *aporos* (EM), and in relation to non-entities (HI). We are exposed to seeming and can get trapped in the usual way of looking at things. The sense that we make of things is thus always finite and fragile. In being exposed to entities in their seeming and in depending on tradition and accustomed ways of making routes to entities, fallen Dasein in each case takes things for granted, makes assumptions, takes shortcuts or the easy path. It usually discovers entities in such a way that it does *not* reach a genuine understanding of them. Thus "Dasein's understanding in *das Man* is constantly *going wrong* in its projects, as regards the genuine possibilities of being" (SZ174). Ontic untruth affords "constant confusion, and hence, the possibility of aberration and mistakes" (EM115/83). We "can be mistaken within the being of entities, and at times, that is, continually [. . .] must be mistaken within being, so that [we] take nonentities to be entities and entities to be nonentities" (HI87/108). Cut off from that upon which it projects, Dasein in each case always risks a projection that breaks down as a discovery of the entity. We are always at risk of error, and familiarity is always capable of being breached or slipping away. Most breakdowns in meaningfulness will be simple mistakes, like Jentsch's tree/snake. Some will produce the uncanny feeling in one or more of the ways I discussed in Chapter 1—particularly if they are breakdowns that reveal the role of ontic untruth in the constitution of familiarity. This is how the uncanny feeling keys us into our essential uncanniness and how it is a consequence of this deeper being uncanny.

Insofar as it always involves ontic untruth, seeming and the possibility of error, our comportment towards entities can be understood as 'risk': "To the extent that the human being is 'together' with non-entities, so that it takes non-entities as entities, it has entrusted entities to the danger of annihilation, put them at stake. Such comportment toward entities is *tolma*, risk" (HI89/110). *At stake* here are entities, as that which present themselves as what they are. In risk, entities show up in a way that is in tension or at odds with what they are. This tension is the counterturning captured in the term 'non-entities.' Heidegger's vocabulary of annihilation is melodramatic, and his description of this phenomenon from the side of entities makes it seem as if the human being is negatively impacting a world that otherwise would be better off. But the point is that the human being is so constituted (i.e., uncannily) that when things show up meaningfully, it is possible for the meaning to twist itself away from the entity. That is, it is possible for the entity to be presented in a distorted way: a misre*present*ation. So at risk are not entities *qua* independent of us but entities *qua* showing up to us as what they are. That is, at stake or at risk is our access to entities in their being. This risk stems ultimately from the withdrawal of being. It is in these terms that Taminiaux interprets 'risk' in HI: it "designates a destiny of erring which is necessitated by Being itself defined in terms of an unconcealment which again and again preserves its secret."[10] Making our way through entities towards being, we can be deflected from our path and fail to find that which we seek. We find only error, mistake, confusion, seeming, mere appearance. So this talk of 'risk' is a way of expressing, from the side of entities in their being, the essential counterturning in our quest to become homely in being. This is why Heidegger can go on to say, "Yet because entities themselves play out their own appearances, the human being, in undertaking the risk of becoming homely, must place everything at stake in such a play and therefore encounter *this:* the fact that the homely refuses itself to it" (HI90/111). Being is not immediately available. It, and we, are uncanny.

Being *Hupsipolis Apolis:* Metaphysics and Transcendence

From the fact of uncanniness we can deduce a variety of finitudes in human making-intelligible and in intelligibility. All possibility of error, all need for revision, and all threat of collapse are consequences of being's uncanniness and in particular of the fact that the human being, as uncanny, must fall and relate to being through entities (that is, the fact that being is always the being of an entity). This in turn follows from the fact that entities show up only if being absences.

But while being's absencing means that the human being relates to entities, absencing is also being's way of *presencing*. So the human being always relates to entities *in their being*. Even as directed towards the ontic, we remain ontological. If we focus on this fact, then a different part of the story comes into view—not a variety of finitudes but a variety of transcendences or transcendings. These follow from the most fundamental transcendence: being open to being's presencing, which in the previous chapter I called 'seeking the homely' or 'faring forth into the sea'. Since they are consequences of this fundamental transcendence, the variety of human transcendings that now become perspicuous are varieties not of

---

[10] Taminiaux, "Plato's Legacy," 39.

being open to being *per se* but of moving *beyond* entities to being. As moving beyond *(meta)* entities *(ta phusika)* to being, the human being is the meta-physical entity.[11]

The human being 'oscillates' (FCM6)—or, better, *is the oscillating*—between falling and transcending, between being directed to the ontic and being open to the ontological. This is an uncanny counterturning. Further, just as falling itself contained an inner counterturning (between *pantoporos* and *aporos*), so too our metaphysical character contains an inner counterturning. We see this in the next strophe of the ode, which pivots from the non-entities and risk that characterize falling to the metaphysical counterturning of being *hupsipolis apolis:*

> Between the ordinance of the earth and the
> order ordained by the gods he ventures:
> Towering high above the site, forfeiting the site
> is he for whom non-entities always are
> for the sake of risk. (HI59/72)

To be *hupsipolis apolis* is to rise high above the site and thereby to lose the site. The phrase is formed in the same way as '*pantoporos aporos*', and Heidegger reads it in a similarly strained way to afford it its uncanny, counterturning structure. Some readers of EM and HI take the *hupsipolis apolis* figure to be the uncanny human being itself, and in doing so conflate uncanniness proper with one of its existential consequences.[12] Part of the difficulty in interpreting what Heidegger says is that (as with being *pantoporos aporos*) there are a variety of different but related phenomena that Heidegger seems to be trying to capture. But he seems more confused about these than he did when working with being *pantoporos aporos*. The task is to tease out the different manifestations of our metaphysical character. How do we go out beyond entities to being?

In EM, Heidegger implies that *hupsipolis apolis* human beings are metaphysical in a reasonably recognizable sense. They are world-historical creators, who question the world into which they are thrown and "rise high in historical being as creators, as doers" (EM163/117). Such world-historical creative figures (attempt to) found new constellations of

---

[11] For one instance among many of Heidegger interpreting 'metaphysics' in this way, see FCM39.

[12] For example, Fried: "Heidegger is fascinated with line 370 of this passage, and particularly with the phrase *hupsipolis apolis*, which he deems Sophocles's deepest characterization of human Being." Fried, *Heidegger's Polemos*, 140; see also the discussion in the following pages.

intelligibility, and for Heidegger they are poets, thinkers, or statesmen. Paradigmatically, the world-historical creator 'rises high' in the *polis* in the sense that she masters (by revising) *dikē*, the order of the world. Jesus and Socrates are plausible examples of such creators. If the creator does not rise quite so high, she perhaps creates new *poroi* or paths to entities. She "dares the surmounting of being" (EM172/123) just like all human beings but in a more profound and more creative way. While all human beings surmount being in the sense of revealing entities, figures like Dante and Newton plausibly surmount being in the sense of revealing entities *in new ways*. This would be the stronger reading of the claim that the human violence-doer is one who "sets out into the un-said, who breaks into the un-thought, who compels what has never happened and makes appear what is unseen" (EM172/123). Whether laying out new paths or opening a new world order, the *hupsipolis apolis* human being is ontologically creative. She institutes new ways of disclosing and in doing so "risk[s] the assault of un-entities, *mē kalon*" (EM172/123). She risks getting entities wrong.

As an uncanny structure, such 'rising high' in the *polis* simultaneously turns and produces its counter-essence. It is "[t]o tower into the heights of one's own essential space and thus govern that space, yet simultaneously to plunge downward into its depths and be lost in that space" (HI87/107). To be *hupsipolis* is to be *apolis* (without site, losing the site)—but again, not in a way that is a straightforward negation or lack. In opening up a new world, creators necessarily break up or out of the old, transcending and transgressing their previous constellation of intelligibility. They are *apolis* insofar as they do not quite belong, either in the 'old' world that they supersede or in the 'new' one that they found since "*as* creators [they] must first ground all this in each case" (EM163/117). The creator is an untimely, transitional figure. Situated between epochs, she lacks a proper history: "The higher the peak of historical Dasein rises, the more gaping is the abyss for the sudden plunge into the un-historical, which then only flails around in a confusion that has no way out and at the same time has no site" (EM172/123). Commentaries are not generally clear on whether this situation makes the *hupsipolis apolis* creator inherently uncanny, makes her feel uncanny, or makes her appear uncanny to others.[13] But this question misses the point. Being untimely

[13] For example: "He is a creator, and yet his creation is brought about at the expense of an essential solitude—the solitude of those who have elevated themselves to the vertiginous height of the summits blown by the great cold winds and by the transparency of the skies. Because of his very nature, the creator cannot be at home in the time of his today. He is

does not make a creator uncanny; it makes her *apolis*. The creator is uncanny insofar as she is counterturningly *both hupsipolis* and *apolis*.

Heidegger's vision of the *hupsipolis apolis* figure in HI is very different. Here, he does not mention creative individuals at all. Beistegui suggests that this is because of a change in Heidegger's understanding of the *polis* and of history (based on a change in his understanding of the human in relation to being). At the same time, he argues that the HI picture is not so much a change of view as an attempt to fully ontologize the reading of the ode.[14] This latter claim is certainly true of HI. Another difference is that while the EM reading has the human being deploying its disclosive powers to surmount being and to bring about a particular world order *(dikē)*, the HI reading emphasizes the fact that the human being is itself implicated in the order of things. The human being is not merely that for which things are ordered but is itself ordered by this ordering. So the *polis* is here understood not only as the clearing within which a particular world order takes hold but also as "the way the revealing and concealing of order occur such that in these occurrences the historical human being comes into its own essence and especially into its counter-essence."[15] The focus on the implication of the human being in *dikē* affects how we read being *hupsipolis apolis*.

Consider the gloss on being *apolis* in the *Parmenides* lectures, which begins with a clarification of *dikē*: "But the 'order' meant here is not the counter-essence to just any sort of 'disorder' we might imagine. We mean 'order' as an indicating, demonstrating, assigning, and at the same

---

always beyond, in a time that negates and opposes the present time. Hence the situation of the creator is one of exile, of unfamiliarity, of *Unheimlichkeit*, even though his creation is precisely such as to contain the promise of a new and more proper dwelling for the historical Dasein. The very possibility of an authentic dwelling presupposes a thrownness out of the familiar into the vertiginous abyss of the uncanny. Such is the reason why, to his contemporaries, to the *Hierigen* and the *Jetzigen*, the creator himself appears to be *unheimisch*—strange, uncanny: monstrous." Miguel de Beistegui, *Heidegger & the Political: Dystopias* (New York: Routledge, 1998), 102.

[14] Ibid., 129. According to Beistegui, in EM "Heidegger sees history, along with the *polis* as the site of its unfolding, as the happening of a conflict or a confrontation between man, essentially determined on the basis of *technē*, and the whole of being (or *phusis*), essentially determined as *dikē*." Ibid., 122. In HI, "*polis* still 'means' *die Stätte*, the place, the site or the scene of the historical happening of man, yet history is here more specifically determined as man's encounter with the truth of beings as a whole, and not so much as the happening of this particular conflict between the ordering power of *phusis* and the violence of machination. More than the scene of a titanic and indeed tragic conflict between opposing forces, the *polis* is now seen as the *polos*, the pole *(der Pol)*, the whirl *(der Wirbel)*, or the hinge around which everything—beings as a whole—revolves." Ibid., 136.

[15] Heidegger, *Parmenides*, 95–96.

time arranging and 'thrusting' order. It is to this that the human being has to be ordered, and so it is precisely out of it that it [sc. the human being] can err into the path of disorder, especially when the assignment conceals itself and falls away, withdrawing the human being from the *polis,* tearing it away from it [sc. the *polis*], so that it [sc. the human being] becomes *apolis.*"[16] With the emphasis on *dike* as "what is ordered to the human being [. . .], what befits the human being and orders it," the human being's relationship to the *polis* is always a relationship to that which orders it: its essence, as a historical destiny.[17] Accordingly, Heidegger in HI understands the *hupsipolis* human being as "tower[ing] into the heights of one's own essential space and thus govern[ing] that space" (HI87/107), with "the supreme heights of mastery of the site of its history" (HI89/110). This mastery cannot be creative but must be a matter of fulfilling the essence that is destined to the human being. This essence can be thought at two levels of abstraction: (i) becoming Da-sein and so coming to be the *polis qua* clearing or site and (ii) fulfilling the particular historical destiny of one's people and so coming into one's order in a particular *polis* or world. That Heidegger leans towards the latter is confirmed by his emphasis in HI on the historical essence and destiny of the German people and how they come to inhabit it. (Note also that such 'coming to be homely' in one's historical essence requires a poet or world-historical creator—for the German people, Hölderlin, and for the Greeks, Sophocles.)

Precisely in coming to fulfill its essence and in that sense 'rising high in the site,' the human being must also be *apolis.* What does this mean? Being *hupsipolis apolis,* on this reading, concerns our relationship to the 'order' of the world *(dike).* We have an assignment, a place, within this order and our destiny is to occupy it. We become *apolis* when we fall into disorder, "plunge downward into its depths," and are "lost in that space" (HI87/107), reaching "the most profound depths of the forfeiture of this site" (HI89/110). This happens, I take it, "when the assignment conceals itself and falls away, withdrawing the human being from the *polis.*"[18] Our ordering to our essence is concealed from us. We misunderstand what or who we are and fall away from ourselves. We thus fail to become what we are—failing to accord with our historical destiny.[19] This may

---

[16] Ibid., 92–93.

[17] Ibid., 92.

[18] Ibid., 92.

[19] Fried has a different reading of the disorder mentioned in this passage from the *Parmenides.* He reads it as the actual collapse of order: "The polis is the abode of Dasein and a site for the polemos of the truth of Being, not because it institutes an enduring political

be associated with decline, of the sort that Nietzsche describes when he accuses German 'clarity of presentation' of degenerating into a mediocre, 'English' calculative rationality.[20] But not being what one *is* is also necessary, at least at the beginning: "In the beginning of the history of any humankind, the destiny fittingly destined for that humankind is indeed assigned to it. What has been assigned is in coming [*im Kommen*]. What is coming is still veiled and equivocal. For this reason, we cannot immediately delimit unequivocally or clearly attend to whatever it is that is fitting. In the beginning, a historical humankind is unable to move freely within the open and ordered possibilities of its essence. It is still closed off from that destiny that is fittingly destined for it. And it is thereby in a certain manner excluded from the origin of its own essence. The historical humankind in question is not yet intimately familiar with the unfolded and essential fullness of its destiny, is not 'at home' in it" (HI130/162–163). Heidegger discusses this kind of being unhomely or being *apolis* at length in HI, and he does so because he has a particular interest in the situation of the German people and in the articulation of German culture by Hölderlin. Germany's destiny is very much a live question at the time of these lectures (1942), and the reading of Hölderlin—and the detour through Sophocles—is supposed to clarify Germany's historical situation (although it is unclear to me precisely how it does so, given that HI fully ontologizes the reading of the ode).

However, notice that the counterturning between the granting of a historical destiny and its occlusion is unlike the other counterturnings that we have considered. It follows from the counterturning in being: being's absencing means that *dikē* can be concealed from us and, as a result, that we can fail to see what we are. But such seeming is a consequence of being

order, but rather because it holds itself open to 'calamity' *(das Unheil)*—that is, to the dissolution of instituted order and to demolition of the meaning of beings and the sense of Being that go with that order. In such calamitous transgression brought on by the apolis figure, everything is *aus den Fugen*, out of joint: the articulated cosmos of meaning dissolves in the face of a new founding, or else collapses entirely into oblivion." Fried, *Heidegger's Polemos*, 142. In contrast, I take this kind of collapse either to apply to the experience of the world-historical creator or to follow as a consequence from being *pantoporos aporos*. I do not see how it can apply to a people's coming to fulfill its historical destiny.

[20] For instance: the German spirit is essentially characterized by a 'clarity of presentation': "the ability to grasp, the designing of projects, the erection of frameworks and enclosures, the construction of boundaries and divisions, dividing and classifying." Martin Heidegger, *Elucidations of Hölderlin's Poetry*, trans. Keith Hoeller (Amherst, NY: Humanity Books, 2000), 112–113. But according to Nietzsche and Heidegger, this clarity has degenerated into a dull, mediocre (English, utilitarian) calculative rationality, governed by the technological attitude; see especially Martin Heidegger, *Introduction to Philosophy: Thinking and Poetizing,* trans. Phillip Jacques Braunstein (Bloomington: Indiana University Press, 2011).

pantoporos aporos and cannot belong intrinsically to being *hupsipolis*. Heidegger makes this clear in attributing such 'disorder,' or loss of the essence, to the withdrawal of being *via* seeming: "disorder" and "disaster" "belong to the *polis* because every unconcealment of entities stands in conflict with concealment and accordingly also with dissemblance and distortion."[21] This is not a downfall that we experience *by virtue of* rising high in the site. If this is what Heidegger has in mind in HI for being *hupsipolis apolis,* then he has failed to hit on a counterturning structure.

It is possible that Heidegger reads being *hupsipolis apolis* in this way in order to make sense of the way in which the ode posits being *hupsipolis apolis* as a consequence of risk:

> Towering high above the site, forfeiting the site
> is he for whom non-entities always are
> for the sake of risk. (HI59/72)

Heidegger, of course, has associated risk and non-entities with being *pantoporos aporos.* The claim in these lines is thus that "[i]nsofar as the human being ventures forth and is everywhere underway, it exceeds the site of its historical essence" (HI89/110–111). How can we make sense of the idea that being *hupsipolis apolis* follows from being *pantoporos aporos* in this way? One option is to understand being *apolis* as having one's own essence concealed from one: "In risk, however, the human being risks not only this or that, but always and in the first instance itself, indeed not only itself as an individual, but itself in its essence" (HI95/118). Understood at the historical level, this amounts to the occlusion of a people's historical destiny. Understood at the level of Dasein itself, it is the idea that Dasein is uncanny: its essence or ground is concealed from Dasein by virtue of the very act of disclosing it. On this reading, the claim is simply that being *pantoporos aporos* follows from being uncanny, which of course we have already seen to be the case. Being *hupsipolis apolis* does not thus appear to add anything new, and it is not a properly counterturning structure.

A more promising approach—which I think the text will bear, at least in part—is a resolutely existential-ontological interpretation of the *hupsipolis apolis* figure. This gives us a third dimension to our transcending or metaphysical nature. What is significant about the *polis* on this reading has nothing to do with it being the site of *dikē*, either as something creatively instituted (first reading) or as something to which we are ordered

---

[21] Heidegger, *Parmenides*, 91.

(second reading). Instead, the *polis* is understood as the site of openness: the clearing *per se*. Consider this passage: "The human being is then related in an exceptional sense to this pole, insofar as the human being, in understanding being, stands in the midst of entities and here necessarily has a 'status' in each case, a stance in its instances and circumstances" (HI81/100). The human being is special among all the entities that turn around the pole of the *polis* since it is the human being to whom this pole is manifest and from whom it withdraws. We have seen this before. The human being itself *is* the site, or the *polis,* in a deep sense and as such it is the most uncanny of all entities. It looms and stirs *(ragend sich regt)* and so *is* in the manner of *pelein* in a superlative way. The ode expresses this superlative condition using the metaphor of height, saying that the human being (on Heidegger's translation) *hochüberragend die Stätte*: rises high in the site. Notice the recurrence of *ragend* here, repeated from the opening line and repeating our being in the manner of *pelein*. So the repetition in *hupsipolis apolis* brings out the comparison with other entities, by pointing out that as a consequence of being superlatively uncanny we *are* in a way that is unlike other entities in the open site. Specifically, we (counterturningly, uncannily) move beyond entities to being.

This access to being, in the midst of entities, is transcendence, metaphysics, or philosophizing. Recall that, like the term *'hupsipolis,'* 'metaphysics' uses a somewhat spatial metaphor to grasp what is special about Dasein: it is the entity that goes beyond *(meta)* entities *(ta phusika)* to being. In FCM, Heidegger calls this a "turnaround" *(Umwendung)* (FCM39): we turn away from entities and towards being. He also describes this movement as an urge, a restlessness, a being driven (FCM5), and a demand (FCM6). Following Novalis, he calls it a 'homesickness' (FCM5). We have an urge "to be at home everywhere" (FCM5), where this means "to exist among entities *as a whole*" (FCM8)—to understand entities in their being. This homesickness, the drive beyond entities to being, is the immediate ontological-existential consequence of our openness to being's presencing, our seeking of the homely. So 'metaphysics,' 'philosophizing,' 'transcendence,' and 'rising high in the site' all name the happening of the understanding of entities in their being.

By calling such transcendence or going-beyond-entities 'metaphysics' or 'philosophizing,' Heidegger is not saying that it is something that only certain (academic) people do in certain (intellectual) endeavors. Philosophizing or metaphysics at its most general is what makes us distinctively human: our making things intelligible. To be a case of Dasein *just is* to philosophize. "[P]hilosophizing fundamentally belongs to each human being as something proper to them" (FCM13); it is "a fundamental occurrence within human Dasein" (FCM9). This is what in Chapter 2 I called 'originary angst.' We can also explicitly perform the move beyond entities to being, and this is what in Chapter 2 I called 'the mood of angst.' In the mood of angst, falling is disrupted and we move beyond our everyday immersion in entities to explicitly hook into the ontological. From the perspective of our immersion in entities, angst or philosophizing can be described as the experience of the extraordinary within the ordinary, as Heidegger does in *Parmenides:*

> But where [. . .] Being comes into focus, there the extraordinary announces itself, the excessive that strays 'beyond' the ordinary, that which is not to be explained by explanations on the basis of entities. This is the uncanny [*Ungeheure*], literally understood and not in the otherwise usual sense according to which it rather means the immense and what has never yet been. [. . .] The uncanny is also not what has never yet been present; it is what comes into presence always already and in advance prior to all 'uncanninesses'. The uncanny, as the Being that shines into everything ordinary, i.e., into entities, and that in its shining often grazes entities like the shadow of a cloud silently passing, has nothing in common with the monstrous or the alarming. The uncanny is the simple, the insignificant, ungraspable by the fangs of the will, withdrawing itself from all artifices of calculation, because it surpasses all planning. The emergence and the concealment that dwell in all emerging entities, i.e., Being itself, must therefore be astonishing to common experience within the everyday dealing with entities, if this does manage to get Being actually in focus, though it always has some view of it. The astounding is for the Greeks the simple, the insignificant, Being itself. The astounding, visible in the astonishing, is the uncanny, and it pertains so immediately to the ordinary that it can never be explained on the basis of the ordinary.[22]

The term translated here as 'uncanny' is '*Ungeheure*' (which, incidentally, Hölderlin used in 1804 to translate Sophocles's '*to deinon*' and which Heidegger says captures part of the sense of his '*Unheimlichkeit*' (HI70–71/85–87)). Unlike the *Unheimliche*, the *Ungeheure* is not counterturning; it is merely outside or beyond. Heidegger's point in the *Parmenides* passage is that, from the perspective of our ordinary, everyday dealings with entities, being appears as extraordinary. Philosophizing is the move towards this extraordinary realm.[23]

[22] Ibid., 101.

[23] As best as I can tell, it is along these lines that Cavell interprets Heidegger's talk of 'uncanniness.' See Stanley Cavell, "The Uncanniness of the Ordinary," *In Quest of the Ordinary: Lines of Skepticism and Romanticism* (Chicago: University of Chicago Press,

I have yet to explain what it is to be *apolis* on this third reading, whether being *hupsipolis* means being metaphysical in general, experiencing angst, or explicitly philosophizing. How does the move towards the extraordinary from within the ordinary count as counterturning and so as an uncanny structure? Recalling my discussion of angst, we might think that the motion that turns counter to these metaphysical or anxious steps is falling, which as we know from SZ is grounded in original angst and disrupted by the mood of angst. But while transcendence and falling are, at the most general level, counterturningly related (in the sense that the human being is ontico-ontological), we are dealing here with specific kinds of transcendence. The counterturning—which, recall, must be *inner*—must be more intimately related to the transcendence in question. Thus the counterturning relationship here does not correspond to the revelation/withdrawal structure that I brought out in analyzing the mood of angst.

We get a first glimpse of the turn from being *hupsipolis* to being *apolis* in the claim that philosophizing is an *extraordinary* move towards the extraordinary. Consider this description of philosophizing in EM:

> At the outset we spoke of a question: "Why are there entities at all instead of nothing?" We asserted that to ask this question is to philosophize. Whenever we set out in the direction of this question, thinking and gazing ahead, then right away we forgo any sojourn in any of the usual regions of entities. We pass over and surpass what belongs to the order of the day. We ask beyond the usual, beyond the ordinary that is ordered in the everyday. Nietzsche once said (VII, 269): "A philosopher: that is a human being who constantly experiences, sees, hears, suspects, hopes, dreams extraordinary things . . ."
>
> Philosophizing is a questioning about the extra-ordinary. Yet as we merely intimated at first, this questioning recoils upon itself, and thus not only what is asked about is extraordinary, but also the questioning itself. This means that this questioning does not lie along our way, so that one day we stumble into it blindly or even by mistake. Nor does it stand in the familiar order of the everyday, so that we could be compelled to it on the ground of some requirements or even regulations. Nor does this questioning lie in the sphere of urgent concern and the satisfaction of dominant needs. The questioning itself is out-of-order. It is completely voluntary. [. . .] Philosophizing, we can now say, is extra-ordinary questioning about the extra-ordinary. (EM13–14/10)

1994), 153–178, and "Night and Day: Heidegger and Thoreau," *Revue Française d'études Américaines* 91 (2002): 110–125. The latter text discusses FCM and HI.

Philosophizing is the extra-ordinary move beyond entities to being, and it is itself extra-ordinary in that it recoils on itself and is out-of-order. What Heidegger seems to have in mind here is that the philosopher is in the same sort of position as the untimely creator. This philosophical move must, in fact, be the condition of possibility of the world-historical creator's act of creation. Such creation will thus always be either poetic-philosophical or philosophical-poetic (or perhaps even political-philosophical or philo-sophical-political). Further, a people can only be moving towards fulfill-ing their historical destiny if they have access to their essence and so are metaphysical or transcending in the basic sense of being ontological. We can thus array these varieties of transcendence—each of which can be of-fered as an interpretation of being *hupsipolis*—in a chain of ontological dependence. The philosopher's *apolis* status, then, is the deepest version of the untimeliness and strangeness of the creator. The philosopher is not between two worlds, as the creator is, but is simply out-of-the-ordinary. In moving out beyond the realm of the everyday (being *hupsipolis*) the phi-losopher becomes out of place in it *(apolis)*. The philosopher is a strange and unhomely figure, which Plato captures when he describes Socrates as *atopos* or out-of-place: a stranger wherever he goes.[24]

But there is a further sense in which philosophical questioning 'recoils' on itself and so is uncannily counterturning. Philosophizing recoils on itself in that it turns on itself and takes itself as its own object. As Hei-degger put the 'recoiling' earlier in EM: "this questioning necessarily re-coils back from what is asked and what is interrogated, back upon itself. [. . .] It runs up against the search for its own Why" (EM6/4). In seeking its own 'Why,' metaphysical questioning is seeking its source in the ques-tioner; it thereby places the questioner in question. This move is familiar from Heidegger's own recoil in SZ from the question of the meaning of being to the interrogation of the questioner who poses it (SZ7, 13). We see it also in FCM's characterization of philosophizing as 'comprehen-sive questioning': "Metaphysics is a questioning in which we inquire into entities as a whole, and inquire in such a way that in so doing we our-selves, the questioners, are thereby also included in the question, placed in question" (FCM9). The same sentiment, in nearly the same words, is expressed in the roughly contemporaneous WM: "[E]very metaphysical question can be asked only in such a way that the questioner as such is also there within the question, that is, is placed in question" (WM82).

When philosophizing thus turns on itself and attempts to illumi-nate itself, it withdraws from its own grasp. It thus presents itself

[24] This theme comes up repeatedly, especially in the *Phaedrus* and the *Apology*.

"ambiguously": "[H]ow and to where can metaphysics as philosophizing, as our own human activity, withdraw from us, if we ourselves are,
after all, human beings? Yet do we in fact know what we ourselves are?
What is man? [. . .] If we know so little about man, how can our essence
not be alien to us? How can philosophizing as a human activity fail to
conceal itself from us in the obscurity of this essence?" (FCM4). Philosophizing fails to achieve its own reflexive self-grasp; it always comes up
against and stumbles on the question of human nature or the question
of the being of the questioner. It seeks its own ground but always fails
to understand itself. So in the experience of philosophizing we encounter
our own self-opacity. This is the revelation of thrownness in the mood of
angst: the confrontation with the veiled 'whence' of Dasein, in which the
human being is "attacked by the fact 'that he is what he is'" (FCM21).[25]
The self-opacity produced in the transcendental move is a consequence
of the fact that the human essence is essentially withheld, and so it is a
consequence of uncanniness—further, one in which our own essential
uncanniness is revealed to us. (I will return to this in Chapter 5.) We can
also conclude that the possibility of the mood of angst has its ground in
our fundamentally uncanny nature—that is, in uncanniness as an aspect
of originary angst.

So philosophizing has an uncanny, inwardly counterturning structure.
The human being is *hupsipolis* in that she transcends entities towards
being. She is *apolis* in that, in so transcending, she encounters the obscure whence of thrownness and so the inexplicability of her own being
as transcending. This transcendence and its counterturning can be expressed at different levels. First, at the level of originary angst, the human being *is* the self-veiling self-encounter: the metaphysical entity that
always has itself in question or is always an issue for itself in its very being (compare SZ12). Second, in the mood of angst (as we have seen) the
human being encounters her fundamental self-opacity in the disclosure of
her thrown being. Finally, the experience of explicit philosophizing will
be an existentiell modification of the mood of angst and so will involve

[25] Heidegger cautions us against understanding this encounter as placid: "[I]n the philosophical concept, man, and indeed man as a whole, is in the *grip of an attack*—driven out
of everydayness and driven back into the ground of things. Yet the attacker is not man, the
dubious subject of the everyday and of the bliss of knowledge. Rather, *in philosophizing
the Da-sein in man launches the attack upon man.* Thus man in the ground of his essence
is someone in the grip of an attack, attacked by the fact 'that he is what he is', and already
caught up in all comprehending questioning. Yet being comprehensively included in this
way is not some blissful awe, but the struggle against the insurmountable ambiguity of all
questioning and being" (FCM21).

the same difficulty in accessing Dasein's being. This is the methodological difficulty that forces Heidegger to analyze angst.

As explicitly philosophizing or as experiencing angst, we might transcend or become *hupsipolis* in an ontologically creative way and so become a creator or reviser of our understanding of being. We are then *apolis* in the sense of being untimely. Finally, a people as a whole might be striving towards fulfilling their essence in the sense of their historical destiny *(hupsipolis)* and find that they lose hold of this as it is concealed (although this is not clearly being *apolis* and so not clearly counterturning).

Just as Heidegger's various interpretations of our being *pantoporos aporos* can be read as detailing the various ways in which we are counter-turningly falling *(ontico*-ontological) and so finite, his readings of our *hupsipolis apolis* nature together show us a variety of ways in which and levels at which we are counterturningly transcendent or ontico-*ontological*. To put the two together: we are ontico-ontological—oscillating between falling and transcendence or entities and their being—in a way that turns counter to itself at each turn. We are thus turnings within turnings. And we are this because we turn, or 'venture,' "[b]etween the ordinance of the earth," understood as being's concealment, "and the order ordained by the gods," namely being *qua dikē*.

The Closing Words

What are we to do with, or as, such an uncanny entity? At the close of the choral ode, the uncanny human being is expelled from the hearth:

> Such shall not be entrusted to my hearth,
> nor share their delusion with my knowing,
> who put such a thing to work. (HI59/72)

Heidegger repeatedly insists that the hearth is being (HI109/136, 112/140, 114/143, 118/147, 120/150). It is that in relation to which we are homely (HI105/130, 107/133, 115/144).[26] So the closing words remind us that

---

[26] Note that Heidegger describes the hearth in terms of the two dimensions of *pelein*—constancy and change—using the familiar spatial and motile metaphors: "The hearth is the site of being-homely. *Parestios* (from *para* and *hestia*): *hestia* is the hearth of the house, the locale at which there stand the gods of the hearth. What is essential to the hearth, however, is the fire in the manifoldness of its essence, which essentially prevails as lighting, illuminating, warming, nourishing, purifying, refining, glowing" (HI105/130).

the human being, as uncanny, is excluded from the hearth in the sense that it does not have straightforward access to being but is always exposed to concealing. This exposure, as we have seen, puts the human being in a condition of 'delusion,' whether this refers to our openness to concealment or to its consequences in falling and seeming.[27] In hearing the closing words, then, we grasp ourselves as uncanny.

The closing words also open us to more or less proper ways of being the uncanny entity. They express our essential uncanniness in such a way that "the inner essence of *being properly* unhomely [*das innere Wesen des* eigentlichen *Unheimisch*seins] is first determined" (HI115/143). The closing words accomplish this by implicitly rejecting improper or unowned *(uneigentlich)* uncanniness and pointing towards proper or owned *(eigentlich)* uncanniness. They call us to be owned—to be homely *in our unhomeliness.* They do this, Heidegger says, by "let[ting] *being* unhomely become worthy of question" (HI115/143). As we will see in Chapter 5, uncanniness is inherently worthy of question. But what is in question here is *being* uncanny in the sense of being the uncanny *entity.* The closing words raise the question of *how* to be the uncanny entity, and they do so by implicitly presenting two figures who seem to be exempt from the expulsion from the hearth and so outside the *deinon:* Sophocles and Antigone.

In EM, Heidegger takes the closing words of the ode to express the Chorus's rejection of the uncanny human being, who does not accord with the everyday, common sense understanding of the human being (EM175/126). In HI, Heidegger rejects this kind of reading: "Assuming that what speaks in this choral song is human mediocrity in its avoidance of everything essential, then it would be impossible for the most profound insights into the human essence also to be pronounced by these same mediocre characters, and indeed in such supreme knowing and such dignified telling" (HI97/121). If the ode does indeed demonstrate

---

[27] Julian Young has a slightly different reading which, I think, is ultimately consistent with mine: "The penultimate line's distinction between 'knowledge' and 'delusion' pertains, Heidegger suggests, to what is 'fitting' or 'proper' in action. According to the Greek conception, the human will is always to act from that knowledge which is proper to the hearth (i.e., *Heimat*). Yet it is also always liable to action that constitutes a 'counterturning'. This, as we have observed, is not 'sin'—willful transgression, in the Christian sense—but, rather, a mistaking of what the chorus calls 'non-beings' for beings, a risk that is written into the 'site,' since truth, as appearing, contains within itself the possibility of delusive appearance. It follows, according to this tragic yet magnificent vision of the human condition that life itself is a 'risk' (or 'venture,' *Wagnis*). One lives with a constant vulnerability to factual and ethical 'delusion.'" Julian Young, "Poets and Rivers: Heidegger on Hölderlin's *'Der Ister,'"* *Dialogue: Canadian Philosophical Review* 38:2 (1999): 407.

a profound insight into the essence of the human being, then those who speak in it must have a special status. Who, then, speaks? Obviously, it is the Chorus: the Theban elders. But from where do they speak? And who are they if they are in a position to pronounce the expulsion from the hearth?

In order to grasp the human being as *deinon* in the way that they do, the speakers must have more than human knowledge: "Such a word must know more, that is, here [*hier*] something more essential, than the mere fact that the human being is the most uncanny of all entities" (HI105/131). In particular, such knowing must know being since it pronounces an expulsion from being: "That knowing, however, that expels the most uncanny one from the hearth can itself know of the hearth only if it stems from a belonging to the hearth" (HI106/132). Heidegger's logic here seems very suspect. Why should knowing the human being's exclusion from being require a special knowledge of being? Indeed, have we not just attained such knowledge ourselves, without thereby ceasing to be uncanny? But Heidegger's claim is that the closing words do not merely report an expulsion but perform the expelling. Only an 'insider,' as it were, can expel from the hearth, and uncanny human beings like us are not insiders.

The speakers of the closing words must have seen beyond the *deinon* to being and so be exempt from the expulsion from being. They cannot be uncanny—or at least, they cannot be so in the usual way. The speakers have some kind of ontological knowledge that somehow escapes concealing or is exposed to it in a different way. I argued in Chapter 3 that there is no knowledge of being without uncanniness, but I did not there take account of the position of the world-historical creator. For the speaker of the closing words is properly the poet (HI118/148), who in writing this choral ode is engaged in an act of world-creation or world-founding: the origin of Western Dasein. By poetically projecting the human being as uncanny, Sophocles first "provides the authentic *Greek* definition of humanity" (EM161/116). Greek tragedy in general and Sophocles's tragedies in particular 'authentically found' Greek being and Dasein (EM154/110). The choral ode especially, in projecting the human being as uncanny, poetizes "the highest thing that the poet must poetize" (HI121/151–152). This makes the choral ode "the supreme poetic work of what is supremely worthy of poetizing" (HI121/152). As the poet who founds Greek Dasein and its uncanniness, Sophocles himself must be in some sense outside this humanity. If he is *deinon,* he must be so in some special way.

In the closing words, Sophocles expels Dasein from the hearth—which is to say, he establishes Dasein as excluded from being or uncanny. The contrast in these words is thus between the 'delusion' of uncanny Dasein and Sophocles's 'knowing' or 'belonging to the hearth.' This latter is the special access to being that the world-historical creator has. Dasein's delusion is then the delusion that it is getting to being. The delusion is thus the same as Dasein's expulsion from the hearth. According to Heidegger, having this explicitly pointed out to us helps us to see something: "This rejection tells us that the uncanny one has an essential relation to the hearth, but it is that of forgetting and blindness, as a result of which he or she is unable to have being in view or in thoughtful remembrance [*Andenken*]" (HI109/135–136). That is, the contrast with the poet's knowledge makes clear that we are open to being but in the mode of being closed off. The closing words thus do not merely announce Dasein's alienation from being but also announce its essential belonging to being. This amounts to a call to take this over and so to be ownedly uncanny.

Like Sophocles, Antigone is often taken to be exempt from the rejection announced in the closing words. Antigone has attempted to bury her brother, the traitor Polyneices, whose burial Creon (ruler of Thebes) has forbidden. On many readings of the ode, the closing words implicitly denounce Creon's hubris and so do not apply to Antigone. Although Heidegger explicitly rejects any reading that posits Antigone as the "innocent" heroine in contrast to a "guilty" Creon (HI52/64), he nonetheless raises the question of Antigone's exemption: "Does Antigone stand outside the relation to *deinon?* Is this tragedy supposed to present a figure who in fact remains untouched and untouchable by the *deinon?*" (HI97/121). This seems impossible; no human being could escape uncanniness. Antigone, like Sophocles, must be uncanny in some special way.

Antigone is, in fact, the supreme uncanny (HI104/129); she "exceeds every other being unhomely" (HI103/128) because she is *"intrinsically unhomely"* (HI104/129). But this does not mean that the closing words do, in fact, apply to her. Antigone is both *deinon* and exempt from the closing words—exempt "not because she stands outside of the *deinon,* but because she properly [*eigentlich*] is the most uncanny in the supreme manner" (HI117/146). Antigone's supreme uncanniness is her becoming homely within being: "What if that which were most intrinsically unhomely, thus most remote from all that is homely, were that which in itself simultaneously preserved the most intimate belonging to the homely? What if this alone, of all things, could be unhomely in the proper sense?" (HI104/129). An intensified way of being unhomely amounts to a way of becoming homely by an uncanny, counterturning logic. At its most extreme, being unhomely turns counter to itself and becomes a becoming homely. But since the *counter-* of the turning is not a straightforward negation, becoming homely is not simply opposed to being unhomely. Rather, becoming homely is a way of being unhomely. Thus Heidegger frequently speaks of becoming homely in being unhomely, where this means not that we get comfortable with our uncanniness but that we are simultaneously and counterturningly becoming homely–being unhomely. Being unhomely or uncanny is not the opposite of becoming homely but its condition: "[b]eing unhomely shows itself as a not yet awakened, not yet decided, not yet assumed potential for being homely and becoming homely" (HI115/144). Becoming homely is not an overcoming of uncanniness but that in which being unhomely is first accomplished or comes into its own. In this, owned uncanniness manifests an uncanny, counterturning structure.

By pointing to two figures who might be uncanny in a special way, the closing words suggest that there are different ways of being uncanny and that it is our task to distinguish them: "The closing words conceal within them a pointer toward that risk that has yet to be unfolded and accomplished but that is accomplished in the tragedy as a whole, the risk of distinguishing and deciding between that being unhomely proper [*dem eigentlichen Unheimischsein*] to the human being and a being unhomely that is inappropriate [*uneigentlichen*]" (HI117/146). The decision between owned and unowned uncanniness takes place in the tragedy as a whole because it takes place in the figure of Antigone (HI117/146). The HI interpretation of the closing words forces Heidegger to discuss Antigone and so parts of the play other than the choral ode, neither of which were relevant to the EM analysis of the ode. Antigone exemplifies owned uncanniness, and the claim is that she does so by raising the very question ("the risk of distinguishing and deciding") that the closing words raise: what are the different ways of being as the uncanny entity? What is it to be ownedly uncanny?[28] To see how she raises this question, we need to follow Heidegger in turning from the choral ode to the rest of the play, considering Antigone and the way in which she is ownedly unhomely ("*'eigentlich' unheimisch*" (HI117/146)).

Expressions of Antigone's Owned Uncanniness

It is surprising that Heidegger offers a concrete figure of ownedly being uncanny, since he nowhere else gives an example of an owned person. It

---

[28] For an examination of how Antigone's ownedness differs from ownedness on other interpretations of Heidegger, see my "Authenticity and Heidegger's Antigone," *Journal of the British Society for Phenomenology* (forthcoming).

is also surprising that he chooses Antigone. Antigone is both a woman and a literary character, and Heidegger does not otherwise engage philosophically with either women or literary characters. It is perhaps not as surprising that Heidegger might choose to discuss *Antigone* in 1942, given the political climate at the time.[29] *Antigone* is often read as a political drama, in which Antigone distinguishes herself as an exemplar of individual resistance to state injustice. Antigone's attempt to bury Polyneices in defiance of Creon's edict is an expression of familial or religious duty that is inherently and tragically in tension with performing her civic duty. Creon eventually realizes that he is wrong to condemn Antigone to death but not before Antigone—sealed in a cave—commits suicide. Her betrothed, Haemon, kills himself from grief—as does, in turn, his mother, Eurydice, Creon's wife. Creon is left, as befits a tragedy, bereft of wife and son. It seems that the *polis* cannot accommodate Antigone's loyalty to the religious or familial, which is outside the *polis* and yet still takes place within it.[30]

Heidegger is not especially concerned with Antigone's resistance to Creon, her particular allegiance, or the nature of her commitments. Heidegger understands Antigone entirely in terms of her relationship to being. The reason is that the *polis* for Heidegger is not anything political; it is the clearing or open site. To read *Antigone* as a 'political' drama in Heidegger's sense is thus to read it as a story about cases of Dasein and their relation to being, including their own uncanniness. What is special about Antigone is how she stands in the *polis* as the uncanny entity—her distinctive way of being *hupsipolis apolis* and *pantoporos aporos*.

Recall that Heidegger describes the *polis* as both a pole and a swirl. The former names being as *dikē* or world, and we relate to it in being *pantoporos aporos:* falling or counterturningly discovering entities. The latter names the clearing as that which presences and absences—and that means being as *phusis,* uncanny presencing and absencing. The uncanny entity is exposed to this 'swirl' and so is *hupsipolis apolis:* counterturningly transcending or metaphysical. In her famous appeal to the divine

---

[29] Young explores the political dimension of Heidegger's reading in his "Poets and Rivers: Heidegger on Hölderlin's '*Der Ister.*'"

[30] Readings that run basically along these lines include those in Judith Butler, *Antigone's Claim: Kinship between Life and Death* (New York: Columbia University Press, 2000); G. W. F. Hegel, *The Phenomenology of Spirit,* trans. A. V. Miller (Oxford: Oxford University Press, 1977); Luce Irigaray, "The Eternal Irony of the Community," trans. Gillian C. Gill, in *Feminist Readings of Antigone,* ed. Fanny Söderbäck (Albany: State University of New York Press, 2010); Jacques Lacan, *The Seminars of Jacques Lacan. Book VII: The Ethics of Psychoanalysis 1959–1960,* trans. Dennis Porter (New York: W. W. Norton and Company, 1992).

law, Antigone appeals to the *polis* in both these senses. She says of Creon's command against burying Polyneices:

> It was no Zeus that bade me this,
> Nor was it Dike, homely amongst the gods below,
> who ordained this law for humans,
> And your command seemed not so powerful to me,
> That it could ever override by human wit
> The immutable, unwritten edict divine.
> Not just now, nor since yesterday, but ever steadfast
> this prevails. And no one knows from whence it once appeared. (Lines
>   450–457; HI116/145, translation modified)

Although Heidegger speaks of the "law of the dead" and the "law of the living" (HI101/126), he emphasizes that this law does not refer to "the prevailing or ancient cult of the dead, or the familial blood-relatedness" (HI116/144). It does not refer to any particular social norms or traditions but to what ultimately grounds these standards: "What determines Antigone is that which first bestows ground and necessity upon the distinction of the dead and the priority of blood" (HI117/147). The law to which Antigone appeals in this passage is that which first makes burial and bloodlines matter at all. It is the law of being (HI118/147, 120/150).

'The law of being' can be heard as either a subjective or an objective genitive. As a subjective genitive, the law of being is the world. It is the set of meaningful relationships that governs how things hang together meaningfully and so that governs entities (like dead bodies and blood relationships) with regard to whether and what they are. This is being in the sense of *dikē*, as ordering and articulating or as 'fittingness.' When we dwell in a world, we inhabit a constellation of intelligibility that orders intelligible things and provides an unwritten, hidden law for human sense-making. Insofar as we stand in a world, we stand under this law. In Antigone's world, for example, we can isolate 'the law of the dead and the law of the living' as that portion of the system of meanings that governs what it is for something to be intelligible as living or dead. According to this law, living bodies should be above ground while dead bodies should be below ground. Thus dead bodies are *to be buried*. We do not create or control such laws of intelligibility; they are destined to us.

The 'law of being' in the sense of the objective genitive refers to the "essential ground" of what is thus destined to us (HI100/124). In this sense, the law of being is the law or logic that governs any world, governing how intelligibility happens. It answers the question, How does any world *work* or *happen* as a world? How does *die Welt weltet?* As we know, this law or logic is the logic of uncanniness: presencing by means of absencing. Being is granted in such a way that it is withheld from us, and this in multiple senses or at multiple levels: the world or *dikē* backgrounds itself, presencing never comes to presence, and the logic of this presencing through absencing is itself inherently mysterious (as we will see in Chapter 5). So while we are subject to the law of being, we do not always have access to it, and we do not know "from whence it once appeared" or precisely how it works.

The law of being in the sense of the objective genitive is the *polis qua* the swirl—the presencing and absencing of the open site. The law of being in the sense of the subjective genitive is the *polis* as the pole, around which entities gather and which determines them as the entities that they are. So Antigone's appeal to the unwritten 'divine' law is an appeal to the *polis*. In this appeal, Antigone "tells of where she belongs, tells of whence she knows herself to be greeted" (HI115/144). Antigone is determined by the *polis* and so is distinctively 'political.'

Antigone's ownedness is a particular way of being the uncanny entity, and this means a particular way of bringing herself to presence as an entity within the *polis*. As we have already seen, Heidegger says, "[t]he human being is [. . .] related in an exceptional sense to this pole, insofar as the human being, in understanding being, stands [*stehen*] in the midst of entities and here necessarily has a 'status' ['*status*'] in each case [*jeweils*], a stance [*Stand*] in its instances [*Zuständen*] and circumstances [*Umständen*]" (HI81/100). To bring or come to a stand is, for Heidegger, to presence as an entity (see, e.g., EM107/78, 75/54, 182/131). Dasein presences as an entity by self-disclosing and so by relating to (its own) being as uncanny. Different ways of relating to (Dasein's) being as uncanny are different modes of self-disclosure and so different ways of taking a stand as an entity: different statuses or stances. These ways of standing are the owned and unowned ways of being the uncanny entity. An unowned way of taking a stand will presumably be presencing (and so self-disclosing) in a way that involves semblance or seeming, while the owned way of taking a stand will presumably be presencing (and so self-disclosing) in a way that lets Dasein's uncanny essence fully presence by self-absencing.

Heidegger distinguishes ways of bringing entities to a stand in the *polis* that allow them to stand steadfastly *(beständig)* and constantly *(ständig)* in their appearing from those that bring entities to appearing under seeming and so in an "un-constancy" *(Unständigkeit)* (EM172/123). When the entity in question is Dasein, these and linguistically or conceptually related terms express ownedness and unownedness.[31] The unownedly uncanny person is one who "lets" herself be "driven about amid entities, without any constancy [*unstet*]" (HI117/146), while the ownedly uncanny person "sways back and forth and yet stands [*hin und her schwankt und doch steht*]" (HI52/64). As Heidegger goes on to explain, "What truly stands steadfast [*Ständige*] must be able to sway within the counterturning pressure of the open paths of the storms. What is merely rigid shatters on account of its own rigidity" (HI52/64). Heidegger is here talking about the play *Antigone* itself rather than the owned person, but the characterization applies equally to both. Notice three things about this description of ownedness.

First, standing steadfastly as 'swaying back and forth yet standing' is a compressed expression of what the verb '*pelein*' says: constancy and change. Thus Heidegger uses the term 'steadfastness' to describe being as uncanny—for example, when he describes Hestia, the goddess of the hearth, as the "most steadfast [*Ständigste*]," "the middle of all steadfast constancy [*Beständigkeit*] and presence—that which essentially prevails in being, that which the Greeks experience in the sense of constant presence" (HI113/141–142). So too, Antigone (on Heidegger's translation) says of the law of being, "ever steadfast [*ständig je*] / this prevails [*west*]" (lines 456–457; HI116 / /145). To 'stand steadfast' is to *be* in the manner of *pelein* and so to *be* as uncanny—to be the uncanny entity ownedly.

Second, the quote suggests that there is a third possibility in addition to standing steadfastly and being inconstant: being rigid and so shattering. This is presumably an unowned way of being the uncanny entity. Third, notice that that in relation to which one stands or presences steadfastly— "the counterturning pressure of the open paths of the storms"—is being's uncanny presencing and absencing. That Heidegger addresses being by speaking of storms should not surprise us, since it echoes the poetic projection of being as the sea in the choral ode ("He ventures forth on the foaming tide / amid the southern storm of winter / and crosses the surge / of the cavernous waves" (HI58/72)). The idea of standing firm in the storm and not being rigid might also be familiar: it is a principle theme in *Antigone*.[32]

---

[31] Compare: "*The constancy* [Ständigkeit] *of the Self,* in the double sense of steadiness and steadfastness [*beständigen Standfestigkeit*], is the *authentic* counter-possibility to the non-Self-constancy [*Unselbst-ständigkeit*] which is characteristic of irresolute falling. Existentially, '*Self-constancy*' signifies nothing other than anticipatory resoluteness" (SZ322).

[32] We might also recall Heidegger's non-standard translation of a phrase from Plato's *Republic* at the end of the Rectoral Address: "*ta . . . megala tanta episphalē. . . .* All that is great stands in the storm." Martin Heidegger, "The Self-Assertion of the German University

Surprisingly, Heidegger does not note this—even though his description of rigidity sounds like a paraphrase of Creon's insight:

> Don't forget: The mind that is most rigid
> Stumbles soonest; the hardest iron—
> Tempered in fire till it is super-strong—
> Shatters easily and clatters into shards. (Lines 473–476, Woodruff
>   translation)[33]

Creon goes on to accuse Antigone of arrogance and boasting but we suspect that in this passage he is unwittingly describing himself. Haemon confirms this when he later criticizes his father using the image of a tree or boat in a storm:

> But a wise man can learn a lot and never be ashamed;
> He knows he does not have to be rigid and close-hauled.
> You've seen trees tossed by a torrent in a flash flood:
> If they bend, they're saved, and every twig survives,
> But if they stiffen up, they're washed out from the roots.
> It's the same in a boat: if a sailor keeps the footline taut,
> If he doesn't give an inch, he'll capsize, and then—
> He'll be sailing home with his benches down and his hull to the sky.
>   (Lines 710–717, Woodruff translation)

The obvious interpretation of these claims about rigidity and flexibility is moral-psychological: we should be less rigid in holding onto our values and in refusing to listen to and learn from others. We should find a middle path of flexibility, adaptability, and compromise—a path between the only two options that Creon sees: "Giving in would be terrible. / But standing firm invites disaster!" (lines 1096–1097, Woodruff translation). Both Creon and Antigone must learn this lesson; both can be faulted for their stubbornness.[34] The seer Tiresias provides additional evidence for

---

and the Rectorate 1933/34: Facts and Thoughts," *Review of Metaphysics* 38:3 (1985): 480, Greek transliterated.

[33] Sophocles, *Antigone,* trans. Paul Woodruff (Indianapolis, IN: Hackett Publishing, 2001). I use Woodruff's translations throughout the remainder of this chapter when I discuss passages that Heidegger does not translate. I indicate when I do so thus: (line xx, Woodruff translation). Woodruff's translations are much more colloquial than Jebb's, and for this reason I have chosen them to help me to give an accessible picture of Antigone and her ownedness.

[34] For a reading that blames both Antigone and Creon for the same stubbornness, see Martha Nussbaum's reading in *The Fragility of Goodness: Luck and Ethics in Greek Tragedy and Philosophy* (Cambridge: Cambridge University Press, 2001).

this interpretation in what appears to be a straightforward statement of the message of the play:

> It's common knowledge, any human being can go wrong.
> But even when he does, a man may still succeed:
> He may have his share of luck and good advice
> But only if he's willing to bend and find a cure
> For the trouble he's caused. It's only being stubborn
> Proves you're a fool. (Lines 1024–1029, Woodruff translation)

Heidegger's reading takes up these ideas (without acknowledgment) and gives them an ontological spin. The storms that we must weather are not the vagaries of life and fortune. Our rigidity is not stubbornness and our flexibility is not compromise. The storms are the presencing and absencing of being: the *polis* as a swirl. Amidst these storms, and so in the *polis,* we must take a stand: bring ourselves to presence as an entity in the open site. There are three modes of doing so: we can be rigid and shatter, we can be driven about amidst entities, or we can stand steadfastly. The interpretive challenge is to determine what these look like. I will argue that these ways of standing are (more or less plausibly) manifested by Creon, Ismene, and Antigone, respectively. The former two are unowned and the latter is the owned way of being the uncanny entity.

In addition to implying that Antigone, like *Antigone,* stands steadfastly, Heidegger specifies Antigone's relationship to the law of being or *polis* using the vocabulary found in the opening exchange between Antigone and her sister Ismene. Ismene counsels Antigone against attempting to bury Polyneices, saying:

> Yet to commence in pursuit of that remains unfitting, against which nothing can avail. (Line 93, HI99/123)[35]

Heidegger takes Antigone's angry reaction to her sister's charge to confirm Ismene's description of her as 'commencing in pursuit' of that "against which nothing can avail."[36] Antigone then repeats the description in different terms:

---

[35] Woodruff translates: "But it's the highest wrong to chase after what's impossible"; Jebb translates: "A hopeless quest should not be made at all." Sophocles, *Plays: Antigone.*

[36] "Ismene indirectly pronounces the essence of Antigone, that is, in such a way that Antigone, in countering, affirms that which her sister has rejected" (HI102/126).

Yet leave this to me, and to that within me that counsels the dangerous and difficult: to take up into my own essence the uncanny that here and now appears. (Lines 95–96, HI99/123)[37]

This is a repetition because "the uncanny that here and now appears" is the same as that "against which nothing can avail." This is what is destined to us (HI100/124, 102/126), over which human beings have no control (HI101/125) and which "appears of its own accord, no one knows wherefrom" (HI117/146–147). It is "that which concerns her dead brother, namely the law of the dead, and thereby the fundamental law of the living" (HI101/126)—the law of being. Antigone's owned standing steadfastly consists in 'commencing in pursuit of' or 'taking up into her own essence' the law of being.

Heidegger points out that this 'pursuit' *(thēran)* echoes the 'pursuit' in the first antistrophe of the ode (HI102/126), which describes the human being as one who "pursues [*thēraō*] the animals of the wilderness" in order to tame them (HI58/71). As we saw in Chapter 3, this taming is bringing being to presence in entities. There is a limit to this: being cannot be surmounted or tamed entirely, in the sense that it cannot be brought to full presencing since it withdraws. So if pursuing the law of being is this kind of pursuit, then it is an attempt to attain full and transparent intelligibility—bringing presencing to presence, foregrounding the world, or laying out the logic of the uncanny. This is not possible; the pursuit cannot succeed. Thus Heidegger also notes that the law of being "resists the entire *mēchanoen* that is named explicitly in the second antistrophe of the choral ode as the work of the human being who ventures forth in all directions" (HI101/126). As we will see, this is a reference to the fact that the human being cannot prevent death, where 'death' means being's withdrawal or absencing. We cannot overcome the withdrawing of being; the overwhelming cannot be completely surmounted (EM172/123). As we saw, *technē* always 'shatters' against being in its withdrawal (EM174/124). Any attempt to master being fails.

But to 'commence in pursuit' is importantly different from merely 'pursuing.' 'Commence' translates '*archē*,' which means "beginning, point of departure, origin, rule" (HI100/125).[38] Heidegger wants to preserve all these senses, and he seems to take such commencing to belong in a sense

---

[37] Woodruff translates: "So you just let me and my 'bad judgment' / Go to hell"; Jebb translates: "But leave me, and the folly that is mine alone, to suffer this dread thing."

[38] "*Archē* means that from which something proceeds, namely, such that that from which something proceeds is not left behind but determines and prevails in advance out beyond everything proceeding from it. *Archē* means at once beginning, point of departure, origin, rule" (HI100/125).

to the object of Antigone's pursuit. He says that she "pursue[s] that against which nothing can avail as the point of departure governing everything" (HI102/127). This suggests that the goal is not to capture the law of being and bring being to full presence but to pursue being as one's own origin or starting point. This would mean bringing oneself to presence as an entity in such a way that one is determined or governed by the law of being—and so in such a way that one is uncanny. It is a kind of self-disclosure, or a way of standing as the open entity in the midst of being's storms.

Ismene's phrase thus says the same as Antigone's claim that she suffers *(pathein)* the *deinon*. Heidegger translates this as 'taking up the uncanny into her essence,' explaining: "[p]*athein* does not mean the mere 'passivity' of accepting and tolerating but rather taking upon oneself—*archēn de thēran* [commencing in pursuit], making it through to the end, that is, properly experiencing" (HI103/128). Antigone takes the *deinon* upon herself; she appropriates it. This amounts to taking on, taking up, or taking over what is destined to her as a human being (HI117/147, 109/136). She "takes this upon herself into her ownmost essence" (HI102/127). We might say that Antigone submits herself to being governed by the law of being. She takes this law as that from which she starts in all things. This is "the proper relation to the *deinon*" (HI103/128).

So being uncanny ownedly can be expressed as suffering the *deinon*, commencing in pursuit of the law of being, or standing steadfastly. This is all that Heidegger tells us about Antigone's ownedness. What he gives us is not especially helpful, and it does not fulfill the promise that his appeal to Antigone made: that of offering a concrete picture of ownedness. We shall thus have to depart from Heidegger's text in order to see what owned uncanniness looks like and how Antigone manifests it. The crucial clue is that Antigone's being determined by the law of being is her relating to the *polis* as a swirl *(phusis)* and pole *(dikē)*. This interpretation of Antigone's appeal to the 'divine law' gives us a connection to being *hupsipolis apolis* and *pantoporos aporos*. What we need to determine is thus how Antigone is ownedly *hupsipolis apolis* and *pantoporos aporos*. This will show how Antigone is supremely uncanny and will allow us to see how this supreme uncanniness turns counter to itself and becomes a homeliness in being.

Being *Pantoporos Aporos* and *Hupsipolis Apolis* Ownedly

As the subjective genitive, 'the law of being' is *dikē* or the *polis* as a pole: the articulated space of meaning in terms of which entities are discovered and which Heidegger calls 'world.' To ownedly relate to being in this sense is to submit oneself to the world or law of intelligibility in which one finds oneself, and so to take it as one's governing principle. We can see this manifest in Antigone's suicide and especially in her attempt to bury Polyneices. Both fall under 'the law of the dead and the law of the living,' which are the ways of making sense of the dead and the living embodied in the various (familial, religious, civic, sanitary, and so on) practices of the community. This law includes a law of proper placement: the dead go below ground, while the living dwell above ground. Thus when Antigone is buried alive, she cannot intelligibly remain both alive and below ground. She must join either the living or the dead—the former, by escaping, or the latter, by committing suicide. Seen in this light, Antigone's suicide stems from and reflects her ability to discover entities as the entities that they are. Similarly, burying Polyneices's body—that is, placing it appropriately: below ground—is how Antigone makes Polyneices intelligible as dead. Dead bodies are *to be buried*.[39] This is less a practical imperative than an ontological one. The body should show up as *to be buried*. To the extent that it does, Antigone respects the law of being.

So what is distinctive about Antigone is not that she performs some particular admirable action or acts for some particular reason. Rather, she lets entities be the entities that they are. Antigone respects the law of being by discovering the dead body as what it is. But this cannot be all that her ownedness consists in, for it seems that her sister Ismene also discovers entities as the entities that they are. Ismene does not attempt to bury Polyneices because of the way that she discloses *herself*: as a woman and civil subject. She says, "We are women and we do not fight with men. / We're subject to them because they're stronger, / And we must obey this order, even if it hurts us more" (lines 62–64, Woodruff translation). What, if anything, distinguishes Antigone from Ismene?

It is tempting to say that the difference is a matter of how identities or values are ranked. Ismene is well aware that Polyneices should be buried, but being a woman and being law-abiding are more important to her or more fundamental to her identity than is the obligation to bury her brother. On the Heideggerian reading, however, the difference is not

---

[39] This is true even of the body of a traitor. Woodruff explains: "To be denied the full ritual of burial is shameful, a grievous penalty for a traitor and his family. Normally, however, the body of a slain traitor would not be left as carrion for wild dogs and vultures. Sometimes relatives were allowed to give it a burial outside the city, or sometimes the body was thrown into a pit or into the sea. Either of these methods, while leaving the sting of shame as a penalty, would save the land from the pollution of rotting flesh." Paul Woodruff, "Introduction to *Antigone,*" in Sophocles, *Antigone,* x.

about competing self-understandings so much as it is about where these self-understandings come from. In discovering entities, including herself, Ismene is *aporos* in a way that Antigone is not: she is wholly determined by tradition.

To understand this, we must distinguish tradition from the law of being or the world.[40] There is a difference in principle between the intelligibility articulated in the world or *dikē* and conventional or traditional intelligibility. There is also, of course, a connection: traditions embody or take over the law of being. So what is required by the law of being is sometimes the same as what is expected by tradition. But often it is not, and that is because we are *aporos*. Our ways of discovering entities turn counter to themselves and become ways of covering over *(pantoporos aporos)*. This is to say that our routes to entities become ruts (EM168/121). Traditional or conventional ways of making sense of things no longer genuinely reach those things.

Recall that 'being *pantoporos aporos*' can mean several different things: discovering entities and being at home among them—but not getting through to being (i.e., being ontico-ontological) (HI); discovering entities in a familiar world—but getting stuck in well-worn routes and so failing to reach the entities themselves (EM); discovering entities—but under the guise of seeming (risk) (HI, SZ). All human beings are *pantoporos aporos* in the sense that we are ontico-ontological, and everyone makes mistakes and confronts semblances sometimes. We are all also at risk of falling into a discovering rut, since we all inhabit worlds with traditional understandings of being. There is no escaping *das Man*. But one way of being *pantoporos aporos* is taking over one's ways of discovering (one's 'routes') from the tradition in such a way that this tradition becomes the only authority, at the expense of the law of being that it is attempting to express. One need not be determined by *das Man* or enmeshed in tradition in this way. Someone who thus lets herself be governed by *das Man* does not attempt to get out of discovering ruts—in fact, she does not recognize them as ruts. We could put this by saying that she self-discloses as *pantoporos,* able to discover entities by traditional means, but not as *aporos.* In not grasping how

---

[40] Heidegger nowhere draws this distinction explicitly but he implies it in SZ (for example) when he says, "Dasein is inclined to fall back upon its world [. . .] but also [. . .] Dasein simultaneously falls prey to the tradition. [. . .] When tradition thus becomes master, it does so in such a way that what it 'transmits' is made so inaccessible, proximally and for the most part, that it rather becomes concealed. Tradition takes what has come down to us and delivers it over to self-evidence; it blocks our access to those primordial 'sources' from which the categories and concepts handed down to us have been in part quite genuinely drawn" (SZ21).

discovery thus turns counter to itself and blocks its own path, she does not grasp her own uncanniness. She is uncanny but in such a way that she is 'shut out of (her) being' (EM168/121): unownedly uncanny.

Ismene is determined by tradition in this way. It is from the conventional ways of understanding entities that she derives the ranking principle that places her status as a woman and civil subject above the need to bury Polyneices. Ismene is unownedly *pantoporos aporos*. Put differently, she brings herself to a stand as the uncanny entity in such a way that she is "driven about amid entities, without any constancy" (HI117/146). To be driven about amidst entities is to be driven about by tradition—to let the well-traveled and well-worn traditional routes to entities guide one's discovery. When one follows the beaten path, it is the path that does the driving. In SZ, Heidegger describes a person who is at the mercy of tradition in this way as someone who is 'dispersed': "Everyday Dasein has been dispersed into the many kinds of things which daily 'come to pass'" (SZ389; see also SZ129). As thus dispersed, Dasein lacks constancy.

Antigone, in contrast, is ownedly *pantoporos aporos* because she relates to public intelligibility differently. She participates in traditional intelligibility but can distinguish traditional ways of discovering entities from ways of discovering entities that let the entity appear as it is, given the law of being *qua dikē*. Her discovery is governed by the law of being, rather than by tradition. In this, Antigone still risks her routes becoming ruts or her discovery failing to let the entity show itself as it is; she remains *pantoporos aporos*. But she can recognize when a way of discovering an entity does not genuinely reach it, and she can do so because the authority governing her discovery is the law of being itself.

That Antigone is not determined by tradition is not in this case a consequence of being the *hupsipolis apolis* creative figure who makes new routes to entities. Antigone is clearly not ontologically creative; she does not reconfigure the world. With regard to tradition, Antigone is less Martin Luther than Martin Luther King Jr. . Civil rights activists of all kinds can be understood as aiming not to replace traditional ways of making sense but to draw attention to them in a way that shows how our practices or political institutions fall short of them. Antigone's attempt to bury Polyneices does the same thing for the Chorus: it provides an occasion to remember what is and what matters, and to consider how well tradition and legislation embody that.

But it does not follow that we should understand Antigone's distance from tradition and her commitment to the law of being in Kantian terms. The suggestion would be that Antigone is owned insofar as she acts in light of the law of being rather than merely in accord with it.[41] The law of being *qua* the world is a set of normative standards in terms of which entities are made intelligible in their being. To act in light of this law is to be committed to and take responsibility for these norms, where this includes taking responsibility for their adequacy and so being willing to critique and revise them.[42] On this reading, the owned person is not simply driven about by standards of intelligibility but holds either or both tradition or/ and *dikē* open to question. This may be a way to characterize Antigone's relationship to the traditional embodiment of the law of being, but it does not adequately capture her relationship to the law of being *qua dikē*. Antigone is not governed by the law of being in the sense that she acts in light of it. As Hegel stresses, Antigone has an immediate relationship to norms rather than a critical distance from them.[43] She simply submits to the law of being. On this Kantian picture of ownedness, then, Antigone would be *unowned*.

So how is Antigone determined by the law of being? This is a way of asking how she transcends, or how she is *hupsipolis apolis,* such that she can be ownedly *pantoporos aporos.* In discovering entities, Antigone is of course the philosopher (and so is *hupsipolis apolis*) in the sense that we all are: she transcends entities to their being. The next sense of being *hupsipolis apolis* that I identified was the ontological revelation in angst. Antigone does not seem to undergo anything recognizable as angst; she does not have any ontological insights. I suggest that we introduce a new 'level' of being *hupsipolis apolis* in order to accommodate Antigone, one that stands between ordinary discovery and ontological revelation. This intermediate position is the situation of the everyday phenomenologist—the regular person (perhaps a Black Forest peasant) who lets entities show themselves as they are, from themselves (compare SZ34). Such

---

[41] For Kant's well-known distinction, see Immanuel Kant, *Grounding for the Metaphysics of Morals,* 3rd ed., trans. James W. Ellington (Indianapolis, IN: Hackett Publishing, 1993).

[42] As John Haugeland puts it: "Taking responsibility for something is not only taking it as something that matters, but also *not* taking it for granted." John Haugeland, "Truth and Finitude: Heidegger's Transcendental Existentialism," in *Heidegger, Authenticity, and Modernity: Essays in Honor of Hubert L. Dreyfus,* Vol. 1, ed. Mark Wrathall and Jeff Malpas (Cambridge, MA: The MIT Press, 2000), 72.

[43] See Hegel, *The Phenomenology of Spirit,* especially §429–476. As Rebecca Kukla puts it, "[s]he could not actually recognize their [sc. norms'] claims, because, as transgression was not a disclosed possibility for her, she could not step back from them so as to see them as making a claim upon her, which she had a responsibility to live up to in virtue of her commitment to their legitimacy." Rebecca Kukla, "The Ontology and Temporality of Conscience," *Continental Philosophy Review* 35:1 (2002): 31fn5. However, for a compelling reading of Antigone as autonomous in Kant's sense, see David N. McNeill, "Antigone's Autonomy," *Inquiry* 54:5 (2011): 411–441.

a person discovers entities as the entities that they are on the basis of an openness to being.

In discovering entities in accordance with the law of being, Antigone is ontologically pious or ontologically responsive. She is responsive to what Heidegger names 'the call of being,' which she hears when Polyneices's unburied body calls out, "Bury me!"[44] Responding to this call is hearing it, and hearing the call of being is hearing what the situation calls for or what is fitting *(dikē)*. In thus hearing the call of being and discovering entities in accord with it, Antigone takes the law of being *qua dikē* as her essential starting point. This is being *hupsipolis* ownedly.

Antigone must also be ownedly *apolis*. In what way does Antigone's rising high in the *polis qua* her openness to the call of being turn counter to itself and alienate her from being? I said that to be *apolis* is for philosophizing to recoil on itself, asking after its own why or ground but finding only concealment or obscurity. In the next chapter, we will see several explicitly philosophical ways to experience this recoil. Antigone undergoes it in a much more mundane way. Recall that one of the ways in which being withdraws is that the world or *dikē* backgrounds itself. At the level of the ordinary discovery of entities this means that the meaningful relationships that order things are not immediately apparent to us. This is the kind of withdrawal to which the everyday phenomenologist is characteristically exposed and which makes her *apolis*: she is open to *dikē* and governed by it but it is withheld from her. Here we see Antigone's relationship to the law of being in the sense of the objective genitive: the logic of being, which is uncanny presencing and absencing.

Antigone encounters the finitude of being and so manifests her *apolis* character when Creon calls her to account for herself. Creon demands an explanation of Antigone's comportment towards Polyneices's body. But as the everyday phenomenologist comporting towards entities, Antigone cannot step back to lay out the structure of the Greek world and show how not leaving dead bodies exposed belongs to its network of shared practices and meaningful relationships. Put differently, Antigone cannot give reasons for her comportment because she does not act in light of the law of being, and she does not act in light of the law of being precisely because this law is not directly 'illuminated' for her. It has withdrawn into the background. If someone does not simply *see* (or, to continue the metaphor of the call, *hear*) that Polyneices is *to be buried*, then there is

---

[44] In addition to Heidegger's 'call of being,' we might hear in Antigone's *letting entities be as they are* an anticipation of what Heidegger will later term 'Gelassenheit.'

nothing to do but insist upon it: burying the dead is what we do; this is how things make sense here. Explanation, reason-giving—or, more broadly, sense-making—comes to an end. It encounters its own obscure ground. *Dikē* withholds itself even as Antigone hears its call, and this makes her *apolis*: at the end of explanation.

Specifically, Antigone is ownedly *apolis*. Notice that, although *Antigone* is obsessed with showing and telling, Antigone seems committed to concealment and silence. Confronting Creon, she says, "You've caught me, you can kill me. What more do you want?" (line 497, Woodruff translation), and "Then what are you waiting for? More talk?" (line 499, Woodruff translation). Antigone is persistently reticent—not in the sense that she does not speak, but in the sense that she says little. Not only does she encounter the withdrawal of being and the end of explanation, but she does not attempt to cover this over with chatter or fake appeals. She respects and preserves the withdrawal.

Of course, Antigone could step back from her everyday comportment and take up the position of the reason-giver who appeals to the nature of the Greek world—or even the philosopher of culture, who can give an accounting of the structure of the Greek world. In either, she would be taking up a different way of being *hupsipolis apolis* and so a different way of relating to being and its withdrawal. Antigone appears to do just this when she offers what looks like a reason for her action: an appeal to the law of irreplaceability. She says, "What law can I claim on my side for this choice? / I may have another husband if the first should die / And get another child from a new man if I'm a widow. / But my mother and my father lie in the land of death, / And there is no ground to grow a brother for me now" (lines 908–912, Woodruff translation). Appealing to her brother's irreplaceability seems to explain or ground Antigone's action quite clearly in Greek familial and reproductive practices as they take up and reflect facts of biology. This is true, and I do not mean to deny that Antigone could in principle take up increasingly deep versions of being *hupsipolis* and so give increasingly deep explanations for her discovery of entities. The point is that at every level of explanation, such being *hupsipolis* will turn counter itself and become *apolis*—it will face an obscurity at its ground. That each obscurity (except, of course, the last) might push us to deeper philosophizing does not change the basic structure of being *hupsipolis*: it will always turn counter to itself. Antigone can manifest this at the single level of her refusal to explain her action; she does not need to repeat the same turn to being *apolis* over and over. In fact, this is precisely what her appeal to her brother's irreplaceability demonstrates.

Antigone's appeal to irreplaceability has long puzzled scholars, both because the passage is written in an odd style and because it does not obviously make sense.[45] First, it seems inconsistent with Antigone's earlier appeal to the 'divine' law. Second, it is not an appeal to the right kind of reason. That Polyneices cannot be replaced might be a good reason to fight for his life, but Polyneices is already dead. His irreplaceability hardly seems relevant to whether, now that he is dead, his body must be buried at all costs. Further, Antigone seems to misunderstand what is important about irreplaceability. The problem, presumably, is not that one cannot have another brother, that the role cannot be filled, but that one cannot replace *this* brother—that the role cannot be filled by this particular, singular individual. But such singularity is not distinctive of brothers. What is important about irreplaceability for Antigone if it is not singularity?

If Antigone's appeal to irreplaceability really is unintelligible, then perhaps this is the point.[46] Instead of stepping back and entering the next level of explanation, Antigone gives an incoherent explanation. This incoherence is a form of reticence (and so a way of being *apolis* ownedly) because it indicates the futility of seeking a stable and clear final ground at any level of explanation. At every level or depth of being *hupsipolis*, philosophizing will turn against itself to become *apolis:* it will confront the withdrawal of being and the opacity of its ground.

We can imagine how the series of demands for intelligibility, and attempts to meet them, would go. Antigone could become a reason-giver and appeal to the law of being *qua dikē* as that which determines her. When asked why *dikē* demands burial, she could become the philosopher of culture and locate burial and associated practices in the Greek world. At the next level, she would be called to account for the Greek world: why is intelligibility structured in just this way? Is there some reason that it should be this way, rather than another? And further, how was this constellation of intelligibility granted to the Greek people? Indeed—why are we open to intelligibility rather than not? That is, why is there something rather than nothing? We can go on. How does openness to being work?

---

[45] Jebb reports that "[f]ew problems of Greek Tragedy have been more discussed than the question of whether these vv., or some of them, are spurious." For his own part, he continues, "I confess that, after long thought, I cannot bring myself to believe that Soph. wrote 905–912." Sophocles, *Plays: Antigone*, 164. For a full discussion, see the Appendix to Jebb's translation.

[46] I am grateful to an audience member at a session of The International Association for Philosophy and Literature (IAPL) Annual Conference in 2012, at which I delivered an early draft of this material, for suggesting a version of this interpretation.

Why does being withdraw itself so that the grounds that we seek are veiled from us? Why is the logic of being the logic of the uncanny? How does this logic of uncanniness work? As we will see in Chapter 5, this questioning will ultimately founder on unintelligibility. The ground of uncanniness is veiled. At each level we encounter being's self-withdrawal, which turns our being *hupsipolis* against itself and makes us *apolis*. We are ownedly *apolis* when we recognize and acknowledge that this is the case. Antigone's reticence does just this.

Such owned being *hupsipolis apolis* can be contrasted with Creon's unowned way of being *hupsipolis apolis*. Heidegger barely mentions Creon, but we can give a somewhat figurative reading of his character that rounds out the picture of ownedness and unownedness. Creon is ruler of Thebes, as his name indicates (*kreōn:* ruler, lord, master). Creon thinks that intelligibility can be legislated. His law-making is an attempt to create new routes to entities. With his edict against burying Polyneices, Creon attempts to override the law of being *qua* the world *(dikē)*, according to which dead bodies are *to be buried*. The Chorus supports him in this: "It is up to you: / Make any law you want—for the dead, or for us who live" (lines 213–214, Woodruff translation). This is an unowned way of being *pantoporos aporos,* and Heidegger identifies it as a second way of being unownedly unhomely (in addition to Ismene's being driven about by tradition): "Being unhomely can be enacted in a mere presumptuousness toward entities in order to forcibly contrive from entities in each case a way out and a site. This presumptuousness toward entities and within entities, however, only is what it is from out of a forgottenness of the hearth, that is, of being" (HI115/144). Creon is presumptuous towards entities in that he presumes to dictate their being to them; he will force them to be what he wants them to be. But human power does not extend to the law of being *qua dikē*. One cannot decree what will or will not make sense. Creon may leave a dead body above ground, but he cannot make this the place where a dead body (even the body of a traitor) belongs. Similarly, he cannot make a tomb an appropriate place for a living body. His attempt to create new routes fails.

As Heidegger notes, such ontological hubris stems from a forgottenness of being—that is, it is based on an unowned way of being *hupsipolis apolis*. (Thus Heidegger's only characterization of Creon says that he "in his way also looms high" over the *polis* (HI103/128).) Antigone identifies this forgottenness in her appeal to the law of being, in which she explicitly accuses Creon of failing to comport properly towards being as uncanny. Recall her description of Creon's command against burying Polyneices:

It was no Zeus that bade me this,
Nor was it Dike, homely amongst the gods below,
who ordained this law for humans,
And your command seemed not so powerful to me,
That it could ever override by human wit
The immutable, unwritten edict divine.
Not just now, nor since yesterday, but ever steadfast
this prevails. And no one knows from whence it once appeared. (Lines
    450–457; HI116/145, translation modified)

Antigone points out that human power cannot override the law of being—whether by legislating intelligibility (overruling *dikē*) or bringing
being to full presence against its withdrawal (overruling *phusis*). She says
that we do not know where this law of being comes from, but that it
nonetheless 'prevails steadfast' and so governs us. It is that against which
nothing can avail, over which human beings neither rule nor dispose,
and which is destined or given to us. Creon's mistake is a mistake about
this relationship between being and the human being. He thinks that the
human being is the master of being or that being depends upon human
whim or power. He can make this mistake precisely because being withdraws and so (as it were) governs invisibly. In a sense, then, Creon takes
advantage of being's self-withdrawal without acknowledging it. He is the
lieutenant (lit. place holder) of being who seizes the command.[47]

What might ground such a mistaken understanding of what it is to
relate to being? One possible source is a determination to achieve full
intelligibility—an attempt to pursue the law of being in the sense of
bringing being to full and unreserved presence. This, I suggest, is what
Heidegger names when he mentions a rigidity that 'shatters' *(zerbricht)*
in the midst of being's presencing and absencing (HI52/64). This is one
of the unowned ways of bringing oneself to a stand as the uncanny
entity. Recall that in EM, 'shattering' *(zerbrechen)* occurs when the disclosive powers confront being's withdrawal and so find themselves at
their disclosive limit (EM174/124). Similarly, the uncanny entity will
'shatter' if it comports inappropriately to being's self-withdrawing. A
sense-maker who demands full intelligibility or non-finite sense-making
is rigidly transcendent in a way that neglects or forgets being's self-
withdrawing and so the finitude of sense-making. She will 'shatter'
in the sense that her self-disclosure will break down: she will come
to a self-misunderstanding and so to seeming. Creon manifests this

---

[47] For the image of the human being as lieutenant to being, see WM93.

self-misunderstanding, and it is plausibly based on this kind of rigid determination to achieve full intelligibility.

Antigone, of course, is often understood as similarly rigid. Even Heidegger cannot avoid noting this feature of her: "Antigone knows that no one can take her decision away from her and that she will not flinch in her resolve" (HI102/127). But if Antigone is determined, she is so in a way that is different from Creon's rigidity. To understand where this difference lies, consider Lacan's reading of Antigone. What makes Antigone special for Lacan is that she does not compromise on her desire but pursues it until the end. But this interpretation seems to be in tension with Lacan's appropriation of Freud's Oedipal drama. For Lacan, desire is for an original plenitude (the mOther), and it is impossible to satisfy because of the law against incest. Stubbornly insisting on one's desire—being rigid—is failing to recognize one's finitude, which is (for Lacan) refusing to submit to castration. This leads to neurosis, perversion, or psychosis. If Antigone is to be a heroine of any kind for Lacan, her desire must be understood differently. It must be a way of refusing to compromise on her desire that is not rigid.

The key is that Antigone's desire is not the desire at stake in the Oedipal drama but a manifestation of Freud's death drive. What Antigone desires is not plenitude but death. As Lacan says, she "pushes to the limit the realization of something that might be called the pure and simple desire of death as such. She incarnates this desire."[48] Richardson interprets this desire for death as follows: "To desire death as death is to desire life up to the limit/end that makes it possible for life even to begin to be."[49] I take this to mean that to desire death is not to will annihilation but to will mortality: to desire life in its appropriate finitude. If this is right, then Antigone's uncompromising desire is not a rigidity that refuses to accept finitude but an embrace of finitude.

In Heidegger's language, the point would be as follows. Desire for plenitude is the seeking of the homely or the striving to disclose being. To be rigid is to stubbornly pursue this desire, insisting on full intelligibility. Such insistence refuses to acknowledge being's self-withdrawal and so the fact that seeking the homely always turns counter to itself (i.e., that the human being is uncanny). Full disclosure is impossible. But this does not mean that one should renounce desire entirely. In some mitigated sense, this is what Ismene accomplishes with her surrender to tradition.

---

[48] Lacan, *The Ethics of Psychoanalysis*, 282.
[49] William Richardson, "Lacan and the Enlightenment: Antigone's Choice," *Research in Phenomenology* 24 (1994): 38.

The challenge is to be the entity that *both* erotically strives to disclose being *and* shatters against being's self-withdrawal—that is, to be the uncanny entity as both transcendent and finite, flexibly turning between the two without emphasizing one over the other. This 'middle ground' is not mediocre or moderate but is perfectly balanced on the turn of the uncanny entity's counterturning. This is standing steadfastly amidst being's storms.[50]

To stand steadfastly is to be determined to make sense of things while gracefully acknowledging when sense runs out. It is, that is, to be ownedly *hupsipolis apolis*. We can also see such steadfast standing manifest in Antigone's relationship to death. Recall that the choral ode presents the idea that disclosure shatters against being's withdrawal with the claim that despite being *pantoporos aporos,* the human being cannot prevent death. As we know, 'death' names being's withdrawal. Owned and unowned uncanniness can thus be described as different ways of being towards death.[51] Creon, we might say, flees from death and denies it; it is because he does not recognize being's withdrawal that he can take himself to have authority over intelligibility. Antigone, by contrast, faces death willingly: "I chose death" (line 555, Woodruff translation), she says, and "There's no return; I follow death, alive" (line 810, Woodruff translation). What kind of relationship to being's withdrawal does this manifest?

Heidegger says surprisingly little about Antigone's dying and her death. He insists that when Antigone resolves to suffer the *deinon,* this "is by no means the fearful and inhabitual experience of an early death, which she herself faces with certainty" (HI104/129). But Heidegger does seem to offer what we (but not he) would call an allegorical reading of Antigone's death. He says that "her dying is, if it is anything at all, that which constitutes *kalōs,* a belonging to being. Her dying is her becoming homely, but a becoming homely within and from out of such being unhomely" (HI104/129).[52] Indeed, Heidegger says of the death mentioned

---

[50] We might compare this description of the person who stands steadfastly with Camus's Sisyphus, who must accept his fate while revolting against it. Albert Camus, *The Myth of Sisyphus and Other Essays,* trans. Justin O'Brien (New York: Vintage Books, 1991). We can also compare Kierkegaard's self as the perfectly calibrated balance of necessity and possibility. Søren Kierkegaard (as Anti-Climacus), *The Sickness unto Death: A Christian Psychological Exposition for Edification and Awakening,* trans. Alastair Hannay (London: Penguin Books, 1989).

[51] However, I make no claim as to how being-toward-death should be understood in SZ.

[52] This seems to be Heidegger's interpretation of the difficult lines from Antigone's confrontation with Ismene: "For everywhere shall I experience nothing of the fact that not to being my dying must belong" (HI99/123). That is, Heidegger seems to take this to be Antigone's insistence that her death *will* be her belonging to being.

in the choral ode, which *pantoporos aporos* cannot prevent, that "[i]t is this One to which Antigone already belongs, and which she knows to belong to being. For this reason, because she is thus becoming homely within being, she is the most unhomely one amid entities" (HI120/150).

If death is being's self-concealing or self-withdrawing, then to belong to death is to take over such concealing as one's point of departure or *archē*. Antigone's own death is presumably her own uncanny self-concealing— that is, being's withdrawal insofar as it takes place as the withdrawal of its own being from the human being (which, recall, makes the human being uncanny). So Antigone's death is the absencing or withdrawal in which she presences as the uncanny entity. As we know, such absencing or withdrawal *is* only for a disclosing, so we can also say that Antigone's death or dying is her self-disclosing, in which she presences by absencing from herself and brings herself to a stand as the uncanny entity. What is special about the way that Antigone does this—what is special about the way that she dies or relates to death—is that she recognizes the withdrawal of her being. But this is just to say that she self-discloses as uncanny—or, indeed, that she is ownedly *hupsipolis apolis*. Antigone's dying, then, allegorically presents owned self-disclosure.

We can understand in a similar way Antigone's claim that she is already dead ("Already my soul is dead" (line 559, Woodruff translation)), as well as Heidegger's enigmatic claim that "[t]he sphere proper to standing [*die eigentliche Sphäre des Stehens*] in the excentric middle of life is death" (HI28/33). Dying or being dead is comporting appropriately towards our finitude, so to be already dead or to stand in death is to self-disclose as appropriately finite. This is the proper way of standing or bringing oneself to a stand as the uncanny entity and so in the "excentric middle of life." We can even interpret Antigone's suicide on this allegorical reading. To commit suicide is to actively bring about one's self-concealing or self-withdrawing, where this refers to explicitly raising philosophical questions that bring one face to face with the self-withdrawing of (Dasein's) being. In the long tradition of associating philosophy with death, let us say that Antigone's suicide is an allegorical description of becoming the philosopher.[53]

---

[53] The meaning of 'suicide' here is thus very different from that in the alleged discussion of suicide in EM. Heidegger says that "the uncanniest possibility of Dasein" is "to break the excessive violence of being through Dasein's ultimate act of violence against itself" (EM189/135). This refers to Dasein "giving up its own essence" in the sense of "withholding [. . .] openness toward being" (EM188/135). The situation, as Heidegger describes it, is this: Dasein must disclose being but shrinks back from this in falling and through *das Man*. But "at moments the possibility must flare up that the surmounting of the overwhelming

So owned being towards death is self-disclosing as uncanny: bringing oneself to presence as the uncanny entity, and in such a way that one stands steadfastly. We can see how this makes Antigone supremely uncanny. In self-disclosing as uncanny, Antigone self-discloses as fundamentally alienated from being. But precisely because she has thereby grasped herself in her being, she is in the greatest proximity to being. The self-withdrawal of being means that we are closest to it when we are farthest from it. Ontological distance uncannily turns counter to itself to become an ontological proximity. Thus being supremely uncanny amounts to becoming homely in being.

To recapitulate: self-disclosing as uncanny is bringing oneself to a stand that is steadfast, in which one is counterturningly both falling and transcending. This is to say that being uncanny ownedly is being *hupsipolis apolis* ownedly and being *pantoporos aporos* ownedly. As we have seen, this means being reticently responsive to being, which we saw Antigone manifest in her discovery of Polyneices's body as *to be buried* and in her silence when called to account for herself. More specifically, being *pantoporos aporos* ownedly is discovering entities (including oneself) as the entities that they are, without becoming enmeshed in and determined by tradition. This is possible only if one is ownedly *hupsipolis apolis,* which

---

can be fully and most certainly fought out if the concealment of being [. . .] is simply preserved" (EM188/135)—if being is left concealed. This would be a different way of acquiescing to the absencing of being. To let being remain concealed, Dasein must in some sense cease the struggle to bring being to presence; the *polemos* must enter the mode of 'time out.' Fynsk and Polt both take this talk of self-violence and self-withholding to be a reference to suicide. Christopher Fynsk, *Heidegger: Thought and Historicity* (Ithaca, NY: Cornell University Press, 1993), 125; Richard Polt, "The Question of Nothing," in *A Companion to Heidegger's Introduction to Metaphysics,* ed. Richard Polt and Gregory Fried (New Haven, CT: Yale University Press, 2001), 79. It is, of course—but not to the physical suicide of the human being and not to uncanny self-absencing. Talk of 'self-violence' must refer to disclosure, and specifically to Dasein's self-disclosure. A self-disclosure in which Dasein withholds the site of openness or steps back from the *polemos* is one in which Dasein does not disclose itself as Dasein. So this 'suicide' amounts to an extreme self-misunderstanding. This possibility has an uncanny structure and so is an 'uncanny' possibility. It is intrinsically counterturning: in the act of repudiating itself as the site of openness through self-misunderstanding, Dasein in effect establishes itself as the site of openness. Further, we can see that it is a possibility that follows directly from Dasein's uncanniness, since any self-misunderstanding is an instance of seeming, of bringing oneself to a stand but not as the entity that one is. Dasein "*is* this possibility insofar as it is" (EM189/135) in the sense that this possibility is still a way to be Dasein and not a way to cease to be Dasein. Even in the most egregious self-misunderstanding, Dasein still offers a site to being. It does not have a way to cease to be itself or destroy itself. (We could, of course, commit physical suicide, thus destroying the entities (people) that Dasein needs in order to take place.). Death or suicide is a mode of disclosure—it is a way of living as Dasein, as it were. But this possibility of self-misunderstanding arises because being conceals itself, and so self-misunderstanding belongs to Dasein as an essential and positive possibility.

requires an openness to the call of being that respects its withdrawal through appropriate reticence at the end of explanation. In this way, Antigone is determined by the law of being (in both senses of the genitive)—which is to say, she suffers the *deinon*. Antigone thus brings herself to a stand in the *polis* as the uncanny entity, relating ownedly to the *polis* as both swirl and pole.

Raising the Question of Owned Uncanniness

By the end of the play, Creon comes to recognize his ontological hubris: he has been too rigid and must acknowledge intelligibility as it is given. Meaning is not up to him. "I cannot fight against necessity" (line 1106, Woodruff translation), he says. But Creon does not thereby become owned, since the law to which he gives his allegiance is not the law of being but tradition: "I'm afraid it is best to obey the laws, / Just as tradition has them, all one's life" (lines 1113–1114, Woodruff translation). Creon has surrendered his unowned way of being *hupsipolis apolis,* but he is not yet ownedly *hupsipolis apolis*. As a result, he is unownedly *pantoporos aporos* in the way that Ismene is: determined by the traditional embodiment of the law of being.

Creon might have benefited more from his conflict with Antigone. In resisting Creon, Antigone demonstrates that there is a law of being to which we are subject and over which we do not have control. For those in a position to see, she reveals the world to which we are and should be subject. Antigone's reticent responsiveness to the call of being in effect calls others to be ownedly *hupsipolis apolis*. Antigone also highlights the discrepancy between the call of being and the call of tradition, opening the possibility of being *pantoporos aporos* ownedly. In these ways, Antigone calls our attention to what is and what matters for us, which we have lost sight of. In thus being the everyday phenomenologist and discovering entities as the entities that they are, Antigone calls on others to do the same.

Yet in so calling, Antigone does not offer something concrete to undertake. The picture of ownedness that she gives us does not provide any practical prescription for becoming owned; it may give us a hazy ideal but it does not tell us how to get there or how we will know when we attain it. This is as it should be. If being uncanny ownedly is self-disclosing as uncanny, then it is not a particular action or the result of a particular action. It is a stance that we take up as the uncanny entity. It is a claim that we make about what it is to be us, and which we make only in how we go about being what we are. Making such a claim amounts to drawing the distinction between owned and unowned uncanniness.

If this is right, then to be called to ownedness is not to be given a set of guidelines and encouraged to live up to them. It cannot even be to be given an exemplar, like Antigone, whom we ought to emulate. To be called to ownedness is to be challenged to draw the distinction between ownedness and unownedness—to be challenged to take a stand on what it is to be the uncanny entity and to be so ownedly. We are called to "the risk of distinguishing and deciding between that being unhomely proper to the human being and a being unhomely that is inappropriate" (HI117/146). It is by presenting this *question*—what is owned uncanniness?—that Antigone calls us to ownedness.

Antigone presents us *as readers* with this question insofar as her status with regards to the closing words is ambiguous. The closing words force us to ask whether Antigone and Sophocles are exempt from the expulsion that they announce and so exempt from the *deinon*. In this, the closing words speak from and call us to "the most uncanny risk that risks nothing less than the essence of uncanniness itself" (HI117/146). Risk, recall, is our comportment towards entities insofar as it always involves ontic untruth, seeming, and the possibility of error. In taking on the question of what it is to be ownedly uncanny, we take on the supreme risk: that we will misunderstand ourselves and bring ourselves to presence under semblance or seeming. Such a stand is one of the varieties of unowned uncanniness. In risking unownedness or self-misunderstanding, we risk our essence. The reason is that what is at stake in drawing the distinction between owned and unowned uncanniness is precisely what it is to be uncanny and to be the uncanny entity.

Further, this risk never goes away; we never definitively answer the question of what it is to be ownedly uncanny. Because (our) being always withdraws from us, we are always at risk of misunderstanding ourselves. In other words, because we are uncanny—because, that is, our ground is always in question—what it is to be ownedly uncanny is always also in question. This is so because what is question-worthy about owned uncanniness is the uncanny logic that governs it, and, as the next chapter will show, this uncanny logic is inherently opaque to us. Let me conclude this chapter by showing how the question of owned uncanniness resolves itself into a question about uncanniness itself, which the next chapter will pursue.

Recall that Antigone is exempt from the closing words and so is not uncanny—but only insofar as she is supremely uncanny. Ownedness requires that being unhomely turn counter to itself and become a becoming homely in being. In Antigone's case, I expressed this using a spatial metaphor: Antigone is uncannily closest to being when she is farthest from it. This makes her supremely, and so ownedly, uncanny.

Similarly for Sophocles. Sophocles, of course, is the successful *hupsipolis apolis* creator who founds a new world. He is *hupsipolis* in that he is responsive to being as it is granted to the human being—not to *dikē*, as Antigone is, but to *phusis*. Antigone hears the call to discover entities as the entities that they are; Sophocles hears and responds to the historical dispensation of being—in his case, the call to disclose being as presencing and absencing, and the human being as caught in this uncanny play. His response is his poetic creation: the ode and the figure of Antigone, through which Sophocles first opens the Greek—and so Western—understanding of being as uncanny and of the human being as uncanny and potentially ownedly uncanny (EM154/110, 156/112, 161/116). As a creator, Sophocles is *apolis* in that he is not properly within the world that he founds; he is both inside and outside of it. Since Sophocles founds the human being as uncanny, he must be both excluded from and included in uncanny humanity. Sophocles's *apolis* character expresses itself in the closing words of the ode, where he explicitly pronounces the expulsion that makes the human being uncanny. This act raises the question of his own relationship to this expulsion and thus to the uncanny essence that he inaugurates.

Like Antigone, Sophocles is exempt from the closing words and so is not uncanny—but only insofar as he is supremely uncanny. Consider that Sophocles's position as simultaneously inside and outside uncanny humanity is itself an uncanny position. Sophocles is excluded from the humanity that he founds because he is a creator, but he is also included in it—and is so because it has now been created. Being included by means of being excluded is a way of being uncanny. Thus Sophocles's exclusion from the *deinon* intrinsically turns counter to itself, becoming a way of being included in the *deinon*. Sophocles is counterturningly exempt and not exempt from the closing words, and this is his supreme uncanniness. Heidegger expresses this peculiar position in Antigone's case by saying that she is so *hupsipolis* that she "steps out" of the *polis* (HI103/129) in such a way that she "comes to be removed from all human possibilities and placed into direct conflict over the site of all entities and into a sublation [*Aufhebung*] of the subsistence [*Bestandes*] of her own life" (HI103/128). That being beyond human possibilities could be a way of being human, or that stepping out of the *polis* could be a way of bringing oneself to a stand as the uncanny entity in the *polis*, seems impossible. What is the logic of this sublation? How does exclusion or being unhomely turn counter to itself so as to become an inclusion, or becoming homely? We can put the same question statically in terms of standing steadfastly: how can one *both* erotically will being's disclosure *and* appropriately acknowledge its withdrawal? How is it possible to be maximally transcendent and maximally finite simultaneously?

The question "what is owned uncanniness?" resolves itself into the question "how does the logic of uncanny counterturning work?" We have seen this logic in play at every level of description of the uncanny entity—in its falling transcendence, in its being *hupsipolis apolis*, in its being *pantoporos aporos*, and in its being owned. At the most fundamental level, this logic governs both the human being and being; it is the logic of *pelein*, of uncanny presencing and absencing. I concluded Chapter 3 by suggesting that the account of the human being as uncanny does not obviously make good sense. We come to roughly the same conclusion here: the account of ownedness does not obviously make good sense. There is something about the logic of uncanniness that is questionable. What is worthy of question, according to Heidegger, is the *polis* itself as uncannily presencing and absencing. So let us raise this question of the uncanny.

5

The Question of the Uncanny

THERE IS SOMETHING not quite right about uncanniness. The story of the birth of uncanny human being seems to presuppose its own ending (Chapter 3) and the account of what it is to be ownedly uncanny relies on a 'supreme' uncanniness in which being uncanny somehow turns counter to itself to become a being homely in being (Chapter 4). There is something questionable about the logic of the counterturning involved in uncanniness. How does it work to produce owedness or to produce Dasein itself?

Heidegger locates this questionability in the *polis* itself: the clearing that uncannily presences and absences in the manner of *pelein*. He says that the *polis* is that which is most properly worthy of question (HI80/99) and that what is question-worthy in it is the "veiled ground [*Grund*]" of uncanniness (HI87/107). But Heidegger also claims that the *polis* can never be defined and that it is constantly questionable anew. This is because its question-worthiness is a positive and proper feature of it: "whatever is essential wishes, in itself and of its own accord, to remain within the realm of that which is worthy of question" (HI80/99). The question-worthiness of the uncanny *polis* is not something that we can or should seek to dissolve or resolve. It must instead be "acknowledged and preserved" (HI81/100) in and for "meditation [*Besinnung*] proper, the highest and most extensive" (HI85/105). It is in doing *this* that we become owned—that is, in raising the question of in what ownedness consists, failing to answer it fully, and preserving the questionability of its uncanny logic. The question of the ground of uncanniness can and must receive no answer.

With this, we approach what I characterized in the Introduction as the impossibility of domesticating uncanniness. But claiming that a question cannot be answered is not sufficient; we have yet to *pose* the question of the uncanny and to get clear on precisely what is question-worthy in it. In pursuing the question-worthiness of uncanniness we seek not an answer but a better understanding of the question and its force as a question. The goal is to make uncanniness intelligible *as* unintelligible. The mark of our success will be our confusion: an experience of the pressing question-worthiness of uncanniness. As Richard Polt puts it: "When the topic of one's thought is self-concealing, then there is no difference between seeking and finding: the obscure question, the frustrated search, is itself the most appropriate response to the thing."[1] The closure of the investigation of uncanniness must thus be the openness of a question.

Yet there is a sense in which we will answer the question. For it will turn out that the question of the uncanny is its own answer. Not only are our confusions about uncanniness positive features of uncanniness rather than the result of deficiencies in the investigation, but these in fact constitute uncanniness. It is our inability to understand the ground of uncanniness that is our primary finitude—that which is concealed in our being, the finding of which opens openness. So uncanniness is not only inherently aporetic, it is itself the question that makes us what we are. This is why uncanniness is *most* properly worthy of question and why this question must be acknowledged and preserved. Acknowledging and preserving the question-worthiness of uncanniness is acknowledging and preserving our own being as uncanny. This is why becoming ownedly uncanny consists in "let[ting] *being* unhomely become worthy of question" (HI115/143).

So the question of the uncanny is *of* the uncanny in two senses: it is a question that asks *about* uncanniness and its ground, and it is a question that constitutes our uncanniness. To say that the human being is essentially uncanny is to say that it is because the human being dwells in this question that it is what it is. It follows that if we succeed in experiencing the question-worthiness of uncanniness, we will have let our uncanniness become worthy of question and so will have performed what the closing words of the choral ode call us to do. We will be called to ownedness by having an existentiell experience of our own uncanniness.

---

[1] Richard Polt, *The Emergency of Being: On Heidegger's Contributions to Philosophy* (Ithaca, NY: Cornell University Press, 2006), 17. Heidegger himself makes this point often; for example: "The openness of the open mystery does not consist in solving the mystery, thus destroying it, but consists in not touching the concealedness of the simple and essential and letting this concealedness alone in its appearance." Martin Heidegger, *Parmenides,* trans. André Schuwer and Richard Rojcewicz (Bloomington: Indiana University Press, 1998), 63.

The Ground of Uncanniness: Four Causes

There are many things that we might be asking after when we ask about the 'ground' [*Grund*] of uncanniness, and there are many ways to pose a question seeking one of these grounds. I will approach the issue by means of Aristotle's four causes, all of which are *archai* and so all of which ground.[2] Even if this approach does not exhaust the possibilities for seeking the ground of uncanniness, it will give us more than enough to develop the question of the uncanny.

Uncanniness is presencing in the manner of absencing—the play of unconcealment and concealment, openness and finitude, in which Dasein and being happen. We have already identified the proximate material cause of this play or process, since I analyzed its elements or stages in Chapter 3. We might also ask after an efficient cause, seeking what gets this play or process going or drives it. As a preliminary question, we will need to determine whether this efficient cause is external (i.e., Dasein is made) or internal. If the latter, then the question of the efficient cause should coincide with that of the formal and final causes, since any entity that has its principle of change within itself (i.e., a natural entity) is driven by itself (efficient cause) *qua* its essence (formal cause) towards fulfillment of that essence (final cause). The question of final causality will ask what *telos* governs the play of uncanniness: to what goal it is directed or in what condition it will be when it has become itself. The latter will be the essence of uncanniness: the formal cause. This essence is the logic of the play of uncanniness: how its counterturning works or how it hangs together as something unified. It is in terms of this formal cause that Heidegger himself puts the question of ground: "the veiled ground of the unity of this twofoldness [of the terms of the counterturning] prevails within the uncanny, a ground worthy of question" (HI87/107).

I start with the material cause. If uncanniness is a play, then its material cause will be the stages in the process of the play. The question or problem that we encounter here concerns the impossibility of clearly laying out the different stages as distinct. This problem will lead us directly into the question of the formal cause and how the play hangs together coherently as a unity.

Recall that I concluded Chapter 3 with a question about how uncanniness works. I interpreted the opening strophes of the first choral ode

[2] For the four causes, see Aristotle's *Physics*, especially Book II (*Physics*, trans. R. P. Hardie and R. K. Gaye, in *The Complete Works of Aristotle: The Revised Oxford Translation*, Vol. 1, ed. Jonathan Barnes (Princeton, NJ: Princeton University Press, 1995)).

as telling a story about Dasein's essential origin as the entity that understands being. According to this story, being throws the disclosive powers to Dasein so that Dasein may bring being to presence in the presencing of entities. However, when Dasein brings itself to presence as an entity, it encounters its own thrown ground in being and so its ground in originary concealment (which Chapter 2 identified as the obscure whence of thrownness). This finding of concealment (or the opening up of finitude) is the opening of finite openness. Dasein's uncanniness is this self-enabling, reciprocal interplay between openness and finitude. I concluded Chapter 3 by suggesting that this story is hard to grasp because it says that Dasein comes to its essence only in departing from it. We might then wonder if Dasein has two essences: a 'full' essence from which it departs and a finite essence to which it comes. Put another way: what sense does it make to posit the human essence at the beginning of the story of its own origin? How can original concealment be found or opened if openness is possible only after this, as finite? The problem is that the story is not simply that there is a finitude and then there is openness. Rather, there is an opening finitude that reveals concealment and so that produces openness as finite, thus first allowing the opening finitude or finite openness that discloses concealment. So which comes first?

We find the same problematic structure in the account of primordial temporality in SZ. This temporality temporalizes itself *(sich zeitigen)* or brings itself to fruition in the reciprocal interplay of its three ek-stases (SZ328–329). The three 'dimensions' of temporality are called 'ek-stases' because they are standings *(staseis)* out *(ek)*. Heidegger insists that there is no 'itself' from which the ek-stases stand out (SZ329). Temporality must thus be the dynamic interplay of the three ek-stases in which they stand out from and reach into one another, bringing each other about: a "process of temporalizing in the unity of the ecstases" (SZ329). So where, or in what, does this temporalizing begin? Which of the three ek-stases is the 'first,' the one that starts off the process? Heidegger reserves a certain priority for the futural ek-stasis, because temporality temporalizes itself "in terms of" the future (SZ329). But this means that in owned, primordial temporalizing, the futural ek-stasis has a special role in determining the character of the whole as owned. It does not mean that the futural ek-stasis is the first to operate or that it is more original than the others. The three ek-stases are equiprimordial, equally originary (SZ329). They bring each other about, such that each presupposes and is presupposed by the others.

Dasein's uncanniness has the same structure: the 'future' of Dasein's finite openness first allows, but presupposes, the 'past' of its opening onto finitude. Temporality is thus uncanny. It is likely, in fact, that the temporalizing interplay of the ek-stases *is* Dasein's uncanniness. Both clear the *da* or 'there' (SZ351) and so open the site of openness, and both stand as the principle of unity of Dasein's being (SZ327). Most obviously, both capture Dasein's essential ek-stasis or ek-centricity. These considerations suggest that the temporalizing of temporality is the happening of uncanniness: the reciprocal interplay at the ground of Dasein.[3] At the very least, both have the same problematic structure.

We can also see this structure at work in the plain language version of the story of the origin of Dasein. This is more or less the story of the origin of philosophizing, since (as we saw in Chapter 4) 'philosophizing' is another name for Dasein, the event of understanding being. Saying that originary concealment, as opened, opens up openness (and *vice versa*) is saying that unintelligibility, when encountered, first sparks the effort to make intelligible. This in turn allows unintelligibility to be encountered in the first place. The first part holds because it is only when there is something unintelligible (concealed) that we are moved to make it intelligible (openness). The second part holds because there is unintelligibility (concealment) only *for* an effort to make it intelligible (openness). As we saw in discussing SZ, the whence of thrownness can be obscure only to a finding. So unintelligibility is both the condition and the consequence of the enterprise of making intelligible, and *vice versa*.

No matter how we tell the story, we encounter the same problem. The problem arises because such stories are told linearly, yet the phenomenon in question is not linear. The story told in the ode is not about actual events in time but is a narrative projection of essence. The narrative cannot fall out perfectly as a linear process because it is attempting to express a kind of looping within Dasein's essence. This looping is the reciprocal relation in which Dasein originates or is grounded. But switching from a temporal-causal vocabulary to this spatial or topological vocabulary does not help, for the same problem arises again under the guise of an uncertainty between the inside and the outside. Dasein's essence is to be excluded from its essence—to be what it is only when it is not what it is. This means that it is fully 'in' itself only by being 'outside' of itself. Dasein's interiority is an exteriority or excentricity. As Heidegger puts it, human beings are "in a center outside of themselves, that is, [. . .] excentric" (HI28/32).

---

[3] It would require significant further analysis to determine exactly how to reconcile the two-part interplay of uncanniness with the three-part interplay of temporality, and to express temporality in terms of finitude and openness. (The key to the latter will be the fact that the ek-stases have horizons.)

Put in these terms, Dasein's uncanniness strongly resembles the state of exception.[4] The state of exception is exemplified by the sovereign, who is both inside and outside the law. The extra-legal dimension of sovereignty comes to the fore in moments of crisis, when the sovereign declares a state of emergency and suspends the law. This possibility is constitutive for the figure of the sovereign; there must be an outlaw dimension internal to the law. Giorgio Agamben characterizes this outlaw dimension in more Heideggerian terms as *"ecstasy-belonging"*: a condition in which what is excluded (by the rule of law) is included (i.e., in the possibility of the suspension of the rule of law).[5] It is a condition in which "the outside is nothing but the exclusion of an inside and the inside is in turn only the inclusion of an outside."[6] In Dasein's case, the outside is concealment (or the non-essence) and the inside is openness (or the essence). The inside is produced by the inclusion (finding) of the outside (concealment). So the play of the inside and outside constitutive for the state of exception is seen in the reciprocal relation of the *polemos,* the presencing and absencing of the open site, expressed in spatial terms.

On the spatial rendering, the problem is that we cannot clearly distinguish the inside and the outside. On the temporal reading, the problem is that we cannot grasp uncanniness in terms of a ground and result, a cause and effect, something original and something subsequent. The reason is that the two terms of the originary *polemos* constitute one another. Although each presupposes the other, neither precedes the other. In other words, Dasein is a self-enabling self-relation. Similarly, ek-static temporality is self-grounding: it brings itself about or makes itself possible in its own temporalizing. So the reason that we cannot lay out this process or this topology clearly (formal cause), and so the reason that its elements are difficult to distinguish (material cause), is that it is a self-constituting process. This is a problem of efficient causality.

To say that Dasein is self-constituting or makes itself possible is to say that the elements of the *polemos* arise together in a leap or that originary angst brings itself about. Dasein is a leap that "attains its own ground [*Grund*] by leaping, performs it in leaping" (EM7/5). As Heidegger himself

---

[4] The state of exception was originally conceived by Carl Schmitt in his *Dictatorship,* trans. Michael Hoelzl and Graham Ward (Cambridge: Polity Press, 2014). The concept was taken up and developed by Giorgio Agamben, especially in his *State of Exception,* trans. Kevin Attell (Chicago: The University of Chicago Press, 2005). Compare also Lacan's concepts of *jouissance* and 'extimacy.'

[5] Agamben, *State of Exception,* 35.

[6] Giorgio Agamben, *The Open: Man and Animal,* trans. Kevin Attell (Stanford, CA: Stanford University Press, 2004), 37.

says, "A curious, indeed *unheimlich* thing that we must first leap onto the soil [*Boden*] on which we really stand."[7] This *Unheimlichkeit* of Dasein's *Unheimlichkeit* is the question-worthiness of the efficient causality of uncanniness: how does the leap come about? The question is the same as that expressed by Michael Haar in a slightly different context: "Does *Dasein* have the potential to make itself possible? The idea that it itself makes itself possible is incredible, no less remarkable than that of the *causa sui*. Would *Dasein* be like the Baron von Münchhausen, who took hold of his hair to lift himself into the air? Whence does the possibility—as it is not simply logical, but ontological—draw its power to make possible?"[8] Here the question is about power and so about the efficient cause understood as a source of momentum (rather than a source of direction). Whence the momentum of the leap of Dasein's self-enabling? In the vocabulary of uncanniness, the question is a little harder to put. We can put it generally as, What drives the original *polemos,* making openness finite and finitude open? To be more specific, we would have to ask something like, How does the finding of original concealment have the power of opening up the openness that it presupposes? It is in these terms that the question is most difficult and most intriguing. It amounts to a question about the productive or inclusive power of the *un-* of 'uncanniness,' which I mentioned in passing in Chapter 3 and to which I will return in the next section.

First, let me pause to confirm that the efficient cause that we are seeking is indeed internal to Dasein. For it is tempting to try to provide some external ground for Dasein's self-origination, as Fynsk does in discussing the (strictly analogous) origin of owned cases of Dasein: "Several times up to this point, we have approached the question of the origin of this movement of authentic existence, and though we have seen Heidegger assign something like a spontaneous, autochthonous birth to it, we have also seen that it is caught up in the circular structure whereby it is made possible by what it reveals. This circular structure might lead us to say simply 'it happens' and thus accept this movement of freedom as a 'pure fact' whose origin or impetus cannot be explained. Or we might recognize the other as providing the intervention necessary for drawing Dasein out of its subjection to the they and drawing it before its death."[9] With this 'other,' Fynsk posits an external efficient cause, thus seeming to solve the problem of Dasein's self-origination. I did the same thing in

---

[7] Martin Heidegger, *What Is Called Thinking?*, trans. J. Glenn Gray (New York: Harper Collins, 1976), 41. I have substituted '*unheimlich*' for the translator's 'unearthly.'

[8] Michel Haar, *Heidegger and the Essence of Man*, trans. William McNeill (Albany: State University of New York Press, 1993), 14.

[9] Christopher Fynsk, *Heidegger Thought and Historicity* (Ithaca, NY: Cornell University Press, 1993), 48–49.

suggesting that Creon might have become owned as a result of his engagement with Antigone, or that we might become owned by reading the closing words of the ode. Dreyfus makes a similar move when he grounds the failure to become owned in something like *akrasia*, thereby implicitly grounding success in becoming owned in some kind of rational virtue.[10] Becoming owned thus depends on the actualization of some pre-existing ability to be owned. The actualization of this ability is an efficient cause that is external to the process being explained (although, in this case, 'internal' to Dasein).

What does this move look like in the context of Dasein's uncanny origination? Recall the plain language story of Dasein's origin as the story of the origin of philosophizing. We ordinarily purport to know perfectly well how philosophizing arises and we do so because we implicitly or explicitly posit a prior capacity or desire to make sense of things, which capacity permits us to both encounter unintelligibility and proceed to make things intelligible. We say that unintelligibility (concealment) can produce the act of making intelligible (openness) by actualizing an already present capacity or igniting a pre-existing desire to make intelligible—an external efficient cause. Such an explanation seems to take the mysterious, self-constituting reciprocity of openness and concealment and give it a clear, external efficient cause that can start the process off, thus resolving the problem of the momentum of its beginning.

But this success is an illusion. This strategy pre-emptively closes down the questionability of the ground of uncanniness and does not resolve it. This is clear from the fact that it produces a regress. In the story of the origin of philosophizing, unintelligibility opens openness (i.e., making intelligible) by engaging or actualizing a pre-existing potentiality or capacity. What allows this capacity to be engaged in the first place? According to the story, unintelligibility activates it. But unintelligibility shows up only for the already actualized potentiality to make intelligible. To appeal to a capacity or potentiality is to do nothing more than push the problem further back. If we then attempt to solve the problem by positing a further or deeper capacity, we enter the regress.

The same holds for an account of the origin of owned Dasein that appeals to the intervention of the other or to a pre-existing condition of Dasein. If the other's intervention is to be successful in some cases and not in others, what distinguishes these cases? Whatever it is, this is already the difference that makes for ownedness. What accounts for *this*? If a case of Dasein capable of facing up to angst is to be distinguished from

[10] Hubert L. Dreyfus, *Being-in-the-World: A Commentary on Heidegger's* Being and Time, *Division I* (Cambridge, MA: The MIT Press, 1991), 335.

an akratic case of Dasein, then the former already possesses the difference that makes the difference for ownedness. Appealing to this feature does not solve but only repeats the problem of the ground of becoming owned.

Agamben draws our attention to a similar problem in accounts of the origin of the human being as a linguistic entity. Such accounts try to show how the human being and its distinctive linguistic ability could have arisen from the non-linguistic, non-human animal. They posit a pre-linguistic stage of humanity—an 'ape-man,' a missing link—from which the human being and its language could spring and which would mark the passage from animal to human being and allow for a demarcation of the two. This 'missing link' fulfills the same explanatory role as the capacity for philosophizing or the intervention of the other. Like these, it pushes the problem further back. Positing a pre-linguistic capacity for language does not explain the origin of language, for it presupposes it.[11] The 'ape-man' *already* has whatever it is that makes the difference for language and so is already distinguished from the animal. Thus the ape-man does not explain the passage from animal to human since it is already on the 'human' side of the passage. So, too, a 'man-ape' would always remain on the 'animal' side. Positing these intermediate cases, then, does not draw the distinction between human and animal but presupposes it. It only displaces and defers the distinction.

In this persisting explanatory gap stands a 'zone of indeterminacy' between the human and the animal. Drawing the distinction between the animal and the human involves excluding from the human and including in the animal that which already belongs to the human (i.e., the pre-linguistic capacity). This produces the 'ape-man': a missing link that traverses the boundary between the human and the animal. It does not produce a clear division but only a play of inclusion and exclusion: a state of exception. Any 'missing link' is—like the sovereign, like the

---

[11] Agamben quotes the linguist Heymann Steinthal on this difficulty: "The prelinguistic stage of intuition can only be one, not double, and it cannot be different for animal and for man. If it were different, that is, if man were naturally higher than the animal, then the origin of man would not coincide with the origin of language, but rather with the origin of his higher form of intuition out of the lower form which is the animal's. Without realizing it, I presupposed this origin: in reality, man with his human characteristics was given to me through creation, and I then sought to discover the origin of language in man. But in this way, I contradicted my presupposition: that is, that the origin of language and the origin of man were one and the same; I set man up first and then had him produce language." Agamben gives the following citation: Heymann Steinthal, *Der Ursprung der Sprache im Zusammenhange mit den letzten Fragen alles Wissens. Eine Darstellung, Kritik und Fortentwicklung der vorzüglichsten Ansichten* (1851; Berlin: Dümmler, 1877), 303. Agamben, *The Open: Man and Animal*, 36–37, bibliographical information on 96.

philosophical capacity or Dasein's proto-ownedness—already both included and excluded.[12]

So the attempt to posit an external efficient cause only returns us to uncanniness and does not resolve the problem. This strategy produces a regress that amounts to positing the state of exception at the ground of Dasein rather than a clear demarcation or a linear origin story. Insofar as the state of exception has the structure of uncanniness, this in turn amounts to positing uncanniness at the ground of Dasein. Heidegger wants us to see this as a positive phenomenon—not as the failure of explanation but as the explanation itself. The failure to identify an external efficient cause is a positive result: there is no external efficient cause; there is only uncanniness. The efficient cause must be internal, where this means that Dasein is uncannily self-constituting. As we saw when discussing originary angst, Dasein as angst brings itself about as uncanny and from its uncanniness, in a self-grounding and self-moving leap.

The Efficient Cause: Freud's Un-

We are trying to make sense of a complex origination that happens in a process of simultaneous, reciprocal constituting. The problems that we have encountered amount to unanswered questions, and they are all different ways of stating the question of the uncanny. There are no new problems or new questions to be uncovered, yet it is beneficial to let the question arise in new ways. We need to return to the question of the momentum of the internal efficient cause, which will resolve into a different way of stating the question about the formal cause of uncanniness. This will eventually lead us to the last of Aristotle's four causes: the final cause.

Earlier, I posed the question of efficient causality in terms of power. How does the finding of original concealment have the power to open up the openness that it presupposes? We can pose this question in terms of the word 'uncanniness' *('Unheimlichkeit')*. The *un-* of *'Unheimlichkeit'* is the element that excludes Dasein from its essence or *heim* and so it must be

---

[12] Agamben argues in *The Open: Man and Animal* that, despite himself, Heidegger ends up with just such a picture in FCM. He claims that Heidegger inadvertently posits a state of exception at the ground of Dasein and that Heidegger does so because his picture requires that the human being arise from, and so be grounded in, the animal. Agamben is right that Heidegger posits a state of exception at the ground of Dasein—although he does so quite deliberately. But Heidegger does not take Dasein to arise from the animal. Agamben's argument clearly and illegitimately presupposes that Dasein is 'alive' and that the story of the relation between Dasein and the animal that Heidegger tells in FCM is supposed to be a genetic story. Both of these claims can be shown to be false.

in or through its negating power that original concealment is found and finite openness opened up. What must the negativity of this *un-* be, such that it has the power to bring Dasein to its essence by excluding it from its essence? I put this in Chapter 3 by saying that the finitude in uncanniness is pregnant and enabling: an overabundance. What is the productive power in the un-? How does this negativity work to bring Dasein to its essence?[13] We saw the same question at the close of Chapter 4: how does Dasein's uncanniness have the power to turn counter to itself and become a becoming homely in being? What is the force of this recoil such that it can catapult supremely uncanny Dasein all the way into homeliness? The metaphor of 'power' forces us to express the question in an awkward and strange way. It is less awkward if we think of it as an entirely linguistic question. Asking what the un- *does* is a way of asking how it negates—how it is to be understood in relation to what it modifies. How does the *un-* operate on the 'canny' or '*heimlich*'? The same kind of negation is operative in *a-poros* and *a-polis,* as well as in the un- or non-essence (*Un-wesen* (EM166/120, 168/121)). We saw that these cannot be straightforward negations. So what kind of negations are they? Taking the question of efficient causality in this way brings it close to a question about formal causality, since we are asking after the logic in terms of which the elements of uncanniness (here grasped linguistically) hang together.

To fully understand the specific negativity of the un- would require a thorough investigation of the 'not,' the negative, and the nothing. In SZ, WM, and still in HI Heidegger claims that this has yet to be accomplished.[14] As a result, the explication of uncanniness "must move in

[13]The question of how our finitude can produce our distinctive openness might seem to have the same structure as, for example, the question of how constraint by norms can enable freedom. Both ask how something 'negative' can produce something 'positive.' But we need to be careful that the negativity in question is of the right kind. Consider, for instance, that Robert Brandom resolves the Kantian problem by interpreting the negativity of constraint as the positivity of inclusion in a community and its practices, and freedom as freedom *to* rather than freedom *from.* So what looks like having something taken away from us in a way that makes us come fully to ourselves is actually a situation of being included in a sphere (constraint, community membership) that affords us further, and distinctive, possibilities (freedom *to*). There is no genuine conflict between freedom *to* and constraint, and so no difficulty in grasping how being constrained opens up possibilities for us: we come fully to ourselves only in belonging to a community, and this inclusion involves finitude. This is structurally quite different from the problem that we are facing with the uncanny, since here it seems that we come fully to ourselves only by being excluded from ourselves in the first place. Robert Brandom, "Freedom and Constraint by Norms," *American Philosophical Quarterly* 16:3 (1979): 187–196.

[14]See SZ286, WM95, HI78/96. For an overview of Heidegger's thinking on the nothing which also places it in the context of the history of philosophy, see Richard Polt, "The Question of Nothing," in *A Companion to Heidegger's Introduction to Metaphysics,* ed. Richard Polt and Gregory Fried (New Haven, CT: Yale University Press, 2001), 57–82.

a twilight" (HI78/96). I cannot here fully illuminate the essence of the negative, but I can take some steps forward in exploring the un-, at least as regards uncanniness. As a first step, let me turn to Freud. In his essay on the uncanny affect, Freud explicitly draws our attention to the peculiar way in which the *un-* of *'unheimlich'* negates.

Working through the dictionary entry for *'heimlich,'* Freud finds a curious phenomenon: the word *'heimlich'* semantically "develops in the direction of ambivalence, until it finally coincides with its opposite, *unheimlich.*"[15] The *unheimlich* thus appears to be a species of the *heimlich,* and if this is so then the *un-* certainly cannot negate in any ordinary sense. To make sense of this, Freud makes two moves. First, he identifies two meanings of *'heimlich,'* allowing the *un-* to operate on each. Second, he locates the *heimlich* and the *unheimlich* within the dynamic realm of psychic activity.

First, *'heimlich'* has two meanings. It refers to both the familiar and safe *and* the hidden or secret *(Geheimnis).* In the latter sense, the homely is something disconcerting and disquieting and so approaches the ordinary sense of *'unheimlich.'* The *un-* acts on the stem *'heimlich'* with respect to both of its meanings, in different ways. When *'heimlich'* means the familiar, the *un-* negates it by producing its lack. When *'heimlich'* means the secret, the *un-* removes, undoes, or reverses it.[16] Thus *'unheimlich'* has, in principle (even if not in German), two meanings: the unfamiliar and the revealed secret.

We can see the semantic merging by reading the following chart diagonally: $heimlich_1$ (homely, familiar) approaches $unheimlich_2$ (revealed secret) and $heimlich_2$ (secret) approaches $unheimlich_1$ (unfamiliar). (Freud notes only the second of these.)

$$heimlich_1 \text{ (homely, familiar)} \quad + \quad un{\text -}_1 \quad = \quad unheimlich_1 \text{ (unfamiliar)}$$

$$heimlich_2 \text{ (secret)} \quad + \quad un{\text -}_2 \quad = \quad unheimlich_2 \text{ (revealed secret)}$$

In the case of the uncanny affect, all these meanings are at stake. To explain this, Freud must introduce a dynamic dimension to the story, understanding the *unheimlich* as something that happens or arises. He thus locates it as an event in a story about psychic activity. The story is this:

---

[15] Sigmund Freud, "The Uncanny," *The Standard Edition of the Complete Psychological Works of Sigmund Freud,* Vol. 17, ed. and trans. James Strachey (London: Vintage Books, 2001), 226.

[16] As Krell points out, this is not entirely unlike a negation of the *heimlich qua* the secret. Since it "implies the *revelation* of the unfamiliar, alien and secret," it "does in some sense negate the absolutely secretive, the utterly alien, the wholly unfamiliar." David Farrell Krell, *Architecture: Ecstasies of Space, Time and the Human Body* (Albany: State University of New York Press, 1997), 108.

1.	Some psychic event occurs. By virtue of the fact that it happens to me, it is proper and familiar.	*heimlich₁* (homely, familiar)
2.	If this event cannot be integrated into my sense of self, it is repressed. Repression hides it or secrets it away, negating it in the sense of making it unfamiliar.	*+ un-₁ = unheimlich₁* (unfamiliar)
3.	The repressed is now secret.	*= heimlich₂* (secret)
4.	However, repression is an imperfect mechanism. We cannot succeed in hiding things from ourselves; what is repressed is never truly secret.	
5.	Under certain circumstances, what is repressed can be prompted to reveal itself again.	*+ un-₂*
6.	If this occurs, then what is repressed returns to the conscious mind. It is revealed. But the revelation is also imperfect: what is revealed is not simply revealed but shows up as something hidden.	*= unheimlich₂* (revealed secret)
7.	So when the repressed returns it retains its unfamiliar character and destabilizes the realm of the familiar.	*= unheimlich₁* (unfamiliar)

We can now understand why Freud says that the *un-* is the "token of repression."[17] I take it that "token" is deliberately vague. In this context, the un- that negates *is* repression while the un- that reveals is the return of the repressed. The uncanny is the return *(un-₂)* of the repressed *(un-₁)*; it is the revelation *(un-₂)* of what was hidden *(heimlich₂)* by repression *(un-₁)* of a psychic event *(heimilch₁)*. The outcome of this process is the uncanny affect: the experience of the revelation *(unheimlich₂)* of something previously familiar *(heimlich₁)* as still secret *(heimlich₂)* and unfamiliar *(unheimlich₁)*.

So Freud explains the semantic merging of *'heimlich'* and *'unheimlich'* by distinguishing two senses of *'heimlich'* and, implicitly, two different ways in which the *un-* negates. We have these two different operations of the un- in English—that is, two distinct un- prefixes. Each has a different meaning and so the two operate differently.

I will call the first un- prefix the 'negating un-.' This un- attaches to a noun, adjective, adverb, or participle and expresses negation. This is how we usually think of the prefix: to be unhappy is *not* to be happy, to be non-happy: not to be a member of the set of happy things. The negating un- is equivalent to other purely privative prefixes like the Latinate *in-* and the Greco *a-*, as well as the privative suffix *-less*. All express a lack or absence of what is named in the stem. The benefit of forming words in this way is that it can express a departure from a normal or

---

[17] Freud, "The Uncanny," 245.

proper condition (un-happiness) as opposed to expressing the condition something is in positively (sadness). (I take it that Orwell had this point in mind when he crafted Newspeak, which contains words like 'ungood' rather than 'bad' (and 'unbad').)[18] The emphasis is on the lack of something that is in some sense supposed to be present. The un- marks a deficiency, an imperfection, a falling short, a failure.[19]

The second un- prefix is quite different. I will call it the 'reversing-releasing un-.' This prefix usually attaches to verbs and expresses a reversal, deprivation, and sometimes a release. 'To unlock' is thus to reverse the action of locking: to de-lock. This is not an absence or lack, and it is not the action of producing an absence or lack (e.g., removing the locking mechanism from the object). It is a motion or change that undoes, turns, or reverses. Many of these un- words have the sense of a return to a normal condition. The un- undoes something artificial or imposed, returning what is acted on to a natural or proper state—or at least to a condition of freedom or openness. The object of the verb comes, or comes back, to itself.[20]

So there are two kinds of negation that might be attributed to the un- of 'uncanniness.' One is privative and produces a lack, absence, or imperfection (negating un-). The other is a reversal or turn which is often a return (reversing-releasing un-). Read strongly, the two are quite opposed. The negating un- says that something fails to be what it should be while the reversing-releasing un- brings the thing to what it should be. Of course, this difference is tied in part to the meaning of the stem. 'Uncover' has the positive sense of a return and success only if we think that being covered is something negative and unnatural. There are certainly cases

---

[18] George Orwell, *Nineteen Eighty-Four* (New York: Alfred A. Knopf, 1992), 54. This feature of the negating un- is also perhaps why the concept of the 'undead' is so perplexing when understood in these terms. Human beings who are dead are supposed to stay dead and in not doing so depart from the normal or proper condition (are 'undead'). But the normal or proper condition for human beings is not to be dead but to be alive. Yet 'unalive' does not capture what is significant about the undead! That the undead stand in an uncanny zone of indeterminacy between life and death suggests that the un- involved in the term 'undead' operates in the same way as the un- of 'uncanniness,' which will turn out to be a much more complex negating.

[19] For example: unclean, ungrateful, unwept, unsung, uneaten, unnamed, uncouth, unpleasant, unskilled, unlawful, unexpected, untried, unwilling, untrue, unwise, uncomfortable, unpaid, unscripted, uncertain, unmoored, unread, unborn, unhelpful, unsolicited, unseemly, unplanned, uncool, ungodly. Even more 'positive' words like 'unarmed', 'unending', 'undivided', or 'unaltered' are positive only in particular contexts; these too express a departure from a norm.

[20] For example: unbuckle, uncover, unyoke, unbind, undo, unbend, unlock, unconceal, uncloak, unearth, unclench, unburden, unwind, uncheck, unfold, unblock, unwrap, unbolt. More ambiguous cases include 'unbalance.'

in which this is not so. But it remains a fact that in English, the un- prefix seems to have attached itself to certain kinds of stems in a way that largely preserves the opposition.

(There is likely a metaphysical explanation for the opposition between the two un-'s, and it is perhaps quite Greek in character. The basic difference between the two is that between the absence of a property and the operation of an action on an entity. If a property can be either present or absent and it is absent, then there is a sense in which it can and so ought to be there. The assumption about properties is that they are proper to a thing, such that only by possessing all of its potential properties does a thing reach completeness or fulfillment. Lacking a potential property is thus an imperfection or failure. With actions that alter entities, the metaphysical assumption in play is different. If we assume that the *telos* of any action is the good, then an act of alteration seeks the good. If we can assume that it seeks the good of the entity acted on, then the act will return the entity to its proper condition. Both accounts seem to me to rest on thoroughly Greek metaphysical views. So this is perhaps a helpful way of thinking about why the difference between the two un-'s might strike us as natural and how it might have come to be built into a language.)

The two un- prefixes in English correspond to the two un-'s that we need to posit to make sense of Freud's story:

heimlich$_1$ (homely, familiar)	+ negating un-	=	*unheimlich$_1$* (unfamiliar)
heimlich$_2$ (secret)	+ reversing-releasing un-	=	*unheimlich$_2$* (revealed secret)

So Freud's uncanny affect can be understood as a complex interplay of the two senses of '*heimlich*' and the two senses of '*unheimlich*,' driven by the two different ways in which the un- operates. Basically, the story of the return of the repressed links the two ways of producing the *unheimlich* in a chain of psychic events: something familiar becomes unfamiliar and hidden, only to return to the familiar as unfamiliar. The un- both negates (repression) and releases (revelation). Further, this revelation is disruptive: it negates the familiar. Freud captures all three moments when he follows Schelling in taking the '*unheimlich*' to designate that which "ought to have remained secret and hidden but has come to light."[21]

The true efficient cause of Freud's uncanny affect is the 'certain circumstance' under which the repressed is prompted to return—whatever

---

[21] Freud, "The Uncanny," 225.

entity or event sparks the return, to which the affect attaches itself. But there is nothing similar in Heidegger's picture, so for the sake of allowing Freud's picture to illuminate Heidegger's let me posit that the repressed can return entirely on its own. What allows it to do so is that neither un- entirely succeeds in its operation. First, repression (the negating un-) is an imperfect mechanism. It seeks to effect an absence or lack but can never entirely divest us of something that belongs to us. It is always possible for this privation to be undone or reversed. That is, it is always possible for the reversing-releasing un- to spring into operation, undoing the repres- sion.[22] But, second, the reversing-releasing un- does not operate perfectly either. What is repressed is not simply unveiled; the *unheimlich* secret is revealed or released *as a secret*. The un- does not bring the secret fully into the open, overcoming hiddenness or concealment. It only makes the concealment manifest as such. This is why, finally, this revelation is dis- ruptive: it introduces something still unfamiliar into the familiar. So what drives or permits the arising of the uncanny affect is the imperfect opera- tion of both un-'s. The familiar is never fully repressed and the repressed is never fully revealed.

The Efficient Cause: Heidegger's Un—

To give a Freudian reading of the *un-* of Heidegger's '*unheimlich*,' we would need to distinguish two senses of '*heimlich*,' roughly along the lines that Freud did: the homely and the secret. In the case of our uncan- ny essence, these will amount to the proper or own and the concealed, respectively. The Freudian hypothesis is that the two senses of *un-* will each operate (imperfectly) on one of these senses of '*heimlich*.' When '*heimlich*' means proper, the negating un- will mark its privation: the not own or improper. When '*heimlich*' means concealed, the reversing- releasing un- will undo or reverse it, allowing the concealed to show up as such:

---

[22] There is of course more to be said about why this is so. Thus Anneleen Masschelein explains it slightly differently: "The prefix 'un-' is not merely a linguistic negation, it is the 'token of repression'. This entails that the uncanny is marked by the unconscious that does not know negation or contradiction; even when something is negated, it still remains present in the unconscious. According to this reasoning, the contradiction resulting from negation is not exclusive or binary: denying something at the same time conjures it up." Anneleen Masschelein, *The Unconcept: The Freudian Uncanny in Late-Twentieth-Century Theory* (Albany: State University of New York Press, 2011), 8; see also 36.

heimlich₁ (homely, familiar) + negating un-	=	*unheimlich₁* (unfamiliar)
heimlich₂ (secret) + reversing-releasing un-	=	*unheimlich₂* (revealed secret)

There are, of course, several problems with this approach. They are born of the fact that it changes the subject. Whereas Freud's model is beholden to the meanings of the German terms, the model applied to Heidegger is beholden to his account of Dasein's essence. There is no reason to think that Heidegger's account of Dasein's essence should fit with Freud's analysis of the German term '*unheimlich*.' Accordingly, it is far from clear that the Heideggerian appropriation of the two senses of '*heimlich*' as the proper and the concealed is legitimate, either linguistically or philosophically. It is also not clear that we still see a semantic merging in either direction—which, of course, is the phenomenon that Freud set out to explain. In looking for a semantic merging, however, we do see a crucial feature of Heidegger's picture. While the improper *(unheimlich₁)* does not semantically merge with its opposite *(heimlich₂)*, it does take it as its content. What is improper to Dasein turns out to consist in the concealed. There are also important similarities between Heidegger's picture and Freud's, which we notice when we retell Heidegger's story of uncanniness on the Freudian model:

1.	There is something that is proper to Dasein: its essence.	*heimlich₁* (proper, own)
2.	There is something that is not proper to Dasein: its non-essence.	+ negating un- = *unheimlich₁* (not own, improper)
3.	What is not proper to Dasein is concealment.	= *heimlich₂* (concealed)
4.	However, the negating un- operates imperfectly: concealment is not in fact simply opposed to Dasein's essence. Dasein's essence is to be open or unconcealing, but all unconcealing requires concealment (the withdrawal of being).	
5.	So, when Dasein discloses (and so comes to) its own essence, it reveals that concealment belongs to it.	= reversing-releasing un-
6.	This revelation reveals concealment as such.	= *unheimlich₂* (concealed revealed)
7.	This revealed concealment excludes Dasein from its essence, or makes it finite—including in Dasein's essence the non-essence.	= *unheimlich₁* (not own, improper)

To be uncanny is for the concealed *(heimlich₂)* qua the improper *(unheimlich₁)* to be revealed *(unheimlich₂)* and so constituted as belonging to the proper *(heimlich₁)*—while still being improper to it *(unheimlich₁)*. As on Freud's story, what drives uncanniness is the imperfection of the operation of the two un-'s—here, the facts that the non-essence is never entirely excluded from the essence and that the revelation of Dasein's concealed ground reveals only concealment.

On this telling, Heidegger's uncanny has the structure of Freud's return of the repressed. This is hardly a surprise. It is easy to gloss Heidegger's uncanniness using the general structure of the uncanny that I developed in Chapter 1. Uncanniness is the inclusion (return) of what is excluded or outside (the repressed) as excluded, which disrupts the sphere of inclusion or the inside (familiarity). We can replace the Freudian terms with Heideggerian terms to generate Heidegger's uncanniness: the inclusion (finding) of what is excluded or outside (the non-essence) as excluded, which disrupts (excludes) the inside (the essence).

That Heidegger's story works on the Freudian model suggests that we should hear the un- of 'uncanniness' as both the negating un- and the reversing-releasing un-. It can be difficult to do the latter since 'homely' (*heimlich*) is not a verb but an adjective, which makes the negating un- grammatically more appropriate. Thus we tend to hear 'unhomely' as the lack of a property—indeed, as the lack of something proper. Being homely or at home is proper to us (especially insofar as it is tied to familiarity), and accordingly unhomeliness or uncanniness seems to be an imperfection. Indeed, there are passages in HI where Heidegger suggests that what is at stake in uncanniness is the negating un- alone. These give us reason to doubt that the reversing-releasing un- is involved in the play of uncanniness.

Of course, insofar as it produces a lack, the negating un- cannot be appropriate to Dasein's being. We learn as much in SZ, which defines a lack in terms of the negating un- as "when something which ought to be and which can be is missing," where 'missing' means "not-being-present-at-hand" (SZ283). To describe Dasein with one of these words is to imply that Dasein is missing something that it ought to have. But even—or especially—in its finitude, Dasein is precisely what it ought to be. As Heidegger puts it, "in existence there can be nothing lacking" (SZ283). This is because Dasein is not present-at-hand, but it is also because Dasein is essentially incomplete or essentially finite.

But in HI and elsewhere, Heidegger insists that an understanding of the negative purely as privative is impoverished, suggesting that an alternative interpretation of the negating un- is possible. He accuses Platonic-Christian metaphysics of taking the Greek negation '*mē*' as "the lesser, something that ought not to be" (HI77/95) and in doing so "eliminat[ing] in advance the 'negative' moment in the uncanny" (HI77/95). The "'un-' in the un-homely does not express a mere lack or simply a shortcoming" (HI84–85/104) but "retains its own essence and does not assume the role of something that could or ought to be eliminated and overcome" (HI84/104). Thus we cannot take the un- "in a merely negative way, in accordance with the sound of the word: mere not-being" (HI73/89). What Heidegger most likely means is that the lack should be thought as a positive phenomenon and not merely as a deficiency. He puts the point this way when interpreting Aristotle's notion of *sterēsis*. *Sterēsis* is "an 'absence': a being-present of something of whose presence an absence is constitutive, absence in the sense of deficiency, of lack. This being-there in the sense of lack is completely peculiar and positive. If I say of a human being: 'I miss him very much, he is not there', I, precisely, do not say that he is not at hand, but assert *a completely determinate way of his being-there for me*. Most things, insofar as they are there, are never *fully* there for me, but are always characterized by *absence, by not-being-thus as they genuinely could and should be.*"[23] This is, of course, the familiar Sartrean point that absence shows up to us and so has positive phenomenal content. It must be thought in this positivity rather than as a *mere* lack or deficit. Given this, it seems that what Heidegger is saying in HI is that the un- of 'uncanniness' is the negating un- but that we have to take care to understand this negating properly.

Yet Heidegger's own vocabulary of counterturning and reversal strongly suggests that there is a reversing-releasing un- at work in uncanniness. Heidegger never glosses uncanniness as a lack, positive or otherwise, but always as a counterturning *(Gegenwendigkeit)* or *katastrophē* (counter *(kata)* turning *(strophē))*. As we know, uncanniness is "a counterturning within the essence of the human being" (HI85/105), such that "the human being itself, in its essence is a *katastrophē*—a reversal that turns it away from its own essence" (HI77/94). The notions of reversal and counterturning are thematic in the *Ister* lectures because Hölderlin's poem describes the river Ister as appearing to flow backwards, which Heidegger understands as a "mysterious counterflow" (HI143/178). But even in EM, Heidegger uses the same term to describe the reciprocal relation between being and the human being (i.e., the opening of openness in the finding of original concealment) (EM173/124; *'Gegenwendigen'* is translated in the English text as 'oppositional'). This language also resonates with SZ's talk of falling *qua* the flight from uncanniness as a 'turning.'[24]

[23] Martin Heidegger, *Basic Concepts of Aristotelian Philosophy,* trans. Robert D. Metcalf and Mark B. Tanzer (Bloomington: Indiana University Press, 2009), 210–211.

[24] In fact, Heidegger often uses the vocabulary of turning and turning back to describe Dasein. For example: "Perhaps the essence of man is precisely an intrinsic re-flection, an original turning-towards that is a re-turn, but one that entails the turning away and that which is turned away taking over and gaining the upper hand." Martin Heidegger, *Heraklit*

That uncanniness is a counterturning suggests (as I claimed in Chapter 3) that its un- is the counter-: a reversing-releasing un-.[25]

But if the un- is reversing-releasing, then it is already a mode of openness. Notice that, on the Freudian telling of Heidegger's story of uncanniness, the reversing-releasing un- is the content of the first sense of '*heimlich*': Dasein's own or proper, the essence. Dasein's essence is to be open or revealing; the reversing-releasing un- is this unconcealing.[26] So what is proper to Dasein (*heimlich₁*) is the reversing-releasing un-; the un- is Dasein's *heimlich*. It is not that the *unheimlich* is a species of the *heimlich*, as on Freud's story, but that the power of the un- belongs to the *heimlich* that it modifies. So the un- that opens Dasein's openness is already a mode of openness.

Further, it is already an *uncanny* mode of openness. To see this, consider an alternative reading: that what Heidegger is trying to capture with the notion of turning or reversal is what I have called the 'imperfection' of the operation of the un-'s. As we saw, the negating un- does not simply exclude and the reversing-releasing un- does not entirely unconceal. It is such 'imperfection' that drives Freud's uncanny affect and Heidegger's uncanniness. Recall that Dasein's uncanny exclusion from its essence is not a straightforward privation, as if being excluded from openness rendered Dasein *not open*. Heidegger marks this distinction in HI by contrasting the uncanny human being with the adventurer. The adventurer "remains homeless on account of his lack of rootedness"; he is characterized by a "not being within the homely, a mere departing and breaking free from the homely" (HI73/89). The adventurer is not uncanny but "merely not-homely [*nicht heimisch*]" (HI74/91) in the sense of the negating un-. The uncanny human being is not home*less* in this way; if anything it is home*sick* (FCM5) because precisely in being expelled from the home, the human being remains related to it.[27] This

---

(Frankfurt: Klostermann, 1979), 209. Cited in Haar, *Heidegger and the Essence of Man*, 142–143; English translation forthcoming from Continuum.

[25] Heidegger thinks the un- as the counter- also in his *Parmenides* lectures, in the context of truth: "The opposite to 'truth' is called, briefly and succinctly, 'untruth'. The word 'untruth', and likewise the word 'un-just', do not ordinarily mean for us simply a failure of justice or a lack of truth. Exactly as 'in-justice' is counter to justice, against justice, so is 'untruth' counter to truth." Heidegger, *Parmenides*, 65. However, Heidegger undermines the natural interpretation of what it is to be counter: "[W]e might wonder whether the 'counter' must necessarily have the sense of the purely adverse and hostile." Ibid., 67.

[26] We do not find a corresponding peculiarity on Freud's picture. His reversing-releasing un- may be proper to the psyche but it does not coincide with one of the senses of *heimlich*.

[27] Heidegger draws the same distinction when he reflects on truth, pointing out that the unconcealed is not opposed to the concealed but remains related to it: "And since *lēthē* pertains to the essence of *alētheia*, un-concealedness itself cannot be the mere *elimination* of

persisting relation—that is, the imperfect operation of the un-—seems to be what Heidegger holds is distinctively counter- in our uncanniness. (I also interpreted the un- and the counter- in this way in Chapter 3.)

If this is right, then in order to understand the efficient cause of uncanniness we must understand the 'imperfect' operation of the un-. What kind of negativity is *this*? The only clue that Heidegger gives us is the enigmatic reference to evil in HI: "We approach whatever belongs to the 'un-' [*das Un-artigen*] more closely in recognizing it as that which belongs to evil [*das Bös-artige*], provided we do not conceive of evil in the sense of something morally bad, that is, as characteristic of human activity, but rather as an essential trait of being itself" (HI78/96). This is the only substantive mention of evil in HI, and evil has not arisen explicitly as a theme in either EM or SZ. Heidegger tells us that evil is not a matter of sin: "the 'negative' is different in kind from 'sin', that is, different from transgression or rebellion—understood in a quite specific respect—against a God of creation and redemption, again understood in a specific respect" (HI84/104). Evil may be transgressive or defiant but it is not a defiance against the order of things, the essence, or against destiny. This is not new; we know that Dasein comes to its essence in uncanniness. So evil cannot be an absence of perfection, *nihil privativum*. What then is this evil—and what is it as a positive feature of being?

In his Nietzsche lectures, Heidegger attributes the notion that "evil [is] proper to the essence of Being" to German Idealism, and he quotes Hegel's attempt to posit a negativity that is not simple negation.[28] But it is in Schelling that we find "[t]he greatest attempt in this direction."[29] In his lectures on Schelling's *Of Human Freedom*, Heidegger explains Schelling's account of evil *(Böse)* as malice, arguing that it is to be understood as a reversal or revolt.[30]

---

concealedness. The *a* in *a-lētheia* in no way means simply an undetermined universal 'un-' and 'not'. Rather, the saving and conserving of the un-concealed is necessarily in relation to concealment, understood as the withdrawal of what appears in its appearing." Heidegger, *Parmenides*, 124.

[28] Heidegger, *Nietzsche*, Vol. I: *The Will to Power as Art*, trans. David Farrell Krell (New York: Harper-Collins, 1991), 62. The Hegel quote says that Spirit "is not this power as something positive that averts its glance from everything negative, as when we say of something that it is nothing, or false, and that now we are done with it and can leave it behind and go on to something else; rather, it is this power only insofar as it looks the negative in the eye and lingers with it." Cited in ibid., 61–62. Compare G. W. F. Hegel, *Phenomenology of Spirit*, trans. A. V. Miller (Oxford: Oxford University Press, 1977), 19.

[29] Heidegger, *Nietzsche*, Vol. I, 62.

[30] Martin Heidegger, *Schelling's Treatise on the Essence of Human Freedom*, trans. Joan Stambaugh (Athens: Ohio University Press, 1985), 144.

By way of clarifying malice Schelling mentions disease. Disease makes itself felt to 'feeling' as something very real, not just as a mere absence of something. When a man is sick, we do say that he 'is not quite all right' (*dass ihm etwas 'fehle'*) and thus express the sickness merely negatively as a lack. But this: 'Why is he not quite right?' ('*Wo fehlt es?*') really means 'What is the matter with him, something which has, so to speak, gotten loose from the harmony of being healthy and, being on the loose, wants to take over all of existence and dominate it?' In the case of sickness, there is not just something lacking, but something wrong. 'Wrong' not in the sense of something only incorrect, but in the genuine sense of falsification, distortion and reversal. [. . .] Disease is not only a disruption, but a reversal of the whole existence which takes over the total condition and dominates it.[31]

In this passage, Heidegger begins by noting that the negating un- has positive phenomenal content but switches quickly to a different negativity, which he glosses in terms of domination, distortion, and wrongness. The key concepts, however, are disease and disharmony.

Just as error is sometimes "not a lack of intelligence, but twisted intelligence," so too disease is not a lack of health but a reversal of something.[32] Heidegger turns to the musical metaphor: "What replaces the place of harmony and attunement is disharmony, the wrong tone which enters the whole."[33] Evil is un-settling and dis-placing; it shifts the harmony of the whole into disharmony. This nest of metaphors has, of course, a Platonic source: the *harmonia* of the three parts of the soul makes for virtue—in

---

[31] Heidegger, *Schelling's Treatise*, 143–144. Although these lectures were delivered in 1936, Heidegger had held an advanced seminar on Schelling in 1941, only a year before the HI lectures. Thus Schelling's conception of evil would have been fresh in his mind. Heidegger's notes for the advanced seminar (which are included in an appendix to the earlier lecture course) show that he continues to understand Schelling's concept of evil in the same way: "the most extreme discord and repulsion against beings as a whole and within beings as a whole." Ibid., 177. An extended reading of Heidegger's Schelling lectures in light of the problematic of uncanniness would be most productive—particularly for further integrating the vocabulary of uncanniness into that of being. Derrida points the way for this: "This evil is inscribed in desire, and, like desire itself, it carries in it a motivity, an 'adversed mobility' (*gegenwendige Bewegtheit*): go out of oneself and return into oneself (*Schelling* . . . , p. 150 [p. 125]). The evil of this *Sehnsucht* which gives the impulsion to go out of oneself in order to return to oneself, or to return to oneself so as to go out of oneself, is the essence of spirit of which Hölderlin speaks as poet." Jacques Derrida, *Of Spirit: Heidegger and the Question*, trans. Geoffrey Bennington and Rachel Bowlby (Chicago: The University of Chicago Press, 1991), 80. More generally, the German Idealist tradition is a rich source for further investigation of the phenomenon that Heidegger calls 'uncanniness.' It would be particularly instructive to consider whether this is related to the regular appearance of the aesthetic concept of uncanniness in this tradition.

[32] Heidegger, *Schelling's Treatise*, 120.

[33] Ibid., 144.

contrast to injustice, which is a disharmony and disease.[34] What is most striking and powerful about the musical metaphor in both cases is that something disharmonious or discordant is not so in comparison to a potential harmoniousness. It does not fall short of some standard but is disharmonious on its own terms, in reference to itself. (Imagine strumming a guitar that is quite out of tune; one need not know what it sounds like to play the guitar *in tune* in order to hear that the guitar is currently out of tune.) For something to be disharmonious is for it to be out of tune with *itself*. I argued the same thing at the end of Chapter 2 when I suggested that if (as Dreyfus puts it) there is something wrong with Dasein then this 'wrongness' is not a falling short of some standard of 'rightness.' This is not to divorce all talk of wrongness or disharmony from talk of rightness or harmony. In attributing disease to something, we do implicitly appeal to a condition of health. But, like disharmony, disease or wrongness is problematic *in itself* and not primarily in comparison to something else. (Something of the force of this distinction comes through in the contrast between the colloquial expression 'that is *all wrong* (incoherent)' and the expression 'this is wrong (incorrect)'.) Heidegger gestures towards something like this distinction when he says of guilt that "[e]xistential nullity has by no means the character of a privation, where something is lacking in comparison with an ideal which has been set up but does not get attained in Dasein; rather, the being of this entity is already null *as projection*" (SZ285). Similarly, disease is wrong *as a condition of the body* and not as lacking in comparison to the ideal of a healthy condition.

Invoking evil, understood *via* Schelling, invokes a disharmony or reversal that has a positive phenomenal character. The finitude or negativity in question is not a lack, a gap, absence, or limit. Rather, it must be a modification of the whole that is complete in itself and that has its own

---

[34] The virtuous or just person "puts himself in order, is his own friend, and harmonizes the three parts of himself like three limiting notes in a musical scale—high, low and middle. He binds together those parts and any others there may be in between, and from having been many things he becomes entirely one, moderate and harmonious." Plato, *Republic*, trans. G. M. A. Grube and C. D. C. Reeve, *Plato: Complete Works*, ed. John M. Cooper and D. S. Hutchinson (Indianapolis, IN: Hackett Publishing, 1997), 443d–e. Injustice, the opposite, is "a kind of civil war between the three parts, a meddling and doing of another's work, a rebellion by some part against the whole soul." Ibid., 444b. The term translated as 'civil war' *(stasis)* has the sense of political factionalism, as if the parts of the soul are at cross-purposes. In the *Sophist*, Plato links this term explicitly with disease: "wickedness is discord [*stasis*] and sickness [*nosos*] of the soul." Plato, *The Sophist*, trans. Nicholas P. White, *Plato: Complete Works*, 228b. The notes on the *Republic* 444b in the Perseus Digital Library point to *Republic* 440e and the *Sophist* 228b for comparison. Paul Shorey, *Plato, Republic*, Perseus Digital Library, available at http://www.perseus.tufts.edu/hopper/text?doc=Perseus%3Atext%3A1999.01.0168%3Abook%3D4%3Asection%3D444b

coherence and integrity. What makes it 'wrong' is that it is in some way internally incoherent; its integrity is somehow at odds with itself. So evil is a self-standing condition or arrangement of something that is internally, or on its own terms, reversed, unstable, disharmonious, distorted.

Disease and disharmony are to serve as models for understanding the 'evil' of being and the imperfect operation of the un- of 'uncanniness' (HI78/96). First, what is the evil or reversal in being? It is the counter-turning of being's presencing into absencing. If absencing is like a disease, then it must be understood not as a failure or limit of presencing but as a variety of it. It is the kind of presencing in which presencing comes to pass disharmoniously. Presencing in the manner of absencing is just like the body being arranged (presencing) in a diseased (absencing) way. Presencing in the manner of absencing is of course *pelein,* and so the internal disharmony or discord is none other than the *polemos* internal to being or between being and the human being. Thus evil as a characteristic of being is *pelein* or uncanniness.

So too for the un- of Dasein's uncanniness, which negates or reveals in an 'imperfect' way. This un- must happen in a disharmonious or diseased manner: privation comes to pass in a way that includes (negating un-); unconcealment comes to pass in a way that conceals (reversing-revealing un-). This disease is, once again and of course, *pelein.* So the un- itself happens in any uncanny way. It is already a mode of openness, and it is already a mode of openness that is uncanny. (Note that this uncanny presencing in the manner of absencing differs from *sterēsis. Sterēsis* may be thought as a way of being present by means of being absent, and so is a presencing in the manner of absencing. But it is not an entity's *proper* way of presencing; *pelein* refers to a presencing-by-absencing in which an entity enters fully into presence. In *sterēsis,* the absence remains a contingent imperfection: *"not-being-thus as they genuinely could and should be."*)[35]

The efficient cause of uncanniness is thus uncanniness. If we locate the power of efficient causality in the un- of 'uncanniness,' then (i) this power cannot be simple privation, since it is a mode of presencing; (ii) if this un- is the reversing-releasing un- then its power lies in the *heimlich:* in already being a mode of openness; (iii) and if the power of efficient causality lies in the imperfect operation of the reversing-releasing un-, then it lies in uncanniness. So what drives the production of uncanniness on Heidegger's story is uncanniness itself. To tell the story of how the *un-* operates on the *heimlich,* we must help ourselves to the *Unheimlichkeit*

---

[35] Heidegger, *Basic Concepts of Aristotelian Philosophy,* 211.

that is produced. What makes Dasein finitely open is its already finite openness. This says that Dasein is uncanny because it is uncanny, or that uncanniness is its own efficient cause. Seeking the efficient cause of uncanniness in the power of its prefix returns us to the indissoluble questionability of uncanniness.

The Final Cause: Love and Perfectionism

The last of Aristotle's four causes is the final cause. The final cause is the real or apparent good, which determines and organizes any process that seeks to attain or possess it. To express Dasein's uncanniness in telic terms, we must return to the vocabulary of seeking the homely. We might gloss this seeking as specifically erotic since love—according to Heidegger—"is the essential will for what is of the essence" (HI131/164).[36] That which is properly *of* Dasein's essence, and so that which it seeks or wills, is being (the homely). Being is that to which openness is open, as well as that on the basis of which it is at all (i.e., it is both the whence and the whither of thrownness). To *will* being is to strive to disclose it—to bring it into presencing. This is Dasein's seeking the homely or being the open site.

What is 'of the essence' can be willed only if one does not have it: only if one is excluded from the essence. We might recall here a line from a draft of Hölderlin's "Bread and Wine" which Heidegger discusses later in HI: "Colony, and bold forgetting spirit loves" (HI131/164). Spirit loves colony: that which belongs to it but which it does not have, or that which it has but which does not belong to it (depending on how we understand 'colony'). Being excluded from the essence or expelled from the hearth prompts the will for what is of the essence: love. So Dasein is on the way to its essence. Because it is grounded in an openness to a closedness—because (its) being is withdrawn from it—Dasein is an erotic striving to be itself.

---

[36] Heidegger rarely speaks of love and nowhere does he advance a definitive position on it. But he does seem to have a consistent view on what kind of phenomenon it is. For example: reading Plato, he interprets the love of which Socrates speaks as "the urge toward Being itself." Martin Heidegger, *Plato's Sophist*, trans. Richard Rojcewicz and André Schuwer (Bloomington: Indiana University Press, 1997), 219. More than a decade later, reading Nietzsche, he says, "*Amor*—love—is to be understood as *will,* the will that wants whatever it loves to be what it is in essence." Martin Heidegger, *Nietzsche,* Vol. II: *The Eternal Recurrence of the Same,* trans. David Farrell Krell (New York: Harper Collins, 1991), 207. For an account of Heidegger on love which resembles my own, see Giorgio Agamben, "The Passion of Facticity," in *Potentialities: Collected Essays in Philosophy,* trans. and ed. Daniel Heller-Roazen (Stanford, CA: Stanford University Press, 1999).

Thus far, the picture resembles Plato's account of human nature in Aristophanes's speech in the *Symposium*. Recall that, as Aristophanes tells it, human beings are halved creatures, erotically striving to reclaim their original wholeness. The story ends with Hephaestus offering to weld two halves together, saying, "Look at your love, and see if this is what you desire: wouldn't this be all the good fortune you could want?"[37] Aristophanes seems to think it is, but Plato's rhetorical question should give us pause. It reminds us that even before we were split we were already erotic creatures. In fact, we were cut in half as punishment for our efforts at self-transcendence. So being welded back together will not make us happy or satisfy our desire, because even in our whole condition we were lovers. Our erotic nature is not only a consequence of a punishment but also the cause of it. It occurs both at the beginning and the end of the story.

So too on Heidegger's picture. Dasein strives for being because being is withdrawn from it, but being is withdrawn from it only because Dasein first strives to disclose being. This is the point that we saw earlier in the story of philosophizing: we seek to know because we encounter the unintelligible but we can only encounter the unintelligible because we seek to know. Heidegger seems to make a similar point when he describes love as the prelude, rather than the consequence, of uncanniness. Early in HI when discussing Hölderlin's "Voice of the People," Heidegger notes that the human being loves the rivers, which "tear [. . .] the human being out of the habitual midst of its life, so that it may be in a center outside of itself, that is, be excentric" (HI28/32). The rivers are being, the withdrawing of which excludes ('tears' *(reissen)*) Dasein from its essence. Heidegger goes on to say that love is the prelude to this exclusion: "The prelude [*Vorstufe*] to inhering [*das Innehalten*] in the excentric midst of human existence, this 'centric' and 'central' abode in the excentric, is love" (HI28/32–33). The erotic quest to disclose being (i.e., loving the rivers) must be posited at the beginning of the story of uncanniness (i.e., the story of becoming excentric)—as well as at the end. We encounter again the non-linearity of the story.

We can solve the problem for Aristophanes by distinguishing the original striving to be god-like from the striving to be whole. The former is entirely self-transcending—a striving to be what one is not. The latter is a striving to be what one is. We cannot do this on Heidegger's story, since the erotic striving at the beginning is the same as that at the end: the

[37] Plato, *Symposium*, trans. Alexander Nehamas and Paul Woodruff (Indianapolis, IN: Hackett Publishing, 1989), 192e.

striving to attain the essence or to be what one is. This opens Heidegger's picture to a further worry: the well-known paradox of self-becoming that attends some perfectionist views. Dasein strives for or seeks its own essence, and yet an essence is always something that an entity already is or was *(to ti ēn einai)*. Put differently, the imperative to 'become what one is' seems empty since it calls us to achieve something that has, in some sense, already been achieved. To become something is not yet to be that, so how can one become something that one already is? The very notion of erotically striving for what is of the essence seems incoherent.

There are various ways to make sense of the idea that an entity strives to fulfill its essence or to become what it is.[38] For each, the trick is to find a way in which we can intelligibly be *not* what we are. Aristophanes either solves or covers over the problem with the mythical temporality of his story, which posits our original wholeness as something that we once had but have since lost. Because of the gods' punishment, we were but are no longer in our essence, and this explains why we must strive to attain it. To solve the problem for Heidegger, we would have to make sense of the idea that the non-essence is already included in the essence. But this would be a solution to the wrong problem, for we have left out the most important part of the story—the part of the story that distinguishes the questionability of Dasein's uncanniness from the traditional paradox of self-becoming: Dasein comes to its essence precisely in being underway to it. Dasein is not just self-becoming; it is *essentially* self-becoming.

Dasein must indeed come to be what it is, but—as we know—Dasein fails in this. As Heidegger puts it, Dasein is "that homely that seeks yet does not find itself, because it seeks itself by way of a distancing and alienation from itself" (HI84/103). This is what Diotima's picture of erotic human nature adds to Aristophanes's: what we erotically seek is impossible to attain.[39] As with the desire for self-transcendence at the beginning of Aristophanes's story, Diotima's story posits love not as a striving to become what we are but as a striving to become more than we are. We desire to possess the good in the way that the gods do: immortally.

[38] For a coherent and compelling interpretation of cases of Dasein as self-becoming in SZ, see Iain Thomson, "Heidegger's Perfectionist Philosophy of Education in *Being and Time*," *Continental Philosophy Review* 37 (2004): 439–467.

[39] Compare Lear's deployment of the vocabulary of erotic finitude, which differs from Plato's and Heidegger's because the finitude in question for Lear is not the impossibility of attaining the goal but the lack of direction in the erotic striving (which is in turn based on the inherent instability of ideals). Nonetheless, Heidegger's uncanniness shares with Lear's an erotic passion or commitment, which (as we saw in Chapter 1) we do not necessarily find in other accounts of uncanniness.

But this is impossible for mortal creatures like us. We cannot possess the good immortally, just as Dasein cannot bring being to full presence or fully disclose its own essence. This is impossible because being—and so Dasein—is essentially finite, essentially self-absencing. So our efforts ultimately fail—although, just as on Diotima's picture they nonetheless yield creative products (offspring, poetry, laws, philosophy), on Heidegger's story they allow entities to show up.

But this failure does not simply mean that Dasein fails to attain its essence, for in this very failure Dasein comes to be what it is. Recall that Heidegger describes love as the *essential* will for what is of the essence. If Dasein essentially seeks the homely, then its essence is not that which it seeks but its own unfulfilled seeking. Dasein's seeking or willing *is* its essence. So Dasein's essence is to seek its own essence. This introduces a negative moment into the story of self-becoming: precisely in *not* being itself, Dasein is itself. This is why the story of Dasein's uncanniness is not a story about Dasein fulfilling its essence and becoming itself but a story about failing to be what it is and thereby succeeding in being what it is. Heidegger's perfectionism turns out to be an imperfectionism.

If this is right, then Dasein's 'diseased' or uncanny openness is its own kind of 'health.' Or rather, Dasein has no possibility of 'real health' or full openness. To be 'healthy' or to fully disclose (its) being would be no longer to be Dasein.[40] This point is perhaps implicit in Plato's dialogue but it is most clearly expressed in Shel Silverstein's picture book *The Missing Piece*.[41] The central character is a circle with a wedge missing from it who embarks upon the erotic, Aristophanean quest to find its 'missing piece.' Eventually it locates the piece that completes it but finds that with the missing piece in place it can no longer be the kind of thing that it is or do the things it does. It can no longer talk to worms, smell flowers, play with butterflies, or sing its song of searching. So it surrenders its miss-

[40] Similarly for Freud: the psyche can never be in perfect harmony; to be a psyche is to be a little neurotic. So too, of course, for being as uncanny. Being must presence by manner of absencing. There is no pure presence, no pure unconcealment. Thus Heidegger: "What is counter to *alētheia* is neither simply the opposite, nor the bare lack, nor the rejection of it as mere denial. *Lēthē*, the oblivion of withdrawing concealment, is that withdrawal by means of which alone the essence of *alētheia* can be preserved and thus be and remain unforgotten." Heidegger, *Parmenides*, 127.

[41] Shel Silverstein, *The Missing Piece* (New York: Harper Collins, 1976). It is surprising that this text has not received more philosophical attention. The only philosophical reference to it that I know of is Žižek's brief treatment, in which he reads the story as "narrat[ing] the myth of how the it (the Lacanian lamella) constitutes itself as a desiring subject through a lack." Slavoj Žižek, *Enjoy Your Symptom!: Jacques Lacan in Hollywood and Out* (New York: Routledge, 2001), viii.

ing piece, recognizing that it was most fully and perfectly itself precisely in its state of incompleteness. To complete itself would be no longer to be itself. Similarly, Dasein strives to disclose (its) being but if it were to accomplish this without absencing then it would cease to be ontological entirely. Attaining the *telos* would amount to surrendering it. This shows that Dasein is an entity that fully attains its *telos* precisely in its ongoing quest to attain it.

Thomas Sheehan has analyzed Dasein in these terms, providing also the requisite conceptual background in Aristotle. Although he does not use the word 'uncanniness,' Sheehan is clearly making the same point. His vocabulary also resonates with that with which both Heidegger and I have glossed uncanniness.

> Dasein—the human essence—is whole and complete *in* its incompleteness. Its ontological perfection is to be imperfect, with no prospect of achieving an ideal perfection in the future. Like God, Dasein has always-already come into its own, but its own-ness is its human finitude. Ontologically Dasein is 'frozen' in its movedness or becoming (even though ontically it is always becoming this or that).[42]
>
> Dasein has always already come into its own, and its own is its perfectly imperfect finitude. Human being, therefore, is ontologically bivalent. (a) Insofar as it is *imperfect,* it is a lack; but that lack is also a longing (a desire), and a belonging—even if there is nothing to belong *to* and no 'something else' to long *for.* This means that human being is off-center, eccentric, a protention that is going nowhere—Dasein is essentially self-absent. (b) But insofar as it is *perfect,* Dasein also has presence, although a radically finite presence: not self-coincident but distended; not a unity but parts-outside-of-parts; not a pure mind but a self-concerned body. Yet for all its distension, human being is held together in a tension of difference and synthesis. In fact, it *is* that tension. This self-concerned, self-aware body, this distended tension that ultimately intends itself, is the *world* engendered by human being. In fact it *is* human being itself.[43]

This is a concise summary of Dasein's uncanniness in the Aristotelian language of perfection. Sheehan describes Dasein's 'seeking the homely' and emphasizes that Dasein comes to its essence in failing to attain it. Thus "Dasein's becoming is always an end in itself rather than a step towards a further goal."[44] Dasein's "perfection is to be imperfect."[45]

---

[42] Thomas Sheehan, "Dasein," in *A Companion to Heidegger,* ed. Hubert L. Dreyfus and Mark A. Wrathall (Malden, MA: Blackwell Publishing, 2007), 205.
[43] Ibid., 206.
[44] Ibid., 205.
[45] Ibid., 205.

We can now see that the problem or paradox in uncanniness—understood in terms of the final cause—is that Dasein seems to have two essential *teloi*: its own essence as seeking and its essence as that which it seeks. These correspond to the two essences that we considered positing at the end of Chapter 3: the essence from which Dasein departs (and so which it seeks or loves) and the essence to which Dasein comes (i.e., its essence as seeking or finite). In seeking (its) being, Dasein is not yet itself and so seeks itself. It is finite in an erotic way. And in being essentially this seeking, Dasein is erotic in a finite way. But how can Dasein thus come to its essence by failing to attain it? How can it be most fully at home when it is unhomely? How, that is, can disease be Dasein's most proper health? Heidegger puts Dasein's condition by saying that it is essentially homesick (FCM5): it is essentially a seeking of (its) being. We can put the same point by saying that Dasein is essentially lovesick. Love is Dasein's disease: its internally disharmonious presencing in the manner of absencing.

Uncanniness as Play

Whether we approach it as a material, formal, efficient, or final cause, the ground of uncanniness shows itself to be question-worthy. As a final cause, it is perversely doubled: the essence is the seeking of the essence. As an efficient cause, it is perversely fractal: the un- that drives uncanniness is itself uncanniness. As a formal cause, it is perversely non-linear: an essential story that presupposes that which it sets out to explain. The material cause of uncanniness, then, consists in steps in a process that cannot clearly be laid out because it is doubled, fractal, or non-linear. In every case, the ground of uncanniness shows itself to be question-worthy. It has stubbornly remained veiled. In some sense, this result demands that we surrender the task of grounding. The best answer to the question, "How does (owned) Dasein come about?" or "How does uncanniness work?" is "It just does." This can be an irritating position to be in.[46] To ground Dasein in a self-enabling play between its essential openness and the mysterious concealment at its ground—to leave the whence of thrownness so utterly obscure—is to leave the question of how Dasein's

---

[46] Haar, for example, cannot hide his frustration with being's uncanniness: "We are not allowed to ask why being hides itself, absents itself, or why being's relation to the essence of man has taken 'the shape of withdrawal' *(in der Gestalt des Entzugs)*. We can only take note of it. There is no answer. The only answer is, 'That's the way things are, this is *the enigma of being.*" Haar, *Heidegger and the Essence of Man,* 134. "In other words, being is the alpha and omega. We must not ask where it comes from. It emerges from itself." Ibid., 186.

self-grounding is possible in its urgency as a question. What kind of answer is this?

I have called this question 'the question of the uncanny' and so far have addressed it as a question *about* uncanniness and how it hangs together as a coherent account of Dasein's essence. But it is also a question *of* the uncanny in the sense that it constitutes our uncanniness. It is because the question that we have raised is the one that makes us uncanny that the question of the uncanny is most properly worthy of question (HI80/99). It follows also that the question of the uncanny in some sense stands as its own answer. Finally, it will follow that by posing the question of the uncanny, we existentielly perform our uncanniness and—in principle at least—become ownedly uncanny.

Let me begin with the idea that uncanniness is a play. It is so in at least four senses. First, it is a play of sorts in that it is a performance in which something comes to pass. What 'happens' in it is the human essence. But this essence comes to pass as a play in a more recognizable sense. It is an *interplay* or reciprocal back-and-forth between two terms: openness and finitude, revelation and concealment, the essence and the non-essence. This is the sense in which I have been calling uncanniness a 'play' so far. Insofar as we are investigating it, uncanniness is also a play in a third sense: a performance for which we are the audience. Yet there is also an interplay here too, since there is no stable boundary between performance and audience. In 'discovering' any truth about human nature, we are ourselves both spectator and scene. This self-disclosure is thus theatrical in Samuel Weber's sense. Weber argues that 'theatricality' is the character of a medium that continuously disrupts the distinction between observer and observed.[47] This disruption is not a mere shifting of boundaries but a continuous destabili*zing* of boundaries and so of the self-identity of the terms in play. Similarly, in disclosing our essence as uncanny we are not detached observers who "merely observe [human life] in operation," viewing it "as no more than a curiosity, like the ritual of an alien religion."[48] Instead, as we saw in Chapter 4, philosophizing (as being *hupsipolis*) always implicates us and places us in question (i.e., makes us *apolis*). Indeed, many philosophers take the recognition of our human nature to have a profound impact on our lives. I will return to this in a moment.

---

[47] Samuel Weber, *The Legend of Freud*, exp. ed. (Stanford, CA: Stanford University Press, 2000). See especially the Introduction, "Uncanny Thinking."

[48] Thomas Nagel, "The Absurd," *Mortal Questions* (Cambridge: Cambridge University Press, 1991), 17 and 21, respectively.

Just as we are not mere observers of our essence, so too our uncanny essence is not a fixed essence that obtains independently of our discovery of it. Uncanniness is a play in what is perhaps a fourth, or at least an amplified, sense: it is a *purely* theatrical phenomenon. Uncanniness is *nothing but* the coming to pass (first sense) of the interplay (second sense) of spectator and scene (third sense). Uncanniness is nothing other than play. Recall that uncanniness is the revelation of our ground as hidden from us, which revelation is itself our ground. (I put this in Chapter 2 by saying that the obscurity of the whence of thrownness is itself that whence.) The co-implication of spectator and scene is at work in uncanniness itself—as the play of openness and concealment that it reveals. For there would be no ground to uncover were it not for Dasein's openness to it and no openness without the revelation of the ground as concealed. Spectator and scene, unconcealment and concealment, make each other possible in their self-constituting play. So our uncanny essence is not merely characterized by theatricality; it is *constituted* theatrically. Uncanniness *is* play.

How does our explicit, philosophical investigation of uncanniness impact our uncanny essence? It performs it. Notice that our investigation has failed to grasp the ground of uncanniness, which has—shall we say— shown up to us only as concealed, in its essential question-worthiness. Now recall that to be essentially uncanny is for the ground to show up only as concealed/ment, as obscure or question-worthy. Our question *about* the uncanny is the question in which uncanniness consists.

Let me make the same point again. Consider: what precisely is concealed from openness when it attempts to grasp its ground? What is concealed—what our openness cannot open as (our) being withdraws from us—is none other than conceal*ment* itself, as that which operates to produce our finite openness. So what openness cannot disclose of its essence or ground is how absencing is a mode of presencing—how, that is, uncanniness itself works. What we cannot grasp about our own essence, and so what makes us uncanny, is how our uncanniness works as our essence or ground. This is the question that we have failed to answer in this chapter, and the concealment that we have encountered is the concealment that first makes us uncanny.

To restate the conclusion (but not the argument): consider Heidegger's claim that "[s]o abyssally does the process of finitude"—namely, uncanniness—"entrench itself in Dasein that our most proper and deepest finitude refuses to yield to our freedom" (WM93)—that is, to openness. What withholds itself from openness is precisely its finitude, and this withholding or refusal *is* Dasein's finitude. So uncanniness *is* the mysteriousness, concealment, or obscurity that makes us uncanny and so

produces our finite openness. The mystery at our ground is the mysteriousness of how a mystery could be a ground.

This means that our attempt to understand ourselves as uncanny is
an existentiell performance of our essence as uncanny. It follows from
this, first, that our unresolved question about the ground of uncanniness
stands as its own answer. Failing to understand uncanniness, as we have
done, counterturningly amounts to understanding uncanniness, since this
failure *is* our uncanniness. We have found the concealment or obscurity
that grounds uncanniness: the question of the uncanny. So in one sense,
our question remains unanswered: the ground we are seeking is concealed
from us. But in another sense our question is answered: such concealment
is our ground. The unanswered question uncannily answers itself. The
uncanny remains undomesticated, but we have met it in the wild.

This has consequences for becoming owned. We saw that becoming
owned consists in raising the question of what it is to be uncanny ownedly, or risking the distinction between owned and unowned uncanniness
(being *hupsipolis*). We saw also that this question resolves into a question
about the logic of uncanniness (being *apolis*), since what is question-
worthy about ownedness is the same as what is question-worthy about
our uncanny essence. If the question of the uncanny answers itself, then
our question about what it is to be uncanny ownedly also answers itself,
insofar as it stands as an open question. Becoming owned is not a matter
of finding an answer to the question of what it is to be ownedly uncanny
but consists in raising the question of uncanniness in such a way that it
turns counter to itself and answers itself by remaining unanswered.

This returns us to the question of how investigating our essence can
change our lives. Recall that the existential performance of uncanniness
is productive; it is how Dasein 'comes to be' as open. Just as uncanniness
existentially 'produces' Dasein, so too an existentiell performance of uncanniness will produce an owned case of Dasein. Such an existentiell performance—becoming owned—is precisely what we have just rehearsed.
In asking the question of the uncanny, we have re-enacted within our
lives the event of Dasein's uncanny self-grounding in the finding of original concealment. As we investigate uncanniness, we are seeking our own
essential ground—we are cases of Dasein seeking the homely (being *hupsipolis*). As such, we are essentially uncanny; our seeking turns counter
to itself and we become *apolis*. Such seeking fails because (our) being
withdraws from us: the question of the uncanny does not admit of an answer. Thus our ground is found only as concealed. By thus encountering
what is questionable about uncanniness, we encounter our uncanniness

itself as a question. And by posing this question, we enact our essential uncanniness and become ownedly *hupsipolis apolis*.

So what is at stake in raising and maintaining the questionability of uncanniness is not only our intellectual grasp of Heidegger's concept but also our ownedness as cases of Dasein. And—in one final, counter-turning twist—only as thus owned can we begin to engage in genuine philosophizing or be philosophically *hupsipolis apolis* in the first place. Thus Sheehan: "[O]nly in concrete *existentiell* appropriation of oneself as the act of questioning does questioning find its answer, namely, that the meaning of being is questionableness itself. Only in resolve does one enter *Ereignis*; only by taking up personally one's own movement does one authentically discover the movement that is being itself. The meaning of being, as Richardson has said, is not a doctrine to be learned but a risk to be taken."[49] Our questioning of uncanniness makes us owned, and our ownedness is the condition of possibility of the genuine questioning of uncanniness. Like Dasein itself, owned or authentic Dasein makes itself possible in an uncanny leap.

[49] Thomas Sheehan, "On The Way to *Ereignis*: Heidegger's Interpretation of *Physis*," in *Continental Philosophy in America,* ed. H. J. Silverman, J. Sallis, and T. M. Seebohm (Pittsburgh, PA: Duquesne University Press, 1983), 163. The reference to Richardson is to William J. Richardson, S.J., *Heidegger: Through Phenomenology to Thought,* 4th ed. (New York: Fordham University Press, 2003), 551, where Richardson says, "No, foundational thinking is not a doctrine to be taught; it is an experience to be made—an experience that each must make for himself."

Conclusion

UNCANNINESS IS A reflexive finitude. Dasein, the ontico-ontological entity, is unable fully to disclose its own being—specifically, the why and the how of this very finitude. Uncanny Dasein is thus unhomely in, or excluded from, its own essence—and in such a way that, in being excluded from it, it fulfills that essence. 'Uncanny' is not a way of describing how our ordinary surroundings appear in the mood of angst, or even how "one feels [*ist*]" in angst (SZ188). It is not that one feels uncanny; rather, "[i]n angst one is [*ist*] '*uncanny*'" (SZ188, translation altered). One *is* uncanny in the sense that one discloses one's own uncanny being. One might also thereby feel unsettled or unfamiliar with oneself, but the primary phenomenon is existential-ontological rather than affective.

Heidegger's picture of the uncanny human being is not as novel as it might appear. Michel Foucault finds it already in Kant.[1] As Foucault understands it, Kant's project is to respond to skepticism by grounding the possibility of knowing in the human being. Kant's Copernican revolution yields to the modern episteme (including phenomenology) the task of grasping the human being as both the transcendental ground of knowledge and an empirical object of knowledge: "a strange

---

[1] Heidegger does not himself seem to see uncanny Dasein in Kant's thought. Throughout his Kant book, Heidegger understands the finitude of knowing to be its dependence on the given. Martin Heidegger, *Kant and the Problem of Metaphysics,* 5th ed., enl., trans. Richard Taft (Bloomington: Indiana University Press, 1997), 18, 31, 133, 160, 165, 208, 209. But it is worth noting that the Kant book does at least touch on phenomena associated with uncanniness: concealing (ibid., 23, 163, 165), forgetting (163), untruth (98), the non-essence (151), and privation (152); see also ibid. (153), where Heidegger seems to suggest that Kant's initial assumption that the finitude of knowing is its dependence on the given needs to be revisited. Heidegger even seems to raise the question of the uncanny when he suggests that the question of finitude is hard to pose, that it must be performed or played out, and that it will not be answered. Ibid., 154, 163, 166. But whether this is indeed uncanniness, and whether we are to attribute it to Kant or to Heidegger, remains to be determined.

empirico-transcendental doublet, since he is a being such that knowledge will be attained in him of what renders all knowledge possible."[2] Foucault is quite unclear about just what the finitude here is. It either is or produces some sort of reflexive blind spot that the human being necessarily has by virtue of being both subject and object of knowledge. Foucault describes it thus:

> Man has not been able to describe himself as a configuration in the *episteme* without thought at the same time discovering, both in itself and outside itself, at its borders yet also in its very warp and woof, an element of darkness, an apparently inert density in which it is embedded, an unthought which it contains entirely, yet in which it is also caught. The unthought (whatever name we give it) is not lodged in man like a shrivelled-up nature or a stratified history; it is, in relation to man, the Other: the Other that is not only a brother but a twin, born, not of man, nor in man, but beside him and at the same time, in an identical newness, in an unavoidable duality. This obscure space so readily interpreted as an abyssal region in man's nature, or as a uniquely impregnable fortress in his history, is linked to him in an entirely different way; it is both exterior to him and indispensable to him: in one sense, the shadow cast by man as he emerged in the field of knowledge; in another, the blind stain by which it is possible to know him.[3]

Despite its vagueness, we should hear in this description the thematics of the uncanny.

Is the empirico-transcendental doublet identical to uncanny Dasein? Not if the ontological and the ontic, between which uncanny Dasein oscillates, differ from the transcendental and the empirical. But nonetheless, the shape of the oscillation between the two poles, and the paradoxes and problems to which it gives rise, are the same.

---

[2] Michel Foucault, *The Order of Things: An Archaeology of the Human Sciences* (New York: Vintage Books, 1994), 318. I follow Béatrice Han-Pile's reading of Foucault's interpretation of Kant. Béatrice Han, "Foucault and Heidegger on Kant and Finitude," in *Foucault and Heidegger: Critical Encounters,* ed. Alan Milchman and Alan Rosenberg (Minneapolis: University of Minnesota Press, 2003), 127–162; see also (among others) Béatrice Han, "The Analytic of Finitude and the History of Subjectivity," trans. Edward Pile, in *The Cambridge Companion to Foucault,* 2nd ed., ed. Gary Gutting (Cambridge: Cambridge University Press, 2003), 176–209. Han-Pile claims that Foucault takes Kant to address skepticism by *"inventing a new form of finitude."* "Foucault and Heidegger on Kant and Finitude," 127. Note also that her overall assessment of Heidegger's relation to Foucault's critique is much like mine. Han-Pile suggests that early Heidegger takes on the foundationalist project of modernity and attempts to displace the transcendental/empirical doublet by ontologizing it. Ibid., 144 and 149. However, Heidegger cannot shake the logic of the doublet, and so in his later work he surrenders the foundationalist project. Ibid., 149 and 151.

[3] Foucault, *The Order of Things,* 326.

It is because of these paradoxes and problems that Foucault takes the modern episteme to have failed, on its own terms. The human being cannot coherently be thought as both transcendental and empirical. As we saw in Chapter 5, the attempt produces only paradoxes, doublings, and so the openness of a question. Foucault puts it well, using the vocabulary of the origin: "what we are concerned with here is neither a completion nor a curve, but rather that ceaseless rending open which frees the origin in exactly the degree to which it recedes."[4] Because of this, modernity's project of responding to skepticism by securely grounding knowledge in the human being fails. Transcendental philosophy (according to Foucault) cannot ground knowledge.

But as we also saw in Chapter 5, we can equally say that the grounding project succeeds. I argued that, for Heidegger, the unanswerability of the question of the uncanny is the answer to that question: uncanniness is the non-ground that uncannily grounds. But this amounts to saying that Heidegger follows Foucault in surrendering the grounding project. To rest content with uncanniness at the ground of finite knowing is to rest content without a solid ground. In embracing uncanniness, Heidegger moves from the modern episteme to a post-modern one.

Still, there is an important respect in which Heidegger remains a clear representative of the modern episteme: his insistence on the centrality of the question, What is the human being? This is particularly clear in the Kant book, in which this insistence explicitly drives much of the argument.[5] Indeed, one of Heidegger's standard moves is to lead any philosophical question back to the question of Dasein and its openness to being, and he often criticizes others for not doing this or for not doing it well. In this, Heidegger is thoroughly under the sway of what Foucault calls modernity's "anthropological sleep."[6]

So Heidegger both does and does not go beyond modernity as Foucault understands it. Perhaps we can say that he is a transitional figure on Foucault's account: Heidegger poses the anthropological question that is distinctive of modernity, but he answers that question in a way that surrenders modernity's foundationalist ambitions. Thus uncanniness exacerbates

[4] Foucault, *The Order of Things*, 334. The sentence concludes: "the extreme is therefore what is nearest." We saw this same shape in Antigone's supreme uncanniness: she is closest to being because she is farthest from it.

[5] See, for instance, Heidegger, *Kant and the Problem of Metaphysics*, 145–146.

[6] So much so, in fact, that it is hard to imagine anyone other than Heidegger as the target of Foucault's scathing dismissal of an anthropological sleep that is "so deep that thought experiences it paradoxically as vigilance, so wholly does it confuse the circularity of a dogmatism folded over upon itself in order to find a basis for itself within itself with the agility and anxiety of a radically philosophical thought." Foucault, *The Order of Things*, 341.

rather than resolves the skeptical worry. Because it surrenders the foundationalist response to skepticism, Heidegger's picture does not fail on its own terms and so is not subject to Foucault's critique. Yet uncanny Dasein does to some extent repeat the figure of the human that, according to Foucault, populates post-Kantian philosophy. This is why we have found such rich connections between, for example, uncanniness and the German Idealist tradition, and between Heidegger's uncanniness and Freud's. Indeed, it would be surprising if prior philosophers had no inkling of Dasein's uncanny essence. Given Heidegger's view of the history of philosophy as a series of attempts to articulate our self-understanding as Dasein, we should expect philosophers to have come across Dasein's uncanniness but to have distorted it—perhaps by thinking it in terms of the transcendental rather than the ontological, or by thinking Dasein as consciousness. It is by *adequately* thinking uncanny Dasein that Heidegger would claim to distinguish himself from his predecessors, not by sheer novelty.

(Nonetheless, if we accept Kant's empirico-transcendental doublet as the historical precursor to uncanny Dasein, then we must wonder whether Heidegger is right to locate the birth of uncanny Dasein in Ancient Greece rather than in Königsberg. Is Heidegger projecting a thoroughly modern concept of the human into Sophocles's ode? Resolving this issue would require a full comparison of Heidegger's history of being with Foucault's archaeology of the human sciences.)

Heidegger did not always think uncanny Dasein adequately, but I do claim that he was always attempting to do so. His thought, early and late, has the unity of a continuity. There were of course changes in Heidegger's approach, as well as in his proximate preoccupations. There were also genuine advances and new discoveries. But throughout his philosophical career, Heidegger was driven to understand just the one thing: the human openness to meaning. From early on, he had and gave clear intimations that this openness was uncannily structured. Uncanny Dasein is conceptually present even in SZ: it is implicit in the way that Heidegger deploys the concepts of angst, thrownness, and uncanniness. Insights into concealing and its role in unconcealing shortly after SZ permitted a fuller formulation of uncanniness in EM.[7] The discussions in HI and the *Parmenides* lectures show Heidegger trying to articulate clearly the difficult logic of the uncanny.[8] But he never quite saw

---

[7] See, for instance, WM (1929) (discussed in Chapter 2) and "On the Essence of Truth" (1930), trans. John Sallis, *Pathmarks,* ed. William McNeill (Cambridge: Cambridge University Press, 1998).

[8] Martin Heidegger, *Parmenides,* trans. André Schuwer and Richard Rojcewicz (Bloomington: Indiana University Press, 1998).

or explained all the paradoxes and problems that worry Foucault and that we traced in Chapter 5. This is in part because Heidegger's poetic vocabulary and his mystical tendencies incline him to take the step into silence a moment or two before it is necessary. Nonetheless, I claim that Heidegger was always attempting to think the uncanny. Uncanniness is one formulation (among others, including *Ereignis*) of the single star that guided Heidegger's thought: the turn of the counterturning between presencing and absencing.[9]

While the details of Dasein's uncanniness are torturously fractal (and the process of working them out, fractally torturous), the basic idea can be expressed in relatively plain language: "The human being is in the manner of knowing—and does not know what he himself is. [. . . T]he human being knows and does not know who he himself is; an uncanny judgment. An uncanniness that loses nothing by the fact that those who are the happy-go-lucky human beings have no inkling of it."[10] Afford to this lack of self-knowledge the status of the condition of possibility of knowing at all, and then specify that what the human being does not know about itself is how such self-opacity could be the condition of knowledge, and you have uncanniness. This is what it is to *be* uncanny. This is how the human being is out of step with itself—unstable, out of joint, *unheimlich*.

[9] The reference to a single star recalls one of Heidegger's poems in "The Thinker as Poet." *Poetry, Language, Thought,* trans. Albert Hofstadter (New York: Harper & Row, 1975), 4. The turn in the counterturning *(die Gegenwendigkeit)* between presencing and absencing is the turn *(die Kehre)* that Heidegger identifies as the matter for thought in his letter to Father Richardson. Martin Heidegger, "Preface," in William J. Richardson, S. J., *Heidegger: Through Phenomenology to Thought,* 4th ed. (New York: Fordham University Press, 2003), viii–xxiii.

[10] Martin Heidegger, *Logic as the Question concerning the Essence of Language,* trans. Wanda Torres Gregory and Yvonne Unna (Albany: State University of New York Press, 2009), 24. I thank Andrew Blitzer for directing me to this passage, among many others.

Acknowledgments

Tʜᴇʀᴇ ᴀʀᴇ ᴍᴀɴʏ people whom I would like to thank, for a variety of things. For comments, corrections, and encouragement on the manuscript: Bill Blattner, Arnold Davidson, Stefano Franchi, the late John Haugeland, Jonathan Lear, Eric Santner, Matthew Shields, Nate Zuckerman, and two anonymous reviewers. For research assistance and helpful conversation, both formal and informal: Andrew Blitzer and Oren Magid. For photography: Tucker McKinney. And for mentorship, friendship, and support: Bill Blattner, Stefano Franchi, John Haugeland, Jonathan Lear, and Kevin Thorn. I also thank Shan Wang and Lindsay Waters of Harvard University Press, as well as all my colleagues and students in the Department of Philosophy at Georgetown University. I am grateful to Georgetown University for a Junior Faculty Research Fellowship, which allowed me to make considerable progress on the manuscript.

This book is for my Miette, who was always there.

Index

absurd, the, 37–42, 43, 45–46, 63; feeling of, 37–42, 44, 46, 50, 54, 55, 65, 68
Agamben, Giorgio, 209, 212
alētheia, 98, 116. *See also* truth
angst, 48–49, 59, 68, 77, 80, 81, 84, 86, 88, 93, 94, 96, 98, 100, 129, 171, 174, 211, 241; as Dasein's being, 79–80, 87, 213; and depression, 48, 53, 54, 58, 62; discloses Dasein's being, 48, 50, 51, 52, 53, 65–69, 72, 73, 77, 79, 80, 89; discloses the nothing, 81, 83, 84, 87; discloses thrownness, 72, 73, 75, 77, 79, 80, 90, 92, 173; discloses world, 52, 59–62, 63, 66, 67, 68, 80, 81, 83, 86, 87, 88, 89, 90, 93; disrupts falling, 50–52, 53, 66, 68, 69, 81, 82, 83, 84–86, 94–95, 97, 99, 170, 171; as an existentiale, 79, 81, 84, 86; grounds falling, 81, 83, 84–86, 87, 88, 94, 171; individuates, 53, 66–68, 72–73, 89; latency of, 79–80, 83, 86; methodological role of, 48–52, 67, 174; mood of, 2–3, 48–69, 72, 79–92, 93, 95, 97, 99, 134, 150, 170, 171, 173, 190, 238; originary, 77–92, 93–94, 97, 98–99, 101, 103, 131, 170, 171, 173, 209, 213; world withdraws in, 53, 54–59, 60, 62, 64, 86. *See also* derealization / depersonalization
Antigone (character), 112, 154, 175–202, 211; appeals to the divine law, 179–181, 182, 186, 193, 194–195; appeals to the law of irreplaceability, 192–193; as exempt from the closing words' expulsion from the hearth, 175, 177, 201–202; as *hupsipolis apolis*, 179, 189–194, 197, 198, 200, 202; Lacan's interpretation of, 196; as *pantoporos aporos*, 179, 188,

189, 190; relation to death, 196–199; suffers the *deinon*, 186, 197, 200; suicide of, 179, 187, 198
Antigone (play), 5, 101, 102, 103, 112, 154, 178, 179, 182, 184, 192; Creon (character), 177, 179, 180, 183, 184, 191–192, 194–196, 197, 200, 211; Ismene (character), 184, 186, 187–189, 194, 196, 200. *See also* Antigone (character)
anxiety, 26, 48, 54, 58, 86, 145; choral ode (from *Antigone*). *See also* angst
Aristotle, 63, 206, 213, 222, 228, 232
Auseinandersetzung, 118, 124, 147. See also *polemos*, the
authenticity. *See* ownedness

de Beistegui, Miguel, 147, 165
Blattner, William, 58
boredom, 3, 57, 58, 59
breakdown, 3–4, 29, 34, 35, 36, 44, 50, 53, 57, 60, 61, 62, 63, 64, 69, 79, 134, 161, 195; of tools, 59–61, 68. *See also* angst: world withdraws in

call of being, 191, 200
call of conscience. *See* conscience
Camus, Albert, 37–38, 40–42, 44, 45, 47. *See also* absurd, the
Cavell, Stanley, 41, 43–45, 59, 60
choral ode (from *Antigone*), 5, 101, 112, 123, 127, 130, 132, 134, 135, 140, 148, 150, 154, 155, 156, 158, 159, 163, 165, 167, 168, 169, 175, 178, 185, 197–198, 241; approach to interpreting, 102–105, 107–108, 113, 132, 135, 149, 207, 208; closing words of, 112, 174–178, 201–202, 205, 211;